Breaking Ranks

Breaking Ranks

IRAQ VETERANS SPEAK OUT AGAINST THE WAR

Matthew Gutmann and
Catherine Lutz

UNIVERSITY OF CALIFORNIA PRESS
Berkeley   Los Angeles   London

University of California Press, one of the most distinguished university presses in the United States, enriches lives around the world by advancing scholarship in the humanities, social sciences, and natural sciences. Its activities are supported by the UC Press Foundation and by philanthropic contributions from individuals and institutions. For more information, visit www.ucpress.edu.

University of California Press
Berkeley and Los Angeles, California

University of California Press, Ltd.
London, England

Library of Congress Cataloging-in-Publication Data

Gutmann, Matthew C., 1953–.
   Breaking ranks : Iraq veterans speak out against the war / Matthew Gutmann and Catherine Lutz.
      p.   cm.
   Includes bibliographical references and index.
   ISBN 978-0-520-26637-7 (cloth : alk. paper)
   ISBN 978-0-520-26638-4 (pbk. : alk. paper)
   1. Iraq War, 2003—Protest movements—United States.   2. Veterans—United States—Political activity.   I. Lutz, Catherine.   II. Title.

DS79.764.U6G88   2010
956.7044′31—dc22   2009035375

Manufactured in the United States of America

19   18   17   16   15   14   13   12   11   10
10   9   8   7   6   5   4   3   2   1

This book is printed on Cascades Enviro 100, a 100% post consumer waste, recycled, de-inked fiber. FSC recycled certified and processed chlorine free. It is acid free, Ecologo certified, and manufactured by BioGas energy.

Contents

Charlie Anderson. Photo by Matthew Gutmann.

Ricky Clousing. Photo by Matthew Gutmann.

Tina Garnanez. Photo by Matthew Gutmann.

Chris Magaoay. Photo by Matthew Gutmann.

Demond Mullins. Photo by Matthew Gutmann.

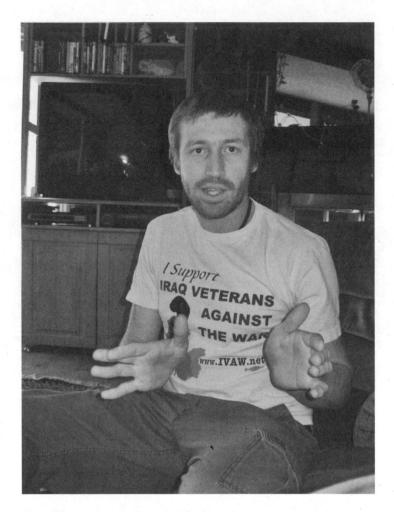

Garett Reppenhagen. Photo by Matthew Gutmann.

Introduction
A Different Kind of War Story

Looking back several years later on his first day at war in Iraq, Navy medic Charlie Anderson sighed and said, "I didn't even know what I didn't know."[1]

The learning curve would soon rise steeply in front of him.

Originally from Rossford, Ohio, Charlie had crossed over from Kuwait in March 2003 with the Marines 1st Expeditionary Force. Like many around him in uniform, he was deeply afraid and intensely intrigued, angry and resigned, excited and ambivalent about the mission he was on. Trained as a Navy corpsman attached to the Marines, he especially relished the idea of helping his buddies if they got hit.[2]

On one of his earliest convoy operations, his unit began taking casualties on the outskirts of Sadr City. Tanks in his battalion moved into forward positions near a small village and began firing at men who, it later turned out, were simply looking for a lost sheep. The fog of war had already descended.

The physical challenges soon followed. Charlie and his unit set up camp next to a garbage dump outside the city. Scorched by the heat, they also had to deal with the reek of raw sewage running down the middle of the road. "You couldn't eat," Charlie said, "because you opened up your MRE [Meal, Ready-to-Eat] and it got covered in flies." Flies apparently do not like coffee, though, and so he and his friends guzzled one cup after another.

Suddenly someone at the back of the column began letting go with bursts of machine gun fire. A disembodied radio voice commanded them to look for a young Arab male wearing black pants, white shirt, and sandals and carrying an AK-47. In other words, almost anybody. One of Charlie's sergeants, who had been telling the younger men a story, opened fire with his weapon, apparently aiming at nothing and no one in particular. Then he went right back to telling his story where he had left it midsentence just seconds before, pausing now and then to sip his coffee.

"A lot of people would think that was cool," said Charlie. "I thought it was scary."

Watching how his leadership approached combat did more than just confuse Charlie. He suddenly felt anxious, anxiety that would become anguish, about what he was doing in Iraq. This event became one in a series of political and moral epiphanies that would change him forever.

His story is one of dozens that we, along with the oral historian Betsy Brinson, gathered between 2005 and 2008 from veterans of the U.S. military who served during the first years of the wars in Iraq and Afghanistan. Like every one of the other veterans, Charlie is an ordinary person who underwent extraordinary transformations. His ordinariness can be seen in the common values and ideas he and so many young people around him carried into Iraq. The astonishing difference was his unorthodox response to what he saw, his unwillingness to simply say, "War is hell!" and leave it at that.

Later that same March day, Charlie's unit received orders to load up and drive into Sadr City. They had high hopes for what was to come. Given the standard American diet of World War II movies, Charlie and his comrades expected that for protecting the population from further depredations by Saddam Hussein they would be celebrated with, he said, "a kind of air of liberation parades in Holland and France." Vice President Dick Cheney had played on such emotions when he announced in 2003 that "things have gotten so bad inside Iraq, from the standpoint of the Iraqi people, my belief is we will, in fact, be greeted as liberators."[3]

But the civilian reception was not what they expected. The thousands of people out in the streets of Sadr City didn't seem excited to see them — except for the children. "There are kids running up and down the sides of streets begging for food. We'd been ordered not to feed them, by the way. I said, 'To hell with that!' I was throwing out pieces of MREs. We just started doing it. We weren't supposed to, but I decided that the generals weren't in my truck and if the generals wanted the order enforced they could come out and enforce it themselves."

And it was not at all a liberation parade or a food giveaway, because they were still supposed to be looking for the "young Arab" male carrying an assault rifle. And there were people everywhere. "You're looking at the kids, at the doorways, at the windows, and the rooftops." Who were each of these people, and what did the expressions on their faces mean? "You're trying to scan the alleys, looking for a guy in this crowd of five thousand that wants to kill you."

Charlie was riding on the passenger side of a Humvee with his weapon in his left hand, safety off, finger on the trigger, pointed at the vehicle's door. With his right hand he continued throwing food out and waving at the kids. After they rounded a corner, the crowd seemed to thin.

In a chaotic instant, all hell broke loose as Marines began shooting in all directions. "We're trying to figure out what one guy is firing at, and he yells, 'Don't ask me what I'm shooting. I'm shooting at fucking people!'"

Charlie turned back to his side of the vehicle. "My heart's going a million miles an hour. I've got the taste of bile in my throat." This was what he'd prepared for when they had used live ammunition in training exercises. This is what more experienced Marines had told him was almost impossible to describe, the terror of a firefight that clamped down and felt as if it were suffocating you. A burst of machine gun fire pierced the air on his side of the road and Charlie dropped down in his seat, but he quickly realized he was now hiding behind a canvas door. Not much good that would do, but somehow he'd forgotten the canvas flap when it mattered.

Everybody else in the vehicle was shooting, so Charlie sat up and started firing too. "I don't even know what I was shooting at. No idea. Can't even remember what's on the other side of that window." But he remembered the strange sensation that the window had appeared "almost like a white movie screen." He had kept pulling the trigger until someone said he could stop. But the U.S. soldiers weren't done. After they had escaped the city and begun driving through the countryside again, their tanks began shooting vehicles on the side of the road to put them out of commission. Then one of the tanks fired into a village up ahead. Charlie's Humvee quickly approached the village through potato fields.

"There's all this pandemonium. Women. Children. They are all running. All I saw were women and kids. I didn't see any men. Doesn't mean they weren't there, just that I didn't see them. And it seems so cliché. But that's really what was happening. Mostly women and children. And a few old men running every which direction screaming and yelling."

The welcoming crowds of Holland and France after D-Day? That picturesque image did not last the day. Those from another war took its place.

"My first thoughts were the black and white photograph of the little girl running down the street in Viet Nam. She'd been napalmed. All her skin's falling off. *That* was what I was thinking about when I saw this all happen."

Imagining how this story would be told somewhere in the future, he asked himself, "Twenty years from now are they going to be talking about the day the Americans came and shot up their village? That's not something I wanted to be associated with."

Five years later, in January 2008, as we sat in his home in the mountains of Boone, North Carolina, Charlie still looked shell-shocked in recounting those operations around Sadr City. Whether he shivered with the winter cold or with the memory of having been a part of the military force that had terrified civilians on the streets of an Iraqi city, he didn't say. The hypervigilance that he had first experienced there was to continue long after his return. Honorably discharged from the Navy with a diagnosis of post-traumatic stress disorder (PTSD), Charlie was still trying to come to grips with his time in Iraq. But regardless of what he and other troops had been ordered to do in the war, he remained convinced that their motivations had been noble. "Most of us thought that we were there to do something good. I don't think anybody joins an army or goes off to war thinking they are going to do evil."

CIVILIANS IN WAR: SOME BACKGROUND LEGALISMS

A civilian is a category defined through the laws of warfare that emerged during the twentieth century's long bloody march. Widely accepted definitions and rules say a civilian is someone who is not a member of any military armed force and therefore is entitled to special protections from violence. Not only should civilians not be shot at, but opposing forces must hold their fire if civilians are highly likely to be hurt.

In a growing number of wars, civilians are seen by military forces as important potential sources of material or political support for their side or as key targets. Civilians can see themselves as neutral or as having political sympathies with either side, so that they may tacitly allow or support the activities of one side in the conflict. These feelings, though, should have no bearing on their legal protections as civilians. Nonetheless, the decisions to wage urban warfare in Iraq and use aerial bombardment put many civilians at risk: officially, in just one year of the war (2007), the United States directly caused between 669 and 756 deaths and was involved in firefights in which an additional 868 to 1,326 Iraqi civilians were killed.[4] The Brookings Iraq Index estimated that overall, by 2008, 113,616 civilians had died as a result of the war. The U.S. Department of Defense public relations operations have successfully convinced the U.S. media, and through the press the American people, that U.S. troops on the ground in Iraq find it is nearly impossible to distinguish a civilian from a combatant and that civilian deaths are an unavoidable if tragic consequence of this or any war. The American public is encouraged to sympathize with the legitimate confusion of U.S. troops when trying to distinguish who is friend and who is foe, as well as with their efforts to do so. So Air Force General Richard B. Myers, then chairman of the Joint Chiefs of Staff, announced in 2003, "There are risks any time you go after any target. But I can tell you, the kind of vetting that the process goes through, from the beginnings of intelligence to the final operation, is exquisite. And we're not going to be perfect. But the success we've had has never been done with more care about bringing innocents into the line of fire. And that will continue. And that's what American service men and women do."[5]

With the absence of strong sanctions against shooting first and asking later, and with such public understanding as Myers and his officers helped to shape, it is certainly reasonable if the troops are guided by the motto "Better safe than sorry," better to be careful and shoot questionable civilians before they have the chance to shoot you. Yet identifying with civilians and their plight has played a role in turning some troops against the war. It was precisely through beginning to grasp the impact of the U.S. war in Iraq on civilians, and to see and register the reactions of Iraqi individuals to the U.S. military and its behavior, that U.S. soldiers were plunged into a series of horrible realizations. The faces and voices and bodies of Iraqi civilians literally caught in the crosshairs exploded preconceptions and prejudices and certainties among certain troops and led them—through a series of epiphanies—from supporting the U.S. mission in Iraq to joining the ranks of the war's most ardent critics.

For those among the troops who brought a measure of idealism to their assignments, the realities of how civilians were treated by the U.S. Armed Forces, and the increasingly hostile reception they received from Iraqi noncombatants, provided a potent challenge that undercut beliefs and morale. Those realities undermined their confidence and loyalty to their mission. For these troops, the war was coming to hold little honor beyond that of helping their buddies get out of Iraq alive.

THE COSTS OF WAR

How does one sum up a war, especially a war that was still under way as this book went to press? Over 650,000 Iraqis killed by violence, malnutrition, and disease in just the first three years?[6] One in seven Iraqis forced to flee their homes and seek refuge elsewhere inside and outside their country?[7] Decimated infrastructure, streets awash with sewage, electricity unreliably fed into homes and businesses more than six years after the invasion? A cultural heritage of museums and libraries looted?[8] Over 4,300 U.S. military personnel dead, 320,000 with brain injuries alone, 900 with amputated limbs, 1,900 with disfiguring burns, 52,000 with PTSD? Suicide rates among Iraq War–era veterans two to four times higher than those of comparable civilians?[9] The sheer scale of the effects at home: 1.7 million American young people deployed to the war zones of Iraq and Afghanistan, a mighty generation's worth of combat experience and, very often, deep trauma? A Pentagon propaganda campaign in support of the war funded by hundreds of millions of dollars and extending to the naming of over forty countries as members of "the coalition of the willing," four of which have no military at all? The $3 trillion conservative estimate of the financial cost, with billions going into the coffers of corporate war profiteers like Halliburton, KBR, Blackwater, ExxonMobil, and Bechtel?[10]

Not surprisingly, many soldiers and civilians began to think that war was good for corporations who wanted to make money and for politicians who wanted to get elected, and that both groups were more interested in profit than truth. In fact, in the years from 2003 to 2007, businesses were awarded war contracts worth $85 billion.[11] Most notoriously, KBR, once a subsidiary of the company that Dick Cheney headed, Halliburton, had taken in over $24 billion since the beginning of the war, with forty thousand employees and subcontractors in Iraq and another twenty-eight thousand in Afghanistan and Kuwait. It is one of three companies that received a phenomenal ten-year, $150 billion contract in 2008 to provide shelter, food, and other basics for U.S. soldiers overseas.[12] And according to an official report on the $117 billion spent—much going through corporate hands—on the reconstruction of Iraq, "The hard figures on basic services and industrial production compiled for the report reveal that for all the money spent and promises made, the rebuilding effort never did much more than restore what was destroyed during the invasion and the convulsive looting that followed."[13] This was not a blunder, though, as much as a planned transfer of wealth to the 150 U.S.

corporations that received billions for their efforts in Iraq, much of it for work that would have been done by Iraqi government bureaucracies and military had they not been disbanded for just this reason in the immediate wake of the invasion.[14]

SIX SOLDIERS: CHARLIE, TINA, RICKY, GARETT, DEMOND, AND CHRIS

But this is not a book about the legalities or statistics of war. It is a book about five men and one woman who enlisted like hundreds of thousands of other young people—to get money for college, to pursue adventure, to serve their country, to find a way to do good in the world, and mostly for a combination of all these things. It demonstrates how multiple and malleable those motives were: they don't match the simple motivations implied by concepts like "the economic draft" or "the patriotism of young Americans," concepts that figure in so many mainstream accounts of the war and its soldiers, whether critical or supportive of the war.

It is a book about how these particular people—unlike many others—came to oppose the Iraq War, often at great personal risk and sacrifice. This book is about the social courage they needed to withstand intense pressures to conform, and the striking and original ideas each developed to understand the war and what it meant. Their critiques are not simple matches to those of the civilian antiwar movement or to our own as authors. Only one is a pacifist. Most say they would fight another kind of war. Some critique the military's actions in Iraq by holding up a positive image of the higher standards of soldiers or Marines of the past. While all of them object to the war on grounds of conscience, most of them do not fit the military's very narrow definition of what a conscientious objector is.

They each created unique moral and political understandings out of a combination of their distinctive and their shared experiences before, during, and after Iraq. They suggest that another definition of patriotism may be needed, as many remain committed to the idea that it is proper and necessary to love America but insist that such patriotism can require a sometimes radical critique of the nation. The yellow ribbon campaigns have tended to silence and harm these veterans. As one dissenting veteran told us, though, on his return home from Iraq (after having to buy his own body armor), he angrily but methodically collected several hundred yellow ribbon magnets off the cars in his city: he saw those car owners' magnet displays as empty posturing by people who were in fact indifferent to the moral problem of the war and its veterans.

Charlie is one of the six veterans whose stories are at the center of this book. The others—Ricky Clousing, Tina Garnanez, Chris Magaoay, Demond Mullins, and Garett Reppenhagen—come from places across the United States—Toledo, Ohio; Sumner, Washington; Shiprock, New Mexico; Pukalani, Hawai'i; Brooklyn, New York; and Fort Bliss, Texas. They come from tight-knit families and dispersed ones. Cities, suburbs, and farms are home to one or another of them. Some are righteous in their religious purpose, others are indifferent or happy secularists. Their faces are those of American ethnic diversity—they have white, Native American, black, and Filipino ancestry. What they share are roots in an American civil religion that preaches the righteousness of what the United States does and stands for, and families that come from the bottom half of the country's wealth distribution.

We did not go looking for a demographically diverse group of veterans. From the over forty interviews conducted by Betsy Brinson, we chose the life stories of Charlie, Ricky, Tina, Chris, Demond, and Garett because we learned the most from them about the process by which a young person's thinking about war and occupation and his or her own values can change. We returned for extended interviews with them ourselves and heard of lives still in the process of being shaped. In the years since returning from war, they had variously gone through divorces, committed themselves daily to activism on behalf of vets or against war, lost some religious faith and engaged in renewed vision quests, taken college courses, sought medical help. Their lives and experiences from childhood until early 2009 are the focus of this book.

A river of news coverage and books over the years of the war has saturated the airwaves, cyberspace, and print media, suggesting that everything about the war is now known and under intellectual control. But media attention has radically thinned out as weariness or disgust with the war and occupation has set in; news stories on the war dropped from an already low average of 15 percent of all stories in mid-2007 to just 3 percent in 2008, according to one study.[15] A miniscule number of stories deal with revolt within the ranks of the U.S. military or with the half-truths and outright lies that recruiters often tell the young people whom they still need to staff the war. Few give accounts of the harsh realities of U.S. military training and deployment.

What the six veterans here tell us is that it is very difficult to swim against the tide of military mobilization and action. They also tell us something about how to explain human cruelty in war and elsewhere, and about how moral restraints are eroded and moral codes reshaped not only in training and everyday life in the military but far earlier as well. As famous psychological experiments on obedience by Milgram and Zimbardo showed, it is difficult *not* to conform to the demands of people constituted as authorities, but when people sense something is wrong many refuse to simply go along. In the following chapters, we see how these individuals came to understand that a problem existed and struggled to identify and correct it, often with tremendous exertion.

As people who have been against the war from the beginning, we, like many Americans, have been deeply discouraged and angry that the war has continued for years and that all desires and efforts to end it have seemed to be for naught. As cultural anthropologists, we also bring a unique perspective to understanding war and the resistance to it. Our field draws attention to the unspoken ideas and values that guide behavior and can make war and occupation seem normal or at least inevitable for many. It also suggests, though, that as important as dominant cultural norms are in shaping what people do and think, those norms are often full of conflict, are ambiguous and contradictory, and are in constant flux. What an anthropological perspective leads us to ask is what those standards, in all their complexity, are and to see some of the same complexity even in dissenting thinkers as they challenge aspects of dominant ways of thinking. The power of the standards—and the power of the authority figures and media outlets that mostly articulate them—mean, however, that dissident voices are less often heard or understood by the public. This makes it all the more essential that their views and experiences circulate as widely as possible.

These six people, like hundreds of other veterans, inspire hope through their creative thinking and their example of commitment to telling the truth as they see it and to activist work, even as their lives are not simple stories of reward or triumph on account of this. We think these antiwar stories need telling. They can counter Pentagon recruitment efforts and let active-duty soldiers exposed to similar contradictions, deceptions, and traumas in their own military work know that their experiences are not just personal, idiosyncratic, or natural and inevitable but rather deeply political, rethinkable, and some of the most important resources for ending the war and preventing future ones.

This book demonstrates the hubris of war, the overweening arrogance that the war's conduct demonstrates when it is made visible by on-the-ground, firsthand accounts like these. Yet even more importantly this is a book about discovery and how young soldiers and Marines came to change their minds about the war and develop a different kind of conviction about how things should be. From a range of perspectives and in complex, often contradictory ways, the six people here share the torment and belief that emerged from their experience and share insightful lessons from their recruitment, training, deployment, and return home. We turn now to the stories of the six veterans, how they came to find themselves in the U.S. Armed Forces, and how they made decisions that led them to enlistment and, ultimately, to war in Iraq.

PART ONE Innocence

ONE Recruiting Volunteers

In junior high school, having a father who was a drug pusher and a weightlifter could be a blessing. When anyone tried to mess with Chris Magaoay, "I flashed my dad's name around and people shut up. My dad was their drug dealer." But when Chris got to high school, some of that reputational protection service began to come apart. Maybe it was because he was just a bit smaller than others, or maybe he experienced the sting of teasing more than they did, but he felt bullied. At home no one understood or could help, especially his father: "My dad was this huge guy who never was scared of anyone and always told me that you can kill anyone if you want to." He didn't want to be a bully or hit back, so he dropped out of school.

Born in 1985 in Wailuku, Hawai'i, Christopher Scott Magaoay lived with a grandmother and an aunt who did housekeeping at the Maui

Seaside Hotel in downtown Kahului. He had also lived with his grand-father, a retired irrigation worker from the Hawaiian Commercial & Sugar Company plantation. His father was in construction for a short while before focusing on drug sales, mainly crystal methamphetamine in the neighborhood, and dipping in himself. "My dad was very abusive. Very. I can remember one time, he got really pissed off and threw me across the room. But that was the drugs getting to him, and I understand that."

When we talked in May 2008, Chris still had his U.S. Marine buzz cut, and it was obvious he was as full of energy and a spirit to tackle what-ever obstacles he encountered as his stories would indicate. Compact and wiry, he seemed to greet the interview with an intensity that was at once earnest and apprehensive. He wanted to find the right way to put things, to make sure we understood who he was and what he'd been through since he'd joined the Marines in the fall of 2004.

The way Chris put it, "I was raised by my entire family. We never had a central core thing. It's kind of the Filipino-Hawai'ian way. You don't have a central parental unit." He went to Pukalani Elementary School and later the Kalama Intermediate School. Chris was only four or five when the First Gulf War occurred in 1990–91. "I heard that the war was coming on the news and I started panicking. My dad told me, 'You don't have to worry. We have two aircraft carriers parked out front.' I didn't know what that meant, but later in school we studied Pearl Harbor, the whole history of Hawai'i and its military significance." In elementary school they had gone on a field trip to the Combined Arms Exercise Cen-ter on the Big Island. He and his classmates even slept overnight in the barracks there and were impressed to see tanks rolling by.[1] It was not surprising, then, that at Henry Perrine Baldwin High School one of the first things he did was join the Junior Reserve Officer Training Corps (JROTC).

Chris stayed at different family homes until one day in ninth grade, December 14, 1999: "I tell everyone that was the day my life took a turn for the worse. I remember the day very clearly. I ran away from home." He had been living that fall with his mother, but she started doing drugs, as she had often in the past, and ultimately was arrested on charges of stealing a car. By December she was about to go to jail. Chris didn't want to live with his dad because he was a drug addict too, "and I didn't want to go through that anymore. I lived on the beaches for about a year. The police would pick me up every so often. That was about until I was fifteen."

To make the money he needed to survive on his own, Chris picked *opihi*, a local snail delicacy, and sold them for twenty dollars a gallon zip-lock bag. For clothing he went to the Salvation Army. But the law finally got a solid grip on him, putting him on probation and sending him back to high school. He went for about two months and then decided to take the GED. His high score allowed him to graduate nearly two years ahead of his class.

Done with school at sixteen, Chris decided he needed a change of scenery. As he was considering what to do, he learned that his girlfriend, Erika Lea, was being molested by her stepfather at home. He wanted to help. As he said looking back later, "I already had the Marine inside of me. Had to save somebody." After they reported him to the authorities, the stepfather was removed from the house, but Erika and Chris remained frightened that he might return in another of his furies. Erika Lea's mother decided to take her to the Philippines and invited Chris to come along. He jumped at the chance to get out of Hawai'i, at least for a while. He went online to order his birth certificate, picked up a state ID, paid $65 for his expedited passport, and received the document without anyone in his family knowing what he was planning.

Within a month of arriving in the province of Luzon in the Philippines, Erika Lea was pregnant, and, remembered Chris, "I had to grow up real fast." Before long, in November 2002, their son, John Luke, was born.

Over the next intense year and a half, he said, "I learned pretty much everything that I know today." He and his wife, wife's mother, and son were all in the Philippines in March 2003 when the United States invaded Iraq. To his shock and dismay, some local people threw rocks at his house because he and Erika were Americans. After a series of bomb attacks on Philippine civilians in which an American missionary was killed, the U.S. Embassy in Manila issued a travel advisory from the State Department to all U.S. citizens warning them that it was no longer safe to be in the Philippines and that those who wished to remain did so at their own risk. "It got pretty rough," Chris remembered, and he called his family back in Hawai'i for help getting home. His great-grandmother sent him the money they needed.

The only problem was that once he arrived back in the United States he was arrested for having "fled the country" while on probation, the sentence he had received for running away from home before. Court-ordered to get a job, Chris found one at the local Kentucky Fried Chicken. After a few months he realized there was no way he could go on working there and began to think about other possibilities. The military was clearly a more than acceptable and somewhat familiar option after his stint in JROTC. On top of that, Chuck Norris had had many fans in his household, and his dad's favorite movie had been *Full Metal Jacket:* "I remember he used to say over and over to himself when he was upset or joking around, '*What's* your major malfunction?!' That's what the drill sergeant screamed at the private who commits suicide in the movie."

His dad, he said, "had the drill instructor mentality that respect comes through fear and pain." Chris did stomach crunches to protect himself from being hit in the gut by his father: "That was his thing. That was his way of punishing, to see you gasp for air."

His mother's stepfather had been a Marine who had fought in the Pacific during World War II. He had stayed on in the service afterwards, finishing up the twenty years needed to retire on a full military pension. Along with the lighter he carried during the war, he'd given Chris a sense that the military life was normal. Chris also had other family who had been in the military, including his father's father, who was "a Filipino traitor in World War II, working with the Japanese army." He recounted this bit of family history with a wry grin, suggesting that even though it had once been very shameful, it was now far enough in the past to have become a joke.

Then there was the other grandfather who loved the TV show *JAG*. "He would get dressed up in his old Charlies [the Marine service uniform], his military dress uniforms, his Dress Blue Deltas, and he'd sit there watching it. God help you when there was a *JAG* marathon on. He used to get his saber out and he'd do drill. I would get a little stick. Here's this seventy-, eighty-year-old man doing his marching drills with this saber, and I'm out there with a stick I found in the yard trying to copy him.

"So I grew up with a lot of military in my life. I wanted to be in the military, but I didn't want to be a grunt soldier. My grandfather used to tell me, 'What's the difference between an officer and an enlisted man? One's a working man.' But I still felt I wanted to be an officer, and since then I've wanted to be one of three things: a JAG lawyer, a fighter pilot, or an officer in the military." And he wanted to set himself up for a career, not just a stint, in the military.

Chris and his elementary school friends played soldier, rolling around in the mud, executing low crawls through the grass, and sneaking up on each other. In junior high, they graduated to tougher assignments: they emulated the 10th Mountain Division by tying a length of rope to a fire hydrant and, without any safety equipment, rappelling down a vertiginous sheer rock cliff into a gully below. (This early reconnaissance came in handy later, in high school, when Chris was able to hide in the same ravine after running away from home.) They were Filipino, Hawai'ian, *haole* (Hawaiian for foreigners), and Japanese kids. The last often pretended they were in the 442nd, the mostly Japanese American infantry unit that remains the most decorated in the history of the U.S. Armed Forces.[2] Many of these same kids joined the military as soon as they could, most choosing to enter the Marine Corps.

Not too long after his return from the Philippines, Chris began talking to military recruiters because, he said, "I was really angry with the way they were treating Americans in the Philippines. I wanted to be patriotic and serve my country." Not wanting to be a regular grunt, he quickly determined that he would need some college credits beyond his GED in order to have the most options open to him. A recruiter even went to see Chris's judge and complain that his probation status was preventing him from joining the Marines. The judge released him.[3]

The way was cleared, but Chris still didn't have the college credits to enter as he wanted. He tried the Army. Then he talked to the Navy guy. No dice. The Marine Corps. Same story. And then the Air Force. No one would take him except at the lowest ranks without at least fifteen college credits. "They told me pretty much, 'Buzz off.' So I just gave up on that, tried to live a normal life like everyone else in Hawai'i. Just stay home and do what you need to."

While he was home in Pukalani, he discovered his girlfriend was cheating on him and they broke up. Then, while "waiting for something to happen in my life," he met a woman online. The only problem was that she was in Mississauga, Ontario, in the suburbs of Toronto. Chris decided he was in love again and flew to Mississauga to meet her in March 2004. Things worked out well. They moved in together and, a month later, got married.

Having temporarily solved the problems of his love life, he was still frustrated that all his efforts to enlist had been thwarted. Determined to sign up for reasons he could not easily explain at the time of our interview, Chris found a way in Canada to get some college credits that promised to help his case for joining the military at a rank higher than the lowest-level private. A few months and a rapid fifteen credits later, he called 411 and asked for the nearest U.S. military recruiter.[4] Directory assistance told Chris that the closest recruiting center was in West Seneca, New York. "So I drove there almost every day for two months straight. It cost me and my wife about $4,000, traveling back and forth, doing all the processing. I was very serious about getting in. And then I joined the United States Marine Corps," Chris told us, pausing over each part of the name of the armed service to which he had pledged his allegiance.

With body bag counts rising in Iraq, plentiful criticism of the war's rationale and prosecution, and relatively better economic prospects at home, many young people had been making other choices.[5] But Chris was one of thousands for whom the military seemed to promise redemption, or at least it seemed like the right move at the right time. In a real sense, the volunteer military is made up of other willing, able, and determined young people like him, though few have to knock so long and hard on the door to be allowed to join the military.

LOOKING FOR THE PARK

Charlie Anderson was picked up by Navy recruiters in a park. It was back in 1995 in Lafayette, Indiana, where he lived with his mother and stepfather. Thirteen years later, as we huddled next to a heater on a cold winter day in his apartment in Boone, North Carolina, Charlie seemed alternately relaxed and anxious as he recounted how he had gotten from Lafayette to Iraq and back. His bushy eyebrows pumped up and down with animation as he described how it had all happened and what it all meant.

When Charlie met the recruiters, his mother was studying for a PhD in English with a minor in women's studies, and his stepfather was working on complex analysis for his doctorate in mathematics. But he was not raised the child of professionals. Born in 1977, he spent his first twelve years in the working-class community of Rossford, Ohio, outside Toledo, where his neighbors and family friends worked in the Libbey-Owens-Ford Glass factory in nearby Toledo or in other factories that supplied parts to the automobile industry in Detroit and Dearborn, Michigan. But as he reached adulthood, those manufacturing jobs were in decline. So Charlie was already thinking in vague terms about enlisting, as friends from school had already done. He was just not sure which branch offered the best prospects. Because "a friend had just been screwed by the Army, I wasn't really interested in them. And the Marines were not really my cup of tea. So here's the Navy and Air Force if I was going to do it. I wasn't really married to any one concept at this point."

As chance would have it, Charlie was on his way to work one day when a couple of Navy recruiters spotted him walking down a Lafayette street. They were out on a search-and-recruit mission for fresh prospects. "I'm literally walking to work. And it's a Senior Chief and a Second-Class or a First-Class. And they wanted to know how to get to the park. Good opening gambit. After I showed them where the park was, they offered to give me a ride to work. And they started talking about the Navy." Charlie got out of their car with a couple of glossy pamphlets and a business card. He gave them his home phone and set up an appointment to talk more.

Then again, it was not so much a coincidence that these recruiters found Charlie, as they were two of some ten thousand who go to work each day to bring in the approximately twenty-five thousand new replacement recruits needed *each month* across the services. They are just part of the marketing mix, along with video games, sophisticated and seductive Web sites, school visits, helicopter parachute drop simulators hauled around in over a dozen $1 million tractor trailers, and ads on the channels that either young people or their parents watch.[6]

The main obstacle turned out to be Charlie's mother. "That's what you want to be when you grow up?" she challenged him "with a fair amount of scorn." In her disapproval of his interest in the military, Charlie's mother was hardly alone. The reluctance of parents to have their children join the military is so widespread, especially as the wars dragged on through the 2000s, that the military has designed special marketing campaigns to attract the parents as "key influencers." The "Navy for Moms" Web site, for example, promoted through outsized posters in many U.S. train and bus stations, gives upbeat answers to "Moms who have questions about Navy life for their kids."

But Charlie's mother could also draw on powerful religious traditions in arguing with him about war and the military. Originally Lutheran, she and Charlie "went Methodist" because they liked the church and "an excellent, excellent minister." Charlie identified with the church as much as with any family ethnic lineage, which included Scot, Irish, Welsh, English, and German ancestry—"I'm Spot the Backyard Dog," he said.

As a kid, Charlie Anderson was always picked last for sports in school: "I was usually the squeak toy. They'd play with me until I squeaked and ran." But when they played war, things were different: Charlie was on the team. In the woods behind his friend's house, the neighborhood boys carried plastic weapons and conducted maneuvers, "what today I would term 'Force on Force.'" Charlie himself had other ideas about how to best play war games, and they did not involve dividing up into opposing army squads. He tried to convince his friends to play shoulder to shoulder on the same team, fighting an "invisible enemy." "You played Army, you played war games." And you religiously watched *G.I. Joe* on television. It was on channel 24, Monday through Friday at 3:30. At the end of the show they would immediately switch to channel 50, out of Detroit, which showed the same episode of *G.I. Joe* at 4:00.

He also watched *The ThunderCats* and *Transformers*, which, he noted, "were more or less the same thing. All of them are violent and all of them are male dominated. I mean, there were women in them, but it was the token girl. There was also the token minority."

"I remember very clearly, boys played with GI Joe and girls played with Barbie. Boys go in the backyard and pretend to kill each other, girls go and have tea parties. And don't do the wrong one! I always played with Barbies with my cousin, and effectively Ken was GI Joe. And one time somebody came over to the house [and saw it], and, man, you would have thought I'd been convicted of espionage." The visitor made quite a scene, Charlie was humiliated, and the lesson about what was expected of boys and combat got stamped into his mind. "It was horrible."

Charlie concluded that preparing to be a soldier does not start where most people think it does. "You might like to think that it begins when the recruiter approaches young people in high school. But the moment you put one of those little plastic army men into a little boy's hand—and it's usually a little boy—it reinforces the concept of that culture." In this and other ways, Charlie thinks of his upbringing in Rossford, Ohio, as "quintessential small-town America."

Military recruiters find many of their prospects in such places, where children are already prepared to see war as a positive. They make frequent appearances at local high schools to which they are individually assigned. There, the Army Recruiting Command instruction manual tells them, they are to "effectively penetrate the school market." They will do so by being "so helpful and so much a part of the school scene that you are in constant demand," thereby achieving "school ownership." They are advised to volunteer to coach school sports teams, eat lunch in the school cafeteria on a regular basis, and use such techniques as reading yearbooks to glean details about a student that allow them to "mysteriously" seem to know the student. The success of this strategy of recruiting teens far before their eighteenth birthday—in some cases as young as fourteen—is one reason why the United States is the only country other than Somalia that has never ratified the Convention on the Rights of the Child, which specifically prohibits such practices.[7] The military is now beginning to use social networking sites as well as video games to draw in recruits;[8] the Marines, for example, had over 100,000 friends on Facebook as of the beginning of 2010.

Eventually Charlie and his mother sat down with the Air Force. It didn't go well. The recruiter didn't look his mother in the eye and evaded some questions. A different experience with the Navy recruiters encouraged his mother a bit and left her feeling that at least they "were being as honest as they could be." So with this distinction Charlie began the process of applying for admission into the Navy. As with Chris, and despite the subsequent recruitment problems in all services, this process proved more difficult than anticipated. In Charlie's case the problem appears to have been doubts the Navy had about his emotional fitness, though it took a little while for him to determine exactly why the Navy needed convincing about his mental state.

First the Navy found out that years earlier Charlie had been to see a psychologist, or a social worker—he couldn't remember. It had occurred after his parents divorced. The Navy recruiters decided that they needed to secure those records to make their own assessment about Charlie's emotional capacity. After they read through his therapist's files, the Navy decided he needed a further psychological evaluation. At first it all left Charlie mystified, but as things progressed it became clear that the Navy was not worried he was crazy. They thought he might have another condition that would prevent him from enlisting and becoming a competent sailor: he might be gay.

The Navy might have come to question Charlie's sexuality, he believes, because of his involvement in a high school teen outreach program of Planned Parenthood and volunteer work he had participated in with an organization called Project AIDS Lafayette, a nonprofit helping people in the area with AIDS: "I got teased relentlessly through my entire time in high school, because if I was working with Project AIDS then I must be gay." Perhaps involvement with such a group during his high school days had raised this possibility with the Navy as well. Or maybe what caused the Navy to flag Charlie's file was that he also had spent time organizing support for a fair housing amendment that sought to add sexual orientation to the list of things one could not discriminate against in a lease.

Whatever the reason, the Navy wanted another psychologist to do a new evaluation of Charlie. As the psychologist was not a regular Navy employee but was hired on contract, he wasn't bound by the military's "Don't Ask, Don't Tell" rule. That policy, dating from 1993, permits gay or bisexual men and women in the military to hide their sexual orientation and prohibits military commanders or recruiters from investigating their sexuality. In any event, Charlie went through the interview and passed with flying colors. He negotiated training for the position of hospital corpsman, a highly desirable MOS (Military Occupational Specialty), in part because, more than many other military jobs, it involves a skill transferable to the civilian world after the military.

As he reflected on this experience years later, Charlie would remember that he had not been all that interested in joining the military. He had pursued it at first out of some curiosity. But when he was not immediately welcomed into the Navy, "it turned into almost an oppositional defiance where 'Now I want it because you're trying to tell me I can't have it.'"

Yet when Charlie signed his first contract on Halloween of 1995, he had higher purposes as well: "I thought that it was a good thing to be doing. I was serving something that was greater than myself. I was serving my country, defending freedom, democracy, and the Bill of Rights." That's how he viewed his decision at the time. Later he admitted, "I had no concept of what any of that meant. I mean, those are all the sound bites that they throw at you, and it's not just the military. You get that from the evening news. You get that from your civics textbooks. You get that from high school history."

THE LANGUAGE OF CHOICE

When Tina Garnanez enlisted in the Army, she joined an active-duty military of 1.5 million soldiers and 1.5 million reserves, and she was among the 39 percent of the force who are Native American, African

American, Latina/o, Asian American, or others the military calls "minorities."[9] While she was thus part of what is sometimes called the racial or economic draft, Tina would tell you nobody made her join. When we talked in Santa Fe, New Mexico, in June 2008, her slim build made it immediately clear that she was a runner-athlete. Her easy laugh was the most striking evidence of how open and sociable she was. Tina wore her allegiances on her arms with multiple bracelets and tattoos. All these, she told us, she would explain in time.

Born in 1981 in Shiprock, New Mexico, and raised in nearby Farmington, she graduated from high school in 2000 and left for basic training two months later. "I knew at a very young age I wanted to join the military. It's just something I always wanted to do." And it was a family tradition. Although none of her five brothers enlisted, all finding work nearby after high school, two of her great-uncles had been Navajo code talkers in World War II.[10] Her grandfather was in the Army. One of her uncles had joined the Navy, her father was in the Air Force, and her cousin Darwin was in the Marines.

She grew up with those five brothers and her mother. "I was really close with my entire family. We all lived in the same area, so we saw each other really often, daily." During the school year they lived in Farmington, in northwest New Mexico, and in the summertime they'd go to Oakspring, in northeast Arizona, "where my grandma lives. That's where we did all the sheepherding, all that fun stuff. When I wasn't in school we'd go out to the reservation and take care of the sheep and goats. My cousins, and my aunts, and my uncles, great-aunts, great-uncles, and my grandparents, we were all very close."

Named for her mother, Flora, and her grandmother, Daisy, Florentina Daisy Garnanez had a tattoo on her right shoulder of a daisy with thirteen petals, one for each of the women in her family she admired, from her great-grandmother on down. Her grandparents all spoke Navajo, as did her mother and uncles, but she understood only "bits and pieces" of the language. While her grandmother had taught Navajo to her younger cousins, she said that she and her older cousins were part of "the experiment: 'If we teach them English first, let's see how they do.' Because my mom went to boarding school for Native kids and she was smacked for speaking Navajo. They didn't want us to go through that. But now with the younger kids, they're teaching them Navajo too."

From the kitchen window of her grandmother's house, you could look down the hill and see the uranium mines where her uncles and Grandpa James had worked. Like many other Native workers there, they had been poisoned by the radioactive ore, and all had died of lung cancer. "They'd come home covered in dust, just coughing all the time. My grandma had six miscarriages. They didn't know how bad the radiation was. They worked without masks. They weren't told, 'Hey, this stuff is hazardous.' They weren't making much money. Lots of widows continue to fight for compensation, and most of the time the government denies their claims, saying, 'You don't have enough information.'"

After attending Apache and Ladera Elementary Schools, Tina headed for Heights Junior High School. "That's where I began my love of running. I mean, it was in junior high that I started thinking, 'Wow! I *really* like this!' I'd always loved running, you know, chasing the goats and stuff." Tina laughed as she recalled, "I'd be with my grandma and she'd see the goats on a hill far away: 'Tina, go get the goats!' and I'd go running to get them. So when it came time for PE in school, it was, 'Doo, doo, doo' — I was running. I was happy." And it sounded like joy in the retelling.

When Tina was growing up, her mother took her and her brothers to church every Sunday and Wednesday, "revivals and camp meetings, and Jesus all the time. She took us to all these different churches, First Baptist and Episcopalian, Presbyterian, First Methodist. Just to get the feel on everything. Then we went onto the reservation and met folks who believed in the Navajo way. She was just letting us see everything that was out there, letting us decide for ourselves."

Farmington High School was a mix of kids, white, Native, Hispanic, black. Tina was in the Dene Club for Native American students and helped organize pow-wows. She ran track and cross-country and participated in Junior Civic Hands. Tina was also in JROTC for all three of her years in high school. "I enjoyed it and I excelled. It was easy for me to do. It was physical fitness also, and a break from sitting in classrooms and staring at a chalkboard all day. I got to run around outside." She was the first student to jump from private to officer in her first year, and she relished the clear markers of accomplishment the military frequently hands out. "It was just wild. By the time I was a senior I was a captain in ROTC."

Each year some three hundred thousand high school students are enrolled in JROTC high school programs. Students wear military uniforms to school, conduct drill and sometimes weapons practice, and take history and military science courses from retired but uniformed veterans. The military has put these programs in over 3,200 high schools around the country and has especially concentrated them in less well-to-do and ethnic minority high schools like Tina's. As a result, they have reaped a striking 45 percent recruitment rate for JROTC program graduates.[11]

Before joining the Army, Tina said, "I lived at high school. I did everything. I'd wake up at 4:30 or 5:00 in the morning, then be at school at 5:30 to do ROTC Scouts, the physical fitness team, until about 7:30. Then go shower and change and go to class at 8:00. At lunch I'd run for ROTC Scouts; they had us do two laps. School got out at 3:10. At 3:30 I had track or cross-country practice. After practice, around 5:00, I'd have some other meeting, like Dene Club. Then get home around 7:00 or so. Then on top of that, for some strange reason, I got a part-time job my senior year, as a hostess at the Golden Corral. I wouldn't get home till midnight."

All her life her family had remarked at what a happy baby and child she was. "I'm an optimist, a very cheerful person. All my life I have been, 'Life is good!' I've got a great family that I love. And I loved school, got As and Bs. I adored being in school, learning. Can't get enough of books." And she wanted to continue her studies. "I wanted to go to college, but how could I make that happen? I was thinking of all my brothers. No one in my family had really gone to college. My uncle and my mom took some classes at the community college. I had no idea how to pay for it. I wasn't aware of all the options available, grants and scholarships. It was just overwhelming and scary."

Although she joined the Army right out of high school and with enthusiasm, Tina was not intending to make a career or go to battle. She wanted money for college and she wanted to test herself against the physical challenges she thought she'd find in the Army. "There was no 9/11, there was no Saddam threat. There really was nothing happening in the world as far as wars. So when I joined I thought I'd do four years and get out. And, if I was really lucky, I wouldn't have to worry about any of that. I was just curious to do my four years and get out with my money for college."

Things were not to end up that simply.

GROWING UP

Although Demond Mullins had been an outspoken opponent of the Iraq War after his return, by the time we caught up with him he had left activism behind for the time being, finished his bachelor's degree, and begun studying for his doctorate in sociology at City University of New York (CUNY). We agreed to meet in one of the CUNY libraries in Manhattan. There Demond recounted how he'd had to drop out of college several years before because he could not pay the tuition, then ended up in Las Vegas as a model, and later joined the National Guard, thinking this would be a financial ticket back to college. When we talked in January 2008, this men's-magazine-handsome man of easy smile and cautious demeanor explained how his road back to college had taken a detour through Iraq.

During his childhood, Demond was often on the move. Born when his mother was just sixteen, Demond was raised by his mother's own legal guardian to the age of seven, when he moved in with his mom and a stepfather he called Pops, who worked as a brickmason. Over the next several years, with his mom and Pops, Demond moved between New York City (Coney Island, and later Bedford-Stuyvesant in Brooklyn) and Virginia Beach, Virginia.

Beginning in fifth grade, Demond was recruited from his public school to attend the Eliot Feld Ballet Tech dance program in Manhattan. That program moved through city schools looking for children with talent, and after auditioning everyone at his school, they picked Demond and four other children. Once he began taking dance classes, Demond found that "all the kids came out of low-income families, so there were lots of [other] kids from Brooklyn. I embraced it. I wasn't insecure about it being a dance school, thinking that it wasn't masculine. I wasn't worried about that as a kid."

With the encouragement of his highly religious mom and stepfather, Demond also began spending two or three hours a day in a local Baptist church in New York. For Demond, that experience was both "like any number of other kinds of 'cultural activities' for kids" and a time of deep commitment. "I was very involved and I was fervently religious until I started to see a lot of contradictions. I was sixteen when I started to move back from the church. I was longing for something. I know it's a good way for kids to learn ethical behavior, though there's other ways to do that, too. Secular ways."

But after Demond had spent elementary school and the first year of junior high in New York City, he and his parents moved to Virginia Beach. There Demond switched from dance to football, which had not even been an option in his poor Brooklyn neighborhood. His high school was now mostly white, and he was one of the only African Americans. He discovered that both the sports and academic programs in Virginia were nothing like those in New York City. "Exactly the opposite. In inner-city high schools they can barely afford books, and the books are all shredded. A lot of the high schools in New York City didn't have football teams, and I wanted to play football." Virginia was also where he developed his taste in music and clothing.

But Pops was facing an uphill struggle to make a living, so after three years his parents returned everyone to New York City, now with Virginia accents. "And when I came back to New York, I hated it because I totally did not fit in. From a place like Virginia Beach, where the beach is five minutes away, the weather's nice, there's grass and trees, and then you go to live in a brownstone in Bedford-Stuyvesant. They're not even comparable. I was really depressed when my parents moved back, and I became really aloof."

He was readmitted to Eliot Feld Ballet school and could by then take his academic courses there as well. With smaller classes than in the regular Brooklyn public schools, he began to really excel academically for the first time. But he was still depressed about the return to New York. With summer money he had earned working on a construction site with Pops in Virginia, Demond had put together a huge and beloved collection of nearly 150 CDs. But Pops was worried about Demond's aloofness and depression, which he attributed to that music. Calling it evil, Pops proceeded to break all but ten of the CDs. By Demond's lights, "You can't do much worse to a sixteen-year-old," so he ran away from home, returned, and ran away yet again.

He did later graduate from high school and was offered a partial scholarship to study at New York University's Tisch School of the Arts. But he was burning out on dance and wanted something more. So he chose to attend Lehman College in the Bronx, where he found he loved being a college student and made the dean's list his first semester. Then he got the bill for the second semester and couldn't pay it. Not knowing whom to talk with about loans or grants, and with nothing available from his family, Demond dropped out and began working.

At first, he modeled for a hip-hop clothing brand, Pure Playaz, and was able to travel with that job to Las Vegas. "I was only eighteen, and I was consumed by it. I met a girl, and that's one of the experiences in my life that I wouldn't trade. I learned a lot from that: how to take care of myself, how to be independent." But being on his own proved harder as time went on. "Modeling wasn't going how I thought it would go. I wanted to go to school," he said, and then repeated, "I wanted to go to school."

He looked into the military and concluded, "Well, I could just join the National Guard. And then that way I can stay home and get the money for school." What could be the downside of that? His recruiter told him, "'No, you won't go to war or anything like that. If the U.S. is invaded, you'll be activated.' So I was all for that." Years later, Demond knew what it meant to be on the other side of an invasion scenario, but at the time, as the recruiter made his pitch in Las Vegas at the end of 2000, it was impossible for Demond—as for so many others—to fully grasp that he could be sent to war. When we talked eight years later it was clear in his words and eyes that he had not forgotten or forgiven the sales pitch that had convinced him to enlist.

After he had signed up for the Guard in Nevada, but before he actually enlisted, Demond requested transfer to the New York National Guard. That way, he figured, he could get back to school and pay all his bills once he was done with his basic training. He was especially eager to take as many courses as he could about U.S. and world history. As he got older, Demond began to notice what was left out and twisted in so many of his high school history classes. "I didn't like the way it was being told, especially as far as African Americans are concerned. Or just the Africans, period."

TRYING TO BE ALL YOU CAN BE

Garett Reppenhagen was a twenty-four-year-old new father when he volunteered, sensing no other reasonable way out of the problems he had: "I was in a rut. I was working three jobs and I couldn't continue to do that. I had to find a way out somehow." When we talked in Colorado Springs in February of 2008, Garett, a tall redhead with a close-cropped beard, conveyed the sincerity and generosity that would probably make him a good teacher someday. Or maybe, Garett might say, that's just how people are who grow up in the mountains of Colorado.

In a sense you could say Garett volunteered for duty the day he was born at the Army's Fort Bliss to a Viet Nam veteran father in June of 1975. Lying across a huge swath of West Texas and eastern New Mexico along the U.S.-Mexican border around El Paso, Fort Bliss itself is easily the size of Rhode Island and, until explosive growth in the 2000s, housed about thirteen thousand troops and their families. It was to become one of the major points from which troops were later to deploy to Iraq and Afghanistan. For Garett's first thirteen years, the only life he and his two brothers knew was on military installations around the United States and in Europe. "I was pretty much daddy's little soldier. I was disciplined. You know, buzz cut, played sports, wasn't allowed a lot of toys, hospital-corner-made beds every morning."

The family moved to Colorado in 1988, but just a few months later his father died of a cancer traceable to his exposure to Agent Orange. Twenty million gallons of that toxic defoliant had been produced by Dow Chemical and Monsanto and sprayed across the South Vietnamese countryside during the war. Garett's father was one of the four hundred thousand exposed U.S. military personnel, and an estimated 4.8 million Vietnamese were victims of the chemical. As a veteran, his dad carried the Viet Nam War in his body until it finally and literally killed him.

After his dad died, things started to go bad for Garett. "Up until that point I was on the football team, getting decent grades. But I felt like I was doing all that because of the authority of my father over me. And once he was gone, I was like, 'Freedom!' I rushed out the door to discover all the things that all the other kids were talking about doing, what this world was that I was missing." He started getting into trouble with the police, hanging around with skater and punk friends, and getting into fights.

"Once I got into sex, drugs, and rock 'n' roll, I looked around and I realized everybody else was just talking about doing it. I was chasing this misconception, and I realized, 'Shit, I'm the only dummy actually doing it.' But by that time I was just tired of school and dropped out and started working." His mother might not have liked what was happening to Garett, but she tried to accept whatever path he wanted to take. "She's always supported me in everything I've done. I always had a place in this house," he said in February 2008, as we looked out his picture window at the foothills of Manitou Springs, just outside Colorado Springs, Colorado. "I always had food to eat. She worked very hard to provide those things for me and my brothers."

But even though it looked like he was headed for a military career, Garett showed little inclination to join any of the armed services after his father died. "I knew what the military life was. I knew what my father had been doing. I didn't want to do that. I think I wanted to be an artist." Yet despite this opposition to enlisting, "I always knew it was there. I knew the benefits." So signing up was always dangling in front of him as a possibility, should the need arise.

When Garett was twenty-four, his daughter Isabelle was born. By the time she emerged into the world, he and his girlfriend had already worn themselves out fighting and decided to split. His responsibilities as a father loomed large, and he realized, "I can't support a daughter—I can barely support *myself* right now." As he looked around for other job options in Colorado and in Kansas, where one of his brothers was living, and failed to find any readily available, the military reemerged as a possibility. "I was familiar with the military lifestyle, at least the garrison lifestyle," he said, "so I was, like, 'I'm going to join the military.' I didn't need a recruiter breathing down my neck and tempting me to join." While it may seem as if benefits for his daughter and a decent salary to support her were central motives for enlisting at this point in his life, Garett insisted, "I never want it to seem like I joined the military and went to war because my daughter was born. Because that's just too much on her, and that's not really the truth," he added, making clear with his manner that when he knew something to be true that was all that counted.

"So I realized that 'Hey, serving my country is at least a way that I can get out of this and still retain some sort of pride and dignity for my decisions. I'll serve my country and I'll get my GI Bill and I'll get out of debt.'" Garett didn't think of his motives for enlisting as particularly patriotic, but he was sure that "I didn't want to rob a bank to get out of debt." And Garett was certainly one of many people, sold massive new amounts of credit in the last two decades, who found a military job a good exit.

George Bush had just come to office, and the Twin Towers still stood in lower Manhattan. Garett figured some peacekeeping missions in the Balkans would not be so bad and knew it was a relatively easy life because he had lived it as a child. He could get GI Bill benefits for his stint, he would not have to pay for housing, and he could put away all his earnings for his new daughter and his college in the future.

His father's military experience in Europe also suggested something even more sophisticated to him. If he could manage to get stationed there, "I thought it'd be camping with the guys in the woods of Europe and, you know, on weekends I'd be off in Paris, drinking wine at some cool café." As it turned out, some of these desires came to be. He explored numerous countries on weekend leaves during the time he was stationed in Vilseck, Germany, for most of 2002, and after that for nine months in Kosovo, before finally being deployed to Kuwait and Iraq in early 2004.

THE FAITH OF AN AVERAGE AMERICAN

Ricky Clousing had a small-town childhood. Born on the Fourth of July, 1982, he grew up in a very close family of six children—five boys and a girl—in Sumner, Washington, a town with a population around 8,500. That "was definitely what shaped me into being who I am. I mean, being from a smaller town, having a big family." There was also a part of his ancestry that intrigued him, and when we talked in Las Vegas in 2008 Ricky said he was trying to find out more about his mother's side of the family, which had some Lakota Sioux links. He knew his father was descended from Dutch immigrants.

Ricky had a soul patch and an easygoing manner. He explained different events in his life in a calm voice, punctuating his points confidently with his hands.

He described his childhood background as "middle-class family living, pretty similar to a lot of average Americans," and what this meant in practice was that his mom waitressed when he was younger and then went to work at a bank, while his stepdad managed a warehouse just outside Seattle. Normal, too, in another way, was Ricky's parents' divorce when he was young. In junior high and high school he was a skateboarder and enjoyed racing BMXs. And he started smoking pot and experimenting with mushrooms. "Well, believe it or not, I was on mushrooms one time and my buddy and I were just talking about the universe and space and everything. There was this crazy situation where I had a deep epiphany about purpose in life. I didn't know anything about God, but from there I started reading into different religions."

A friend of his who had gone to a summer music camp introduced Ricky to his church, and Ricky found a home for his growing spiritual appetite and questions. Looking back on why he joined a Christian Evangelical church, Ricky believed it was simply what had been available to him and that "if I was another person living in a different culture, I

probably would have been a really devout Buddhist or whatever." Over
the next few years Ricky traveled with his church on missionary trips to
Mexico. In particular he enjoyed the travel aspect of this immensely: "It
was great. How many people get to go down to the real Mexico and stay
with families who make you homemade tortillas for breakfast? It was
great."

After high school and a year studying at Green River Community College and loading planes at the Seattle airport, Ricky decided to make
another big change in his life. In August 2001 he enrolled in a six-month
program at a Christian school called the University of the Nations in
Kona, on the big island of Hawai'i. The idea was to do an academic program for three months and then do three months of practical outreach.
He was in Kona on September 11, 2001, and six weeks later he was sent
to Thailand with a group of other students from the Bible school.

"We flew to Thailand in the fall, spent three months there in the
Chiang Mai area, up in the north, working in orphanages. We taught
English in some of the schools, and talked about the Bible and spirituality, and had a workshop with some of the college students there. I
thought it was amazing. It was really one of the most incredible experiences I've ever had. I mean, just being able to witness another culture in
such a personal way and not as a tourist. We stayed in the orphanages.
When we hiked up into villages we had to ride elephants across rivers.
It was straight out like you're talking Indiana Jones to me. We literally
would hike up a hill for an hour and a half and then come up into a
little bamboo village where people were picking berries and threshing
wheat. It was phenomenal. It was amazing to see some of the old Buddhist temples that were thousands of years old." Ricky was in Thailand
until January 2002.

A German friend he'd met at the school in Hawai'i had returned to
Munich, rented a flat, and invited him to come visit. It was a happy coincidence because Ricky's father was in the U.S. military and stationed in
Germany. Ricky had not grown up around his father very much, and although "he wasn't completely absent from my life, he wasn't completely
active either." They had a relationship, but Ricky now saw an opportunity to spend more time together. So he visited his friend in Munich and

stayed awhile with his father. Although he lacked a work permit for a regular job in Germany, his father was able to land him a job on a U.S. Army base.

It was February 2002, and the first waves of U.S. soldiers going to and returning from Afghanistan were pouring through the base. "I talked to all these guys before and after Afghanistan, and I heard their perspective on things. That was the first time I actually contemplated joining the military. I was already trying to figure out what I was going to do, in terms of school and paying for school. Being from a family of six, my mom and stepdad didn't have the means to pay for college." In late June 2002, he went to speak with a recruiter in Germany.

Ricky tossed around several concerns. He wanted to finish college, but he didn't want to go back and jump into a lot of school debt. He also explained to the recruiter that he did not want to be a front-line fighter. Ricky's father was not pushing him to join the military, but he did suggest that if Ricky enlisted he should try to get into intelligence work as Ricky's father himself had done. With all of this, the job of interrogator sounded appealing, so Ricky took the qualification tests, passed, and two weeks later, in July 2002, was on a plane back to the States for his basic training.

Ricky's life had renewed purpose, pride, and excitement: "Not many people get to be trained as an interrogator and learn a foreign language. And meanwhile I would be serving my country and doing something with the patriotism that came with 9/11. I would also have funds for college later. It would be paid for."

A hard part of enlisting, though, was separation from his brothers and sister. So before he deployed Ricky decided to take them symbolically with him in the form of a "VI" tattoo. "I got the Roman numeral six. We've always been very close and they just meant a lot to me." At a family reunion before he left for Iraq, he showed his four brothers and his sister what he had done. Each soon went out and did the same thing. His brothers have their tattoos on the same place on their arm as Ricky; his sister put hers on her ankle, "a bit smaller."

All in all, Ricky saw his decision of entering the military as coming out of his religion and his personality: "My experience and my time in the church made me want to help people even more. I'm definitely a people pleaser. I like to make people happy. So whether I was in Thailand in an orphanage teaching kids English and helping to build roads or I was in Iraq, I wanted to do things—I wanted to do *good* things."

For Ricky and the other five young people, joining the military represented some pragmatism but also no small measure of idealism. Some held substantial hope that they were making their own lives and/or their country's situation better in some important ways. The reality of what would be asked of them would only truly come into view, however, as they entered training for war.

TWO

Training

When the Twin Towers collapsed in a hell of fire and ash, Demond Terrell
Mullins was in Fort Knox, Kentucky, preparing to become a soldier. In
fact, he was "in holding," waiting to begin basic training. "I didn't even
know how to wear a uniform yet. We were being issued gear, but we
didn't know how to wear it because we weren't soldiers yet. We hadn't
even met our drill sergeants." And, he adds, "I was scared shitless."

At first, Demond and the other members of his New York State National Guard unit were told that the New Yorkers among them would
be allowed to go home. But plans changed and they remained in training, with their instructors drilling into them that they were going to war,

and trying to get some of their recruits to move from the Guard into the Regular Army.

After finishing basic, he and his fellow Guard members were sent back to New York City. Since he didn't have to begin full duties for another six months, Demond returned to Brooklyn College for a semester, "trying to use the military benefits, like the GI Bill and things, and tuition assistance. But they had problems with my paperwork and I wound up never getting the GI Bill and never getting tuition assistance or anything." This would be his experience again—and that of many other veterans—when he returned from Iraq.

Demond's unit was activated the following summer. He joined the massive and visible military presence that was to appear on the streets of many U.S. cities, but especially Washington and New York, for months after 9/11. He and his unit did patrols with the city's transit cops. "We were policing all over the city, everywhere. But doing nothing, just standing around, checking people's bags sometimes. I was at Penn Station for a couple of weeks." In teams of two transit cops and one soldier, their job was to observe people in their area. Most of the time the cops and soldiers sat around talking with each other, waiting for something to react to, experiencing the boredom that is a standard part of all military life, even in wartime. While Demond might not have wanted it any other way, he wasn't happy about it. "Nothing ever happened. Nothing ever happened," he repeated and sighed, as if reliving the unbroken boredom.

It went on like that for over a year, essentially punching the National Guard clock to earn money for tuition and other expenses. He continued at Brooklyn College and joined his buddies in the Guard once a month for routine duty. Then, in March of 2004, he was called up for Iraq. "I was teaching a dance class in an elementary school in the Bronx, P.S. 8. And my platoon sergeant called me during the class, and he said, 'I wanted to let you know right away. We're going to Iraq.' And I was like, 'Holy shit!' And I said it loud. And I know the kids heard me say it, but, like, I really tried to quit my job at that moment. After he told me that, and I knew that I only had about four weeks, maybe about a month and a half until I got deployed, so I just wanted to spend the rest of my time spending my money and having fun, because I knew what it was going to be like. I was really afraid. I actually didn't think I was going to make it back home."

His commanders ordered him to report for a Primary Leaders Development Course (PLDC) that trained specialists to become sergeants. Although his test scores put him at the top of his class, Demond was passed over for sergeant in favor of other men with more seniority. "I was really pissed about that. And then in Iraq I was stuck taking orders from guys who didn't even pass this school." As the war wore on, however, and as in most wars, promotion rates throughout the military were to skyrocket, especially in the Army, where, by one officer's assessment, "Basically, if you haven't been court-martialed, you're going to be promoted [from captain] to major."[1]

Despite this setback, in retrospect Demond described himself as going with the flow at that point. He had serious reservations about what people in charge, those in the government and in the military, were saying about Iraq. "I remember things happening along the way. Even in the beginning I didn't support the war politically. Ideologically I didn't support the war." But he found himself in uniform all the same, and scheduled to leave for Iraq in spring 2004.

He laughed when he recounted the scene because, as he pointed out, "I was scared that I was going to war. I signed up to go with the National Guard because I wanted money to go to college."[2] When the orders to deploy came through, "I'm wondering, 'Why the hell did I do it?' I wasn't in the Guard because I loved America so much in my damn bone marrow that I wanted to go out and 'Rah-Rah!' and kill people for America. I wanted to go to damn college, man, and I had no options. Looking back, I now understand that I had very few options."

Nor was dying what Demond feared. "I've never been afraid of death. Death is easy, and I saw that firsthand when I was in Iraq. I was more afraid of wasting my life. That's what I was afraid of. Like if you only get one chance to live and I had just fucked it all over by joining this organization. And now I was going to go fight for something I didn't believe in." And it was not as if he could get support for his deployment from his family. "I started trying to communicate with them before I left, because

I didn't think that I would be making it back home." They drove him to the airport, not talking about how they felt about the war. "I know they weren't proud, because my mom never was, like, promilitary. I wasn't as aware as I should have been," he said, imagining the anxiety his situation undoubtedly caused his family.

LEARNING TO INTERROGATE THE WAR

Off on the Big Island of Hawai'i, preparing to do Christian missionary work on that momentous September day, Ricky Clousing was more outside the whirlwind sweeping up others for a military response to the attacks in New York City. But the violence did play an indirect role in prompting him to join the Army, because after he finished his missionary work in Thailand he ended up in Europe, where he got a job on a U.S. military base in Germany in 2002. There he became inspired to enlist in part through conversations with U.S. soldiers transiting to and from Afghanistan. And it was from these discussions that the idea of joining first germinated. It all happened pretty quickly after he took and passed the tests to be an interrogator. Before he knew it, he was on his way back in the United States for basic training at Fort Jackson, South Carolina.

Motivated by patriotism and the call to serve his country after 9/11, Ricky was also looking forward to learning, as promised, a foreign language, and to receiving funds later for college. All in all, he counted the blessings that came from joining the military. After two months of basic, he was sent to Fort Benning, Georgia, for a monthlong parachute training course at the Airborne School. Then he was sent for what the Army calls Advanced Individual Training (AIT)—in Ricky's case, five months at Fort Huachuca in Arizona, where he learned the arts and military meanings of "interrogation" and "eliciting information" from enemy combatants and the civilian population.

When they started interrogation school, his instructors screened the movie *Spy Game* "to get an idea of the kind of mentality we'd need for the job. They told us to watch and take notes." The movie has many elements they might have watched, as it shows a CIA operative, played by Robert Redford, trying to spy on and interrogate his own colleagues in order to thwart their plans to abandon another CIA agent in the midst of a delicate presidential diplomatic mission to China.

In the first part of the course, soldiers were taught how to talk to subjects brought in for interrogation, how to read their body language, how to direct conversations, and how to ask questions in different "formats" — that is, how to probe the same issue in different ways to verify information and catch people in inconsistencies and lies. The second half of the course was called "collections." In this part, which Ricky thought of as "a pseudo–spy course on how to recruit intelligence," the soldiers were taught how to "recruit sources" to support the military with information, how to analyze whether someone would be a good source, how to maintain people as informants, and more on how to extract information from people.

Ricky described his exposure to the form of torture known as waterboarding.[3] "A lot of the instructors in our course were the first interrogators who had been in Afghanistan questioning guys. They didn't teach us how to waterboard, but we were shown pictures of when our instructors were over there. One of them in particular showed us photos of his time in Afghanistan. You know, with the bags over their heads, and tied up. Nothing like Abu Ghraib, naked pictures, but definitely vulgar photos."[4]

Most Americans at the time, said Ricky, were just bent on "blind retaliation. All they saw is that 'these towelheads are responsible for 9/11, and fuck them!' This was the attitude of a lot of soldiers, too. And it's like a chained dog. A dog builds up all its frustration and anger, and you let him off his chain. And now they're finally in combat with a gun, able to do whatever they want. So we saw pictures, with bags over people's heads, and they were getting waterboarded."[5]

During a field training exercise that had the students practice interrogations for five days in a mock city, the relevance of everything he had been learning became clear. He was in the midst of the exercise, on March 17, 2003, when President George Bush announced that he had just given his forty-eight-hour ultimatum to Saddam Hussein: leave Iraq or else. "I remember feeling a little confused, not sure how we got from 9/11 to Iraq. But I knew I still had many months of school ahead, so I just focused on what my class requirements were."

To Ricky's surprise, he was also able to take classes in a civilian classroom, taking advantage of a partnership between the military at Fort Huachuca and one of the local community colleges. It allowed him to receive college credit for the courses on interrogation, eliciting information, and collection gathering.[6]

Ricky received even more college credits at his next training stop, the U.S. military's Defense Language Institute in Monterey, California. Soldiers spend so much time learning languages there that some even earn associate's degrees. Ricky had studied a lot of Spanish in high school and, even more significantly, had gone for several summers in a row to do missionary work in Mexico. Even so, he was assigned French because he was going to be part of the 82nd Airborne out of Fort Bragg, and the 82nd was responsible for North Africa, where French is spoken in several countries.

French is one of the easier languages to learn and, along with Spanish, German, and Italian, is considered a Category Two language. Category Three includes Russian and other eastern European languages. Category Four languages like Korean, Arabic, and many tribal languages might require fifteen or sixteen months of intensive classes. After five months in the immersion program for French, reading, writing, and speaking French with native speakers for six or seven hours a day, Ricky graduated from Monterey, and in the fall of 2003, after more than fifteen months of training, he shipped out to the 313th Military Intelligence Battalion of the 82nd Airborne Division in Fayetteville, North Carolina. He was assigned to Bravo Company and remained there until he was deployed to the Middle East in the fall of 2004, receiving promotion to specialist just before leaving.

Once a month, Ricky and his fellow GIs participated in airborne training exercises at Fort Bragg. They would link up, manifest, get on the planes, and jump out. Once in the drop zones, they played out scenarios with mock operations through the night. This and other aspects of his training energized Ricky. While he had joined the Army before the war in Iraq, like Demond Mullins and so many other young men and women, he was not just keeping his head down and enduring the stress of getting through various training programs and procedures. He was also proud of the fact that he had become a skilled and competent soldier. He was eager to go to Iraq and apply his training in the service not just of his country but of everyone who wanted to put an end to all the "craziness" happening in Iraq. He had learned intelligence gathering and the more mundane aspects of soldiering like keeping his weapon clean and knowing how to use it when necessary. He was part of a highly disciplined team and felt he had arrived at the right time to be sent to the right place to do good in and for the world.

Most of all, "I really felt like I was on this quest to find out what's going on. When I found out I was deploying, I was actually a little bit excited, like I think a lot of soldiers are, because you train for so long to do a particular job, and then you don't use that skill until you're in a war or sent to a combat zone," he remembered, with some zest. "Fortunately, my skill wasn't just shooting people, so I was excited to talk to people, to interrogate. For once I was going to be able to figure it out." Ricky wanted to be able to formulate his own ideas about the war, and the best way to do that would be to actually be in country and have conversations, even if coerced, with Iraqis.

BREAKING AND MAKING A MARINE

The senior drill instructor looked over the room of recruits and said to the other drill instructors present, "You have 'em," then disappeared. Moments later, the recruits watched as "this huge black guy, about six foot five and 250 pounds, and this little skinny white guy come out. And they start flipping over two-hundred-pound bunk beds like they were pieces of paper. They take big wooden crates with all our stuff in them and just throw them right across the room. They just terrorize us to try to get us used to it. It was a pretty horrifying experience." This was what Chris Magaoay called "the scariest moment of my life," a day in his early training at the Marine boot camp at Parris Island.

Once the site of British plantations, and later during and after the Civil War the home to freed slaves, today Parris Island, near Beaufort, South Carolina, is quarters for thirteen weeks to any man living east of the Mississippi River and every woman from anywhere in the United States who wants to try to become a U.S. Marine. Through instruction in marksmanship, drilling, martial arts, and personal hygiene, Marine boot camp uncovers who among the thousands of men and women who report for duty is good enough to become an "elite warrior," as the Marine Corps would have it. By reputation, basic training for Marines is even more rigorous than for the other services in terms of physical, emotional, and weapons qualifications. It includes "the Crucible," a fifty-four-hour simulated combat exercise—with little food and sleep and forty miles to cover—structured to inculcate teamwork and the ability to endure extreme hardship.

In November 2004, Chris flew out for Parris Island, "the swamp of South Carolina, such a lovely place," he quipped later. At the airport, he and the other recruits got onto a bus at about 1:00 in the morning and drove to Beaumont. He fell asleep right away and awoke to see the sign, "Parris Island Marine Recruit Depot: We Make Marines." They passed through the gate and were driven all around the base in the middle of the night, "so you can't figure out how to escape the place," which was a good idea, he suggested, "because I thought about it later."

The recruits climbed out of the bus in front of some building, and the first thing they saw were the famous yellow footprints that greet all U.S. Marine recruits upon arrival at Parris Island. Someone started screaming at them to stand at attention. "It's the most horrible, horrible feeling. Most people are used to kicking back, nobody yelling at you, nobody hitting you." But the rules, he would learn, were different here.

As Chris recalled, they were told to stand on a yellow line while four points of the Uniform Code of Military Justice were explained: You cannot disrespect an NCO, a noncommissioned officer. You must follow orders. You must not leave the base without authorization. You must train when you are told to; no malingering will be tolerated.

Recruits were processed through Camp Devil Dog, made up to look like a forward operating base so they would get psychologically "adjusted" right away to the idea of combat. "You don't sleep for about three days straight. You just process. It's the phase of breaking you down. Their theory is that if they break you down into a big ball of clay they can re-form you into whatever you need to be." As if to teach the central lessons of military life, the first week at Parris Island did not involve drills but only two things: waiting and getting yelled at.

When you get to Marine boot camp you are told you can wear your wedding ring. You can have two photos of your family. And you can have a Bible. That's it, Chris reported. He brought those things, but they told him to put them away. "They said if they caught me wearing my wedding band they'd cut it off my finger. It was pretty harsh."

As for Marine tough, Chris insisted that despite claims to the contrary the purpose of boot camp was not so much to physically challenge recruits as to teach them discipline and drill, discipline through drills. You stand still at attention for hours on end. You stand in a line and don't do anything. You get ready to eat, then stand and wait. You do march, and swim, and get rifle training. And then you practice standing still some more. Chris did well on his swim qualification—he was from Hawai'i, after all—and was placed in amphibious warfare training.

One combat trainer, Staff Sergeant Rousser, introduced Chris and the other recruits to dead baby jokes. "I never knew they existed. This guy was absolutely nuts. This guy was crazy. He changed morning roll call, when you shout out 'Rah!' or 'Semper Fi!' so we were to scream out, 'Kill babies!'"

Of boot camp generally, Chris said, "At the time, I thought it was the worst thing that could ever happen to me." He especially disliked the physical abuse they meted out. Recruiters had told him, "We do not hit Marines." But when he got to Parris Island he was shown the fine print: a "warning order" from the commandant of the Marine Corps that there would be no hazing in the Corps except for instructional purposes among the recruits. "So they can do whatever they want to you in recruit depot. If they wanted to, they could suspend you upside down by your feet for hours at a time. I've seen them do it. They had one kid try to hang himself by his bootlaces, and the drill instructor just sat there and laughed. Just watched him tie himself up." Luckily, in his panic, the recruit was trying to kill himself by holding the other end of the lace. "So," as Chris ruefully remembered, "it wasn't going to work out."

The drill instructors resorted to almost anything to break down the minds of the recruits. They told Chris that his wife was cheating on him. "I come from a family where nobody messes with you, and I told them, 'Look, you say one more thing about my wife, I'm going to kill you in your sleep.'" He felt justified in threatening the drill instructor "because nobody talks about your wife like that. Nobody should. That's not how you build up camaraderie or loyalty." His drill instructor, however, did not respond well to that. "He tore me apart." He threw Chris around and hit him in the gut with a stick that had "a metal skull like a shifter knob on top of it."

About a month into training, Chris's father had a massive stroke, which by Marine regulations was grounds for an emergency leave. Word from the intensive care unit at the hospital in Hawai'i was that "they weren't planning on him surviving much longer," perhaps two weeks at most. But Chris was denied leave because, he was told, "it wasn't emergency enough." He "requested mast" to talk with his commanding officer regarding his situation. For asking for emergency leave to see his father, Chris was "quarter-decked."

Chris's quarter-decking meant he had to do a series of exercises at superhuman speed: push-ups, crunches, running. He had to do jumping-jacks, spin around, and scream the "Twelfth General Order" — "To walk my post from flank to flank and take no shit from any rank" — until he passed out.[7] When he couldn't move, the instructors kicked him to start again. "They torture you. They don't let you off when you give up." They kept at him until he got second, and third, bursts of energy.

But then he stopped. He announced, "I'm not going to do it." So his drill instructor tied a rope around his waist and lifted him up and dropped him to make it look like he was doing push-ups. "And then," Chris said, "my belt ripped off my trousers – the whole waistline of the trousers which is sewed on ripped right off my body which he had tied it onto. And he [the drill instructor] said, 'Good, the rope gave up. Come here, I'm going to give you flying lessons.'" The next thing Chris knew he was sailing toward an eight-foot-high mirror that shattered when he slammed into it. Chris's shoulders grew stiff as he told this story, making it clear he could still feel the pain of that moment.

Eventually, the senior drill instructor and the chaplain showed up to talk to Chris. They asked about the mirror and were told there had been an accident and Chris was simply assigned to clean up the mess. "I don't even want to know what would have happened if I had said anything to them" about what really happened, Chris said.

While some of the things that Chris's instructors did may seem out of control, much of this is standard operating procedure for the military.[8] It runs its basic training and boot camps this way following decades of experience in producing a mass military, including extensive psychosocial research aimed at creating disciplined, obedient, physically enduring grunts needed to fill the enlisted ranks. Because the military is eager to tap into the bravura posturing of some recruits, exposure to such violence is also intended to push recruits past any resistance they have to actual acts of killing. In his classic book *On Killing,* former Army officer Dave Grossman describes similar military techniques for getting past this resistance and raising what are otherwise low firing rates in combat.

And perhaps the techniques worked even in Chris's case because, despite the outrage he felt at this treatment, after the incident Chris wanted to put it all behind him. He finished boot camp with the others in thirteen weeks and said to himself, "You know what? I'm a Marine now. They were just trying to toughen me up and I finally made it." His father survived too, and now Chris felt he had something—a Marine Corps uniform—that no one could take away from him. Learning about his son's graduation from boot camp and becoming a Marine was, according to Chris, "the only time in my father's life he was ever proud of me."

Chris left Florida, where he had been on leave with his wife, drove her back to Toronto, and headed to Camp Geiger, just south of Camp Lejeune in North Carolina, for combat training. "That was a good time," he thought, though he did have one instructor who told what he saw as sick stories about Afghanistan, about how much fun it was to kill civilians. "He gave us our unofficial Marine Corps motto, 'Kill babies and rape the elderly.' The entire platoon had to scream it at the top of our lungs every morning."

NOT YOUR "TYPICAL JINGOISTIC
MACHOISTIC DUDES"

In August 2001, Garett Reppenhagen signed up for the Army's Delayed
Enlistment Program (sometimes called the Delayed Entry Program),
planning to begin his basic training in October of that year. On September 10, 2001, he packed his truck, planning to move furniture and other
personal belongings from a house he shared with his brother in Wichita,
Kansas, before heading for Cavalry Scout training at Fort Knox, Kentucky. The next morning he turned on the television while he had his
breakfast, and, as he remembers it, started watching some cartoons. A
buddy who had enlisted at the same time as he did called Garett and told
him, "Planes are hitting the Towers. We're under some sort of attack."

With the rest of the world, Garett sat in disbelieving silence watching
his black-and-white TV. "I wasn't sure about anything. I flipped the channels and watched the planes hitting the buildings. Cheerios are dripping
out of my mouth in shock. I just didn't know what to think. I didn't think
we were going to war. Yeah, maybe this is a terrorist attack, but who are
we going to attack? If they're terrorists, it's not like a nation is organized
against us. It's like the Mafia from New York City attacking some building in France and then France going to war with America. I was thinking,
that just doesn't happen." He assumed that the matter would be dealt
with by the CIA and elite military teams from Special Forces.

Trying to figure out what it all meant, and having just sworn an oath
to the military, Garett got in touch with his recruiter. "I wouldn't have
become a Cavalry Scout if I was against going to war," he said, but "going to war for a terrorist attack just seemed too far-fetched." There didn't
seem to actually be a country organized militarily against the United
States. He told the man who had signed his enlistment papers only a
month before, "Look, I am having second thoughts about this whole
thing." The recruiter told Garett that at that point he had no choice, that
he had to report for duty at Fort Knox on schedule in October. He added
that if Garett failed to report he would be considered absent without
leave (AWOL) and in a heap of trouble. In fact, the recruiter lied, as very

commonly happens: the Delayed Entry Program allows you to change your mind, and in 1999, up to a quarter of all those in it did so.[9]

And so Garett reported for duty as ordered. Training in his case combined the normal nine-week basic training with the next stage, Advanced Individual Training, in what the Army calls One-Station Unit Training (OSUT), a special sixteen-week training course for scouts. As for his recruiter, Garett had no resentments: "His name was Staff Sergeant Petty, and once the Iraq War started he joined back up with his old unit, went to Iraq, and was shot in the face guarding a weapons cache. He left a five-year-old son fatherless, so I guess he believed in it. He put his money where his mouth was instead of staying in his cushy recruiter job."

Although he was later to become an accomplished sniper, Garett finished basic training with the lowest score for marksmanship that still allowed a person to pass. His first posting was to Vilseck, Germany, close to the Czech border, in February 2002. In November he was redeployed to Kosovo, where he stayed for twelve months before next heading to Stetten, Germany, in November 2003, to get trained as a sharpshooter at the International Interdiction Course. Throughout his months of training and during his time in western Europe, Garett received continuous indoctrination from commanders and noncommissioned officers (NCOs) about the high purposes of the invasions of Afghanistan and then Iraq. All along, however, he and his fellow cavalry scouts debated the merits of these U.S. military actions.

Because they were all cavalry scouts in a combat arms unit, women were never around on a regular basis. He said he was not sure what it would have been like if they'd had a mixed-gender unit, and while he didn't think any of his buddies would have mistreated a woman, "there's still language, girls are bitches and sluts, and I would tell somebody if he didn't want to do something that he's bitching out." Yet, he insisted, "I wasn't the typical jingoistic macho dude, I didn't ride high on being that kind of person." Garett waved his arms to make clear that he wanted nothing to do with that kind of thinking.

The number one insult that people used was "Yeah, you're a faggot." Garett knew homosexual soldiers. Some he knew were gay because they told him—"I guess they were more comfortable around some of the more open-minded soldiers and they didn't want to hang out with a lot of the regular dudes"—others because when everyone went out to bars in Germany, "they'd definitely go to different bars." But the climate in general included daily put-downs of women and homosexuals.

Like that of every enlisted person in the U.S. military, Garett's training included many such informal but crucial lessons about what a man should be like and how you would be punished if you dared to live your life in any way that challenged that.

ENTERING AN ARMY OF ONE

Charlie Anderson, who enlisted in 1995, hated basic training. From the outset he was angered, like many soldiers, by what he saw as abuses of authority by those ranked higher than he. He connected the small everyday abuses of boot camp with the larger ones of war and the military themselves. And he already engaged in his own protests.

He remembered once trying to lead a cadence, even though the sailors were within earshot of a general. His choice of refrain? Black Sabbath's "War Pigs," which talks about politicians starting wars but never fighting them—that, the lyrics say, gets left to the poor. Charlie remembered that day with pride, though he admitted that this was clearly an act not only of defiance but of minor insubordination as well.

In his spare time during basic training, Charlie read history and philosophy. And just as he had enjoyed tweaking the general on the marching field that day, he also liked to provoke debate "in the face of the Religious Right" who shared the training experience with him. A lot of the people he met in boot camp were devout Christians, and Charlie tried to point out holes in their reasoning from the Bible, though he didn't think he had accomplished very much in the end other than passing the time. And it was not as if he had anything against the Bible himself; in fact, during his years in the military he went through several periods in which he read from the Bible and said prayers every day and attended one or another Christian service as often as he could.

From boot camp, Charlie headed for Navy Hospital Corps training, where he was dismayed to see that the medics-to-be were spoon-fed the information needed to pass their class. "It was a rubber-stamp situation. Unless you really fucked up you were going to pass." Charlie's training included tutoring, in his Petty Officer Indoctrination class, on what were called the "three bedrock principles of Naval leadership." "They were that what you were doing was important, your mission is important, vital to national security; that you will have everything you need to perform your mission; and your family is going to be taken care of. And also, they didn't say this but it was implied, that you are going to be taken care of if it doesn't go well."

Each of these three principles Charlie saw betrayed in Iraq. "If we look at Iraq, that country didn't have WMDs. It was not harboring terrorists. It certainly is today. We didn't have the basic equipment and training and basic skill sets that we needed. News story after news story shows how our families weren't taken care of and we weren't being taken care of. That's betrayal. And then to be told, 'Don't worry about it. Your job is to follow orders. We don't make policy, we enforce it.' It was as though we were absolutely expendable." He was articulating the view that, as veteran and author Stan Goff has said, the military loves soldiers the way Frank Purdue loves chickens.[10] Many were not protected even from each other.

Like Garett, Charlie saw women and gays targeted every day in the military. "People call each other 'Faggot!' Don't be a pussy!' 'What, you got sand in your clit?' 'My bitch grandma runs faster than you, and she's dead!' There's another one about shooting pregnant women: two for one. And about how napalm sticks to kids."

But these experiences could recede behind the indelible Hollywood image of the military. For Charlie and other veterans, movies had been perhaps the most powerful influence working to convince them that they needed to prove themselves in combat. But Charlie was coming to see them in a new light. When we talked in 2008, a new Rambo movie was coming out in the theaters. When Charlie heard that, he thought he was "about to have an aneurysm: 'Rambo Part 76!'" Even when war movies claimed to be more accurate than earlier gung-ho efforts, it all rested on how they were utilized and viewed. "I think *Three Kings* was intended to be antiwar," said Charlie, "but that's not the way it got treated. Just like what happened with *Platoon* and just like *Full Metal Jacket*, which, by the way, Marines almost worship." When he was "on float," stationed on a ship, "you could always tell when we were going into an exercise, because they showed the movie back-to-back-to-back-to-back."

TRAINING FOR THE EMERGENCY

At nineteen years of age, Tina Garnanez reported for basic training at Fort Leonard Wood in Missouri, two months after graduating from high school in Farmington, New Mexico in 2000. Not everyone from her JROTC class in high school went on to enlist in the regular military, but they were all strongly encouraged to do so. One incentive offered to Tina and her fellow cadets was that, on the basis of their experience in ROTC, they would enter the military at a higher rank than other young men and women who had enlisted through normal recruiting channels. In Tina's case that meant enlisting as an E2 while most of the others in her cohort had to start from scratch at E1.[11] After her training, she went to Germany for a year, Kosovo for a year, and then back to Germany. Tina was saving money for college and beginning to enjoy some of the adventures she'd dreamed about back in New Mexico. All in all, it looked as if her plan to put in a few years in the Army was going to work out just fine. She was able to parlay her three years in the JROTC program into the kinds of assignments and training that would satisfy her curiosities and keep her out of harm's way.

But some of the problems she would have became evident immediately when she arrived back in basic training. When drill sergeants yelled at her to shout, "Kill! Kill! Kill!" as she thrust her bayonet at a tire on a rope, Tina said she would yell back, "I don't want to!" Before being deployed to Iraq in 2004, she spent the fall of 2000 getting trained as an emergency medical technician (EMT) at Fort Sam Houston in San Antonio. There, she and the other EMTs were taught basic anatomy and CPR and how to deal with head injuries and other trauma. "All sorts of rigorous and intense medical stuff was thrown at us. We had to learn it all very quickly. A very crash course, nineteen-year-olds sticking each other with needles, learning how to get the IV started.

"A lot of mistakes [were made] when we were doing IVs, practicing, trying to shoot each other in the hands and not getting the veins, and then having to do it again. It was terrifying having to do that to each other. I remember my hand was shaking the first time I had to give an IV. The blood scared me." Most of the two hundred soldiers in her EMT course were women, far more than their one-in-seven numbers in the military overall, which made sense to Tina, as "I really didn't see too many females too excited to go and be mechanics."

While she was stationed as a medic with the 1st Battalion, 44th Air Defense Artillery Regiment in Texas, soldiers came in with "nothing too wild, just little things like headaches and people trying to get out of PT by getting put on sick call." Tina smiled with a knowing grin as she re-called these minor complaints. None of them showed up at clinic with the kinds of injuries, like sucking chest wounds or massive burns, that she would later be expected to treat in Iraq.

How could training, for any of these six people, ever come close to simulating the military and medical arenas they were about to enter? But even before deploying to the kill zones of Baghdad, several of these veterans faced tests in other overseas assignments like Kosovo, where they began to get a taste of what it means to be a member of a foreign occupying army in regular contact with civilian populations.

THREE   First Missions

Three of the soldiers you have met so far went from their training to deployment in the Balkans before they made their way to Iraq. These early missions gave them a comparative advantage when they arrived in the Middle East, for they already had some sense of what a (former) war zone looked like and of what it was like to be a U.S. soldier in action. This was true even if their duties as peacekeepers differed from those they would be given in Iraq. These early missions provided a crucial perspective on every experience they had later in Iraq. The trail of two of the other soldiers, newly trained, led straight to Iraq. Demond Mullins went from patrolling the streets of New York City in September 2004 to Kuwait and on to Iraq for a year. Ricky Clousing left Fort Bragg in the fall of 2004 for Iraq, also passing through Kuwait on the way. We will meet up with them again in the next chapter, after hearing from the other four about their pre-Iraq military missions.

FIRST ENCOUNTERS IN KOSOVO

"I was in my barracks room," Tina remembered, "and my best friend Matt was my neighbor. I'm heading out the door and [I see him] and I asked, 'Hey, what's up, you coming to breakfast?'" Matt told Tina that the World Trade Center towers had been hit. "It just didn't make any sense to me at the time, and I was, 'Oh, all right. Well, I'm going to get some sausage. I'm hungry.'"

She got to her chow hall at Fort Hood in Texas and watched the conflagration on the big-screen television with everyone else. "At first it didn't click, what that meant. Then everything went crazy. Everyone, the commander, everyone's running around all crazy, all the soldiers are running around doing stuff, and I'm like, 'Jesus, that was a big deal!' They started putting up guard duty everywhere and lockdown security and telling us to call our families and get ready for deployment." Much of that day remains a blur for Tina, but she does know she ran around hugging people a lot. The next day the realization that she could be sent to war began to sink in as she was ordered to carry her rifle with her at all times, just as she would later in Iraq.

But instead of being deployed for the front lines of some new war, Tina remained a few more months in Texas and then received her first overseas assignment in Germany. By early 2003, Tina had been sent to Kosovo with the U.S. forces and had stayed a little over a year. As they do for many soldiers, her deployments represented the first time she had ever been outside the United States and been confronted with cultural differences. The people Tina met seemed in some respects rather exotic and at the same time often reminded her of individuals from among her family and friends back home.

In Kosovo, as odd as it might sound, Tina began her first serious study of Native American history. "I was ordering books from Amazon. My deployments were the places where I had the greatest personal growth because I couldn't go anywhere. I couldn't leave the base and go down the street for coffee. I was stuck in my little room. So I bought a lot of books that were mailed to me."

Her motivation for joining the military and working as hard at it as she did was, she said, that "I was always testing myself, wanting to push myself as far as my limits." At least in part that was "striving to be as good as my brothers": the only girl among five boys back home, she endured the constant taunt, "You're a girl, you can't do it." This was only accentuated by being one of just ten women in her unit of four hundred soldiers at Fort Hood. There, Tina said, "I had that mentality of wanting to be as strong or fast enough, and you know, it really bugged me that people had different standards for the guys, and for girls you don't have to do as many push-ups or run as fast."

She became a medic with these same incentives to achieve. But she also saw medical work as a way to deal with her sense that, despite the occupation she had chosen, killing was wrong. "I didn't want to hurt anybody. I wanted to help. I just knew in my heart that I didn't want to do any harm, and I thought, 'Okay, I want to help people. How can I expand on that? Hey! Medics help people!'"

She was in Kosovo in March 2003 when the United States invaded Iraq. Tina remembered watching the U.S. jets and their furious destruction of wide swaths of Baghdad before the ground troops had arrived from Kuwait and thinking, "That was horrible." She did not have to wait for arrival in Iraq to see the effects of such an aerial onslaught. She had seen the lasting results of U.S. bombing of Kosovo a few years earlier: "We bombed the area heavily and they had a civil war. The houses were broken, just falling apart, missing roofs and walls and doors and windows. And people are living in their houses with two or three other families." And when she was there, "there were still bombs, land mines on the side of the road, in fields. It wasn't unusual to hear a farmer talk about going to clear a field for planting, hitting a mine, and losing a leg."

Her contact with Kosovars was limited but rewarding. Outside their post, soldiers mainly just drove through cities in their military vehicles. On base, however, she could get to know some locals, whom she found "friendly and polite." In the translators she found a striking connection to both past and future: "If no one came to the gate with any medical problems I just sat there with the translators. They would talk to me about everything, about their lives growing up, about the history of their people. They would tell me about their family's history, all the way back to Abraham. They were very up to date. Very smart about a lot of things.

We spoke about history and religion. I just loved speaking with the translators because they updated me about things that had been happening
in their country, and why, and what they hoped to see happen there with
their government, and the changes they wanted to make." Not all U.S.
soldiers are like this: sometimes called "barracks rats," or Fobbits, many
can and do spend all their time on U.S. bases with their buddies or in
phone or Internet contact with home, living in touch with the world of
video games, fast food, and English that they came from.

Shortly after the initial invasion of Iraq, while still in Kosovo, Tina
picked up a copy of the U.S. Armed Forces newspaper, *Stars and Stripes*,
with an article on war protests at home, and was happily shocked. "I
loved all the pictures of protesters saying, 'No, we shouldn't be in Iraq.' It
was awesome." Far from feeling angry that U.S. citizens were not showing support for the war and by inference the U.S. troops, Tina realized
suddenly, "'God, I'm not alone in feeling this is wrong and we shouldn't
be there.' Knowing there were people protesting, 'Bring them home!
Bring them home!' gave me so much hope. It was the little light at the
end of the tunnel. It was comforting to me. I didn't think anyone else
was feeling that way. To see the protesters on the streets and angry and
screaming, I was grateful.

"And when I came home to the U.S., it was kind of funny. They would
thank me. Like, 'Thank you for your service.' And I am, 'No, thank *you.*
Thank you for being on the street. Thank you for going to the schools.
Thank you for just saying this is wrong, because I couldn't do it at the
time.'"

GAINING CONFIDENCE

In 2002, Garett Reppenhagen got his orders to deploy to Kosovo. He was
pleased with the posting for several reasons, including that this meant
he was not being sent to Afghanistan. Kosovo was to be a peacekeeping
mission, so not only would he probably have no need to shoot anything,
but even more importantly, from his perspective, "I was proud of what
we were doing in Kosovo. I saw a lot of good things happening." His

recollection of his six months there was that the U.S. forces "were not op-pressing anyone. We were delivering medical supplies and preventing two ethnicities of people from killing each other. We only did that with the threat of arms, the threat of military action and violence." Both at the time and later, he felt it had been a good mission.

Years later, as we sat in his living room with a big picture window looking out on the Colorado Rockies, Garett remembered being assigned guard duties at a wedding between a Kosovar Serb and a Kosovar Alba-nian. Uncles and grandfathers from both sides, he recalled, wanted to prevent the wedding and threatened to stop it. So Garett and his unit set up checkpoints in the town, by the house where the wedding was to take place, and in the muddy fields surrounding it. They were under orders to search everyone approaching the house, and they carried a "wanted list" of people who were to be arrested if caught.

More generally, Garett's task was to police the border between Serbia and Macedonia. Black Hawk helicopters would drop them at the border and they would set up observation posts. He remembered those times fondly as "just camping in the woods. We'd stay out there for a couple of days watching the border trails to see if any smugglers were com-ing across. We got tons of contraband—weapons, ammunition, drugs. We found prostitutes being brought in, like twelve- and thirteen-year-old girls from some country. I was pretty proud, you know? Every night when I went to bed I felt like I was doing a good thing.

"I never had a rock thrown at me in Kosovo," Garett could say by the time he left that country. "A lot of the people in Kosovo wanted us there. They knew why we were there. They remembered the bloodshed, the war, the ethnic cleansing. There were still some Kosovars who didn't want us there. They had their businesses, their Mafia setup, their syndi-cates, their violence and gangs. They were vying for control of certain areas or businesses and we were interfering. Also there were plenty of young people, and it was not very trendy to like the American soldiers, because we were cops, and what kid really likes a cop?

"Morale was generally good. It was still a deployment, and still had the inconveniences of not being home, not having days off, whatever. But we had our little base with our MWR [Morale, Recreation and Welfare], a building where you could go and play pool and watch TV and movies and get on the Internet. It was a small, mile-by-mile square base that we controlled and operated. And I was 215 pounds," he mentioned with a chuckle, now a few pounds lighter and not as bulked up after a few years out of the military and that heavy physical training routine.

Yet the pride in doing a job he saw as righteous and needed—even with all the physical training and game playing in the world—was not enough to keep Garett from being bored a lot of the time. Really bored. To entertain himself, Garett began going to a shooting range on Saturdays and firing off rounds. Though he had been such a poor shot in basic training that he'd almost failed the final marksmanship test, going to the range became the one thing out of his week that he most began to look forward to. At first it was just to occupy himself. Then he began to find his aim and lose his self-doubts. "Going into the military I didn't have a lot of confidence in myself. I was a high school dropout. I thought I was stupid. I thought I was weird. I didn't fit in with the jocks or the other cliques. So when I joined the military and started to learn things like band navigation and driving a Humvee up riverbeds, and rappelling, I was like, 'Wow, you know, I'm improving myself.' I'm doing something that later on I can say, 'Hey, I did all this cool stuff.'"

Going to the shooting range was more of the same, and as the weeks turned into months he steadily improved to the point that when he left Kosovo he was shooting a perfect 40 out of 40, doing two hours of physical training running and working out in the gym each day, and even taking courses in basic English and math at a college level. The courses were taught in a little tent on his base, and his homework was often done while on guard duty. "Late at night we're doing security checkpoint and I'm in the back of the Humvee with a flashlight in my mouth, trying to do math equations." Garett remembered this as the crucial juncture when, as he said, "I was improving my mind and starting to get this confidence, like I was becoming somebody important." Like other young men and women, Garett associated his success in life with success in the military, so that his feelings about becoming a better person were connected to having become a soldier.

In April 2003, his six-month tour of Kosovo was extended by three months because the unit that was to replace his was sent instead to Kuwait. Rumors started flying that his unit, too, was headed for Kuwait and

Iraq in another six months. And sure enough, he soon received a two-week leave to return home to his family in preparation for deployment to Iraq. In many ways, those two weeks back in Colorado Springs were to prove crucial in how Garett viewed his time in Iraq. Whereas before he was deployed to Kosovo he had felt excitement and pride, now more than anything he felt apprehension about being sent off to war in Iraq. "I think that my first gut reaction was, Is this tactically sound?" The rationale for the war at that point was far from clear to him. "I started questioning the whole September 11th—I was trying to get my head around why a terrorist would attack the United States. I thought we were the good guys. We're out there helping people. I didn't understand, so I decided to teach myself. I started asking questions and getting books."

When Garett looked back on his 2003 leave, he found it remarkable that the most memorable part had been his visit to a bookstore. After all, he said with a self-deprecating laugh, "I could hardly read. I was practically illiterate." He was familiar with a used bookstore in town and had gone there in the past for their used CDs. "So I knew the place. I just never really went back into the book sections. . . . So I just said to the lady working there, 'I'm a soldier. I'm going to Iraq and I don't know what I'm getting into. I'm trying to find books about why we'd be attacked by terrorists. How come we're the enemy of so many people now? Can you give me some books that might help me figure this out?' I guess I was looking for history about Iraq, U.S. policy, stuff like that."

She gave him Howard Zinn's *A People's History of the United States* and a book by Noam Chomsky. Another by Kurt Vonnegut. And *Catch-22* by Joseph Heller. "She just said, 'This will help you. You should read it.' She was pretty convincing and a great lady, and I was, like, 'Yeah!'"

That's how Garett ended up carrying a dufflebag full of books back to the Balkans. Though in high school he had barely studied, he had picked up the reading habit through his English and math courses at the tiny base in Kosovo. And the more he read the more he became convinced that the war in Iraq was not being fought for the right reasons. But he was trapped. "I was stuck. I was in the military. I was in the bubble. The military is a closed area, and there is not a lot of outside information coming in. You're reading *Stars and Stripes* and you're watching Armed Forces Network. It's all guaranteed to drive you into a certain mentality."[1]

Not long after he returned to Kosovo in 2003, Garett and his unit received their orders: they had six more months in Europe and then they were going to Iraq. And despite all his reading, "I think why I went is that, by the end of the day, my friends were going. I don't think I would have felt right if I'd been the one guy who didn't go. In a lot of senses it was easier to go. It was the path of least resistance. Sometimes going to war is the path of least resistance." What difference would it make if he agreed with the war or not? "Even if I knew that this war was wrong, I'm still going to end up in Iraq." That said, the more he read, as he learned that there had been no weapons of mass destruction, that Saddam had been caught, and that the United States was still not leaving, the more he wondered, "Why are we going? What's the purpose here?"

He and a buddy began to think about going AWOL. "We had AWOL bags packed with all our possessions that we would need to live in the civilian world. We had these bags and we knew that if any time we wanted to split, we could literally go back to our barracks, take off our uniforms, pick up our AWOL bags, and leave. We'd be off in Europe somewhere. Gone."

Instead, while they were waiting for their specific Iraq assignments, an opportunity arose for Garett. Or, better put, he was offered a new assignment and then had to decide if it was opportunity or lunacy. Eight soldiers were to receive further training as vaunted cavalry scout snipers, and he was the first one asked to join the team. "And I wasn't so sure about it. I had to consult Howard Zinn about that one. So, you know, I was debating it and weighing it, and slowly I saw him asking other people, and them quickly joining, and excited about it, and all these people were my friends, and finally I was like, 'Well, you know, this is a chance. I can learn more skills and better myself. I'll be with my buddies. And do I want some other kid, behind the sight, pulling the trigger on these people, that might not think as rationally as I do? Or do I want the responsibility to do it?' And I debated a lot of different things, but finally I said, 'Yeah. I'll do it.'"

Garett sensed that for him the sniper assignment would become "one of the best parts of my military experience. It was what every GI Joe–loving boy wants to do." All the rereading of Zinn did was make him feel "a little more depressed about making the decision to do all of it." With these mixed emotions, he joined the sniper team at the International Interdiction Course in Stetten, Germany, and got trained in the Alps by a Dutch sniper named Hans. Shooting became ever more a challenge and a game; by the end of the course, he could hit a target the size of a human head at a distance of over 1,500 meters. "I enjoyed shooting, I enjoyed sneaking through the woods. It was fun as training if it were never used practically." That, of course, was impossible, which was why, "when we got to Iraq, I stopped enjoying the sniper business."

In the meantime, he still had a few months left in Europe, and he was determined to make the most of them. After he returned from Kosovo, and while back in Germany again, he and his buddies took off every chance they got, exploring a new country every weekend. They went to Ireland and London, and Garett even dyed his hair green "so they wouldn't think I was a soldier. Every four-day weekend we were, 'What country do you want to go to?' We would just rent cars and drive." Sometimes they didn't even have a destination, but they'd drive and end up in Rome, or Austria, or Switzerland. Prague and Poland. Paris, Denmark, and Norway. Some of the barracks rats resented the fact that they had been sent to Germany and that they were away from their families in the United States. "There was a certain amount of xenophobia, I guess, that goes into prejudice against people. That's why a lot of soldiers didn't leave. They stayed on the base because they were worried because they couldn't speak German. They couldn't speak French. They didn't know how they were going to get along, order food, get a hotel, find their way around towns. We didn't know any of that stuff either, but we were excited to find our way around. It made it even more fun discovering things." Through these travels as well as his reading, Garett said, he was gaining confidence in himself and "developing stories" about himself to explain who he was and what he, as a good man, would do.

ENLISTING AND RE-UPPING

Because Navy corpsmen serve with the Marines and therefore have to be given minimal arms training, from Navy Hospital Corps school Charlie Anderson headed for the Marines' Camp Lejeune. He needed to pick up some basics on how to shoot the enemy, or at least how to throw down protective fire to defend himself and his comrades in a firefight. First rule, shoot three rounds at the individual enemy target. Two bullets should be aimed at "the center mass," that is, the chest, and the other must be directed toward the head.

Perhaps it was precisely because Charlie was so enthusiastic about being in the Hospital Corps and having the opportunities to heal others that this target practice seemed inherently problematic. "I had a little bit of a problem, because I was learning how to kill people up-front and personal." As strange as it might sound to some people, he was certainly not alone, especially with respect to young men and women who had signed up during what they considered to be reliably peaceful times, looking for steady income, college money, and travel and adventure that did not include violence.

So in 1997, two years after joining the Navy, Charlie sat down for the first but by no means the last time to reconsider what kind of a situation he'd gotten himself into. In particular, he thought seriously about applying for conscientious objector (CO) status. He went to the chaplain at Camp Lejeune, assuming that this would be a good person he could talk to about his qualms, which for him were very connected to religious teachings and beliefs. He was disappointed, then, when the chaplain dismissed his questions by informing Charlie that he didn't fit the mold of a CO. Maybe the chaplain was correct, Charlie wondered later, because it didn't take much convincing to get Charlie to drop the subject in public and private.

"The more I thought about it, the more I just decided to go with the flow," Charlie recalled, meaning that for the time being he figured the Navy was as good a place for him to be working as anywhere else. Besides, he was being sent to a shore command and could finish out his time and then be gone. From Camp Lejeune, he was posted to Fort Meade, Maryland, and there he met a woman, fell in love, and got married. Then he came to the end of his contract and had to make another major decision: Should he stay or should he go? Leave the Navy, seek an extension, or just flat-out re-up?[2]

His new wife was in favor of his reenlisting. His mother put a lot of pressure on him to leave. In the end he stayed in the Navy for another stint. "I had my medical officer reenlist me. Right in front of the National Naval Medical Center in Bethesda, Maryland, where there's a stone sculpture of a hospital corpsman. It's very beautiful. He's got a fallen Marine in his lap." The image appealed to what Charlie wanted to be himself—as he put it, a caregiver and nurturer to those in need. The opportunity to heal others was one of the many things that he liked about the Navy, and on a wall in his house in Boone, North Carolina, are plaques and photographs testifying to his dedication to service to others.

Charlie was transferred back to Camp Lejeune, to the 1st Marine Division, in 2000. He saw Marines on sick call, diagnosed them, worked closely with them. One of his first patients at Camp Lejeune this time around was a man who'd just been promoted from lance corporal (E-3) to corporal (E-4), thereby earning him the red stripe that runs up the legs of a Marine's dress blue trousers. By tradition, the stripe gets "pinned" on a man when he is kneed in his thighs until he can no longer walk. "It's an extreme example of how insecure heterosexual men express their camaraderie," was Charlie's analysis. Even though some of his best friendships had been made inside the Marines, he said, "there was this undercurrent of abuse."

Eventually Charlie did get sent to sea for six months, most of which time was taken up with what the Navy calls "Gator Squares," in which the three ships in his readiness group cruised in giant squares through the Mediterranean. "We went to some really great places in Italy, Spain, a really bad port of call in France, and then Malta, which, by the way, is a really beautiful place. Good food, they speak English, beautiful architecture, pretty close to Spain and to Italy. It's great. Where I'd like to retire." Then they ended up off the coast of Croatia for a "dumpex," often the last field exercise of a cruise. It carries this name because "if you haven't used your ammunition and military stores, you have to go on a field exercise to expend down to the bare minimum, what you would need to operate for thirty days under ideal circumstances."

By the end of 2000, Charlie was put ashore with Marines to be stationed in the small town of Slunj, in the mountainous part of Croatia, sent there to train the Croatian army. His commanders negotiated a deal with the mayor of Slunj to allow the Marines to bivouac and train there, and, to ensure that the townspeople would profit from their presence, the agreement required that the Marines spend money in the town when they were not on duty.

But unlike Tina and Garett, Charlie Anderson did not have nearly as positive memories of being a member of the U.S. Armed Forces stationed in southeastern Europe. In fact, he had a series of unpleasant encounters with the locals. Some of those experiences made him question the entire U.S. presence in the region, and others caused him to question which local military forces the United States had chosen as allies—and why.

He remembered one particular incident in town that had left him shaken. It was in May 2001, and he was walking with his buddies through the streets of Slunj. Since the town contained a population of fewer than two thousand people, there were not that many routes to take. Local people were staring at the Marines as they wandered around. They came down one cobblestone street where a little boy was playing with a ball. When it bounced toward him, Charlie picked it up and went to hand it back. But before he could do this, the mother quickly scooped the child up. She crossed the street, put him down on the sidewalk, and began to scold the boy. Then she walked back across the street, snatched the ball from Charlie, wagged her finger in his face, and yelled at him in Croatian.

The Marines went on until they found a bar where they could order pizzas and something to drink. After the meal Charlie went to the bathroom, and his comrades went out to the street to wait for him. As he exited the bathroom and started to leave to join the others, "a man of about forty-five or fifty, six foot, maybe 250 pounds or so, grabs my arm." He was a solid guy with a bit of a gut, wearing an army jacket. His breath smelled of alcohol. "He looks in my face and says, 'American go home!'" Though Charlie pushed the man's hand off his arm, determined to quickly escape and avoid any further confrontation with locals, he still thought to himself, "Actually, that's the smartest thing anybody has said to me in weeks."

When Charlie and the Marines went into town they could see bullet holes in the sides of buildings and burned homes from the recent war. During a campaign to drive the Serbs out, the United States, as part of

NATO, had bombed this area. It had happened so recently that "there was still spent brass and a variety of debris, and of course there were still unexploded land mines." More problematically, Charlie and some of his buddies became aware of the sinister human rights history of the army they were training: the Croatian military had been involved in war crimes in the 1990s and was resisting investigations meant to bring the perpetrators to account.[3]

To the extent that you could guess someone's feelings from how they looked and behaved, Charlie thought people in Slunj were tired of war, of the fighting, and of militaries in general. And they seemed afraid of the Marines.

When Charlie had just gotten back from his deployment in the Mediterranean and was taking an emergency medical technician class at a local community college, someone opened the classroom door and announced that planes had been flown into the World Trade Center and the buildings were on fire. There were also reports that the White House was on fire and that the president was dead.

Like everyone else, Charlie was wondering, "How could this happen? It was more of a shock. I drove home. My wife was three months pregnant and she had the TV on when I got home, and they were showing Palestinians celebrating the attack. And at the time that didn't strike me as strange at all. And as the weeks went by every channel had shows about 9/11; even Animal Planet was showing specials on cadaver dogs. But as I watched I started noticing that the rhetoric coming from my president was the same rhetoric that was coming from Bin Laden. And I was angry. I saw this rhetoric coming out, and I was hearing all about vengeance, how our bombs are going to fall.

"And the major networks started doing these programs, 'America Strikes Back,' 'America at War,' 'America versus Terrorism.' And I'm thinking, what I'm not seeing is 'America Stops and Thinks about Why People Hate Us.'" Charlie felt challenged to think about not only whom the United States had allied itself with in places like Croatia, but who its enemies were and why, as he put it, some people abhorred the United States so much they would celebrate the deaths of three thousand people in the Twin Towers.

For the second time in his Navy career, Charlie began thinking about filing a claim as a conscientious objector. Before long he was actually preparing the forms.

It was 2001, and at that point he had been in the military for six years and was a midlevel NCO. There was much he liked about the military, including the day-to-day tasks he was assigned and the concept of defending democracy. "I liked the idea of keeping my country safe. I liked the idea of being the guy on the watchtower." But he was very ambivalent about specific assignments he and fellow sailors and Marines were expected to carry out, and applying for CO status seemed to him a possible and honorable way to extricate himself from situations he was coming to believe were unjust and immoral. It had become of paramount importance to Charlie to find ways to distinguish the fictions spun out by politicians and military commanders from the realities he had seen on the ground, what rank-and-file troops sometimes call "the ground truth."

In October 2001, a month after 9/11, while he was home on vacation in Toledo, Ohio, Charlie received a telephone call that his leave had been canceled. He was informed that he and his unit needed to get back to North Carolina as soon as possible. This precipitated a crisis. Charlie had to decide whether to go through with his CO claim, which would theoretically prevent his deployment to Iraq, or whether he should once again stifle his doubts and "go with the flow." While he was deciding, he found a Kinko's and got his CO packet photocopied. Later that day, as he sat in a rental car with his wife, she turned to him and asked what he was going to do. Toledo, Ohio, was temptingly close to the Canadian border. He observed calmly to her, "Do you understand that we could be in Canada in forty-five minutes?"

They remained in the rental car a while longer, neither saying a word. "We just sat there and looked at the map a really long time." Then, without any further discussion, his mind made up, Charlie folded up the map and hit the road—heading south to North Carolina and Camp Lejeune. "I seriously thought of going to Canada, but chances are I would not have been able to come back" to the United States. That, for Charlie and many other soldiers, Marines, and sailors, was the clincher. And he did not ultimately file his CO application. But it was about more than not wanting to live in exile for the rest of his life, or the questions he had about being a conscientious objector—whether he was against all war or just the war he saw coming in Afghanistan or elsewhere in the Middle East against the terrorists who had attacked New York City. For Charlie, after so many years in the Navy and a lot of positive experiences together with the negative ones, "It was too painful to tear off all that veneer" of getting justice for the victims of the 9/11 attack. "It was just too much. I couldn't do it. I wanted to, but the hooks were still in me and it was too painful to let them go. Three thousand people had just died. I didn't want vengeance. But I did want justice."

In August 2002, as Charlie remembered it, he started reading up on Iraq. The books he found convinced him that there was no way the United States would actually invade Iraq. But throughout that fall he and his buddies kept hearing rumors of war. It was starting to drive him a little crazy, so Charlie made an effort to stop reading and listening to the news. What good would knowing any more do? And, besides, maybe the talk about war would go away. As 2003 opened, his unit continued receiving very mixed messages. One day they were told by someone who seemed to know what was going on, "You're going." The next day the same person had it on good authority, "No, you're not." Then, again, "Yes, you are," "No way," and on and on.

Charlie remembered living like a regular guy that winter. He played with his daughter in the snow after the New Year as if nothing unusual were about to happen: a normal existence, raising a family and enjoying friends, punching the Navy's clock at work, and trying to save a little money. This was pretty much the life he'd always imagined. Most days the military seemed to be simply a job: at the end of your shift you could leave it and go relax. But then one afternoon in late January, he and five others were told to pack their gear. They were heading for Iraq.

It was hard to break the news to his wife. It was even harder to play with his daughter Abby, because she was just starting to crawl and he knew that that was the last image he could take with him to Iraq. She would surely be walking before he returned. If he returned. His final image before boarding the bus to leave was handing Abby back to his wife. And then that chapter closed, never to reopen.

"I refer to that as the end of my other life. Everything was different from that moment forward." The rest of that night of January 31, he said, "was really immaterial." It was the last day of January, and "They purposefully kept us until two or three in the morning on the first of February. That was a business practice. They didn't want to have to pay us—they didn't want us to leave the United States at the end of January, because if we had, they would have had to have paid us combat pay, imminent danger pay, family separation allowance, and all that stuff. It would have equaled out to about $700 a guy. So they kept us on the tarmac in the cold until the wee hours of the morning, roused everybody up, and put us on an airplane."

OMENS OF WAR

Chris Magaoay, the new Marine from Hawai'i, went on to other Marine bases, including Camp Pendleton in California, where he learned to drive amphibious vehicles (AVs). "I got to run things over," he remembered with pleasure. "I enjoyed that a lot. I got to drive, got to shoot, got to go camping out in the wilderness for two weeks at a time. I don't know if it was being young or naive or the adrenaline rush I got, but driving around in a twenty-six-ton vehicle jumping sand dunes was a lot of fun. I hadn't seen death yet, never seen anyone get shot. It was like a cartoon. Just like in the movies."

Chris wanted to start his military service off in combat and to earn medals. While this came partly out of a desire "to protect my country," his motives, he felt, were more centered on moving forward with and for the Marines: "I loved the Marine Corps. I wanted to go to war more for the adrenaline rush. And it was a personal thing to advance my career." But it seemed to him then, in June 2005, that the war in Iraq was "just a small conflict, like a peacekeeping force." Later, he recognized what he hadn't been seeing on the news: "We didn't see the piles of bodies that they showed in Viet Nam. So it didn't really affect me. I just thought dying didn't happen. Nothing bad was really happening over there."[4]

He then volunteered to be stationed at Twentynine Palms, also in California, where he met a Staff Sergeant Duncan. At first, Duncan frightened Chris with a chest full of ribbons that took up about a quarter of his uniform. Over the course of the next eight or nine months, though, the staff sergeant took Chris under his wing, passing on technical skills like vehicle maintenance and, more importantly, talking to him about personal issues concerning his wife, how Chris should handle his financial debts, and whether he should think about a long-term career in the Marines or cut his losses and get out. Chris saw it as a stroke of fortune that this older man—with the right combination of experience, wisdom, and kindness—came forward to help him think through all sorts of problems, though many people report similar encounters from their time in the U.S. military.

At Twentynine Palms, Chris also met William Abel, a Marine from Georgia who wanted to become an organic farmer and who liked to joke that he'd gotten lost on his way to college. Chris thought that was pretty funny and only later learned that it was a line from *Jarhead*. "He joined the military via the economic draft. Couldn't afford to do anything else with his life." He was the first person to tell Chris about Smedley Butler (1881–1940), a Marine Corps major general and two-time Medal of Honor winner, who famously wrote, after observing the U.S. Marines' role in Central American politics, "War is a racket. It always has been. It is possibly the oldest, easily the most profitable, surely the most vicious. It is the only one international in scope. It is the only one in which the profits are reckoned in dollars and the losses in lives." Chris said, "At first I thought William was crazy for all the things he was saying. But I learned a lot through him. He knew what was going on. That's why he was trying to get out."

William went on "unauthorized absence" to Canada, what the Marines call being UA, but he remained there only a couple of months because he didn't want to stay in Canada forever; he just didn't want to go to war. To ensure that he wouldn't be deployed to Iraq, he first had to work hard to get kicked out of the Marines: it took failing five drug tests and a few trips to Canada to do it. "That's how desperate they were to have people in the Marine Corps." William was one of the large number of first-tour soldiers and Marines who left the military before filling out their labor contract: for the Army, that number was as high as 18 percent in 2005, with the reasons ranging from being physically unable, to announcing one was gay, to showing a "failure to adapt" to military life, to going AWOL.[5]

Chris had similar qualms about going to war, but he describes himself at the time as still highly motivated to be a good Marine. "I thought it was a regular job. Hey, I might want to be an officer one day. I did anything anyone ever asked me to do. They told me to jump off a bridge, I would jump off a bridge." At every juncture he had proved himself as a man and as a Marine. After returning from living in the Philippines to Hawai'i after 9/11, Chris had tried repeatedly to join the Army, then the Navy, the Marines, and finally the Air Force. He couldn't buy his way in. But he'd persisted, even after moving to Canada to get married. His perseverance eventually paid off and he was able to enlist in the Marine Corps.

After his physical and psychological ordeals, his tests of manhood, in boot camp at Parris Island, life in the Corps seemed to smooth out. If you kept your head down and your nose clean it was not such a bad life, he felt, and it certainly was easier than beating the pavement looking for a string of low-paying, dead-end jobs in Hawai'i or Canada. That was until going to Iraq seemed destined to replace his job assignment of repairing engines in the Pendleton motor pool.

Circumstances changed very fast for Chris at the end of 2005, when the rest of his company returned from deployment in Okinawa and they were all told they would be sent to Iraq in September of 2006. This particular unit, before Chris joined it, had already seen a tour of Iraq during the initial invasion, and now "They harassed us, they didn't respect us for what we knew, 'cause, they thought, 'We've been to combat.' They never saw us before. And they pushed us around. There was a lot of yelling and a lot of going home at nine o'clock at night for no reason, just because they wanted us to sweep a piece of concrete that went on for about half a square mile. They wanted us to sweep it all, which is just wonderful. They made us do a lot of stupid things like that." The respect

Chris felt he had finally earned by learning a variety of high-level skills was lost.

And now Chris was to be deployed with them back to Iraq, with responsibilities in Al Anbar province. "And that just shocked me. I had volunteered for the most desolate place in the United States, Twentynine Palms, so that I couldn't get deployed to Iraq. And now you're telling me I'm getting deployed?" If his buddies had qualms about being sent to war, they seldom raised these with Chris. "In the Marine Corps you don't show your actual emotions. You're going to get hazed. You're a tough Marine. I couldn't really tell what anyone else was thinking." The main comment Chris heard from other Marines about going to Iraq was how many "ragheads" each claimed they would kill over there.

And most of them had signed up never thinking they would be sent to war. They figured they would learn and practice a trade they could use after they left the Marines. Chris blames the recruiters for this disconnect between the expectations and realities of military service. "It's called tactical formation of the truth. The way they set themselves up is not lying. They're just not telling you everything. They'll start talking about the chances of you getting shot in Iraq being less than you dying of a DUI. And you're like, 'Okay! Well, that's not too bad!'" They'd make great lawyers, these recruiters, he said, given their ability to "cloud minds and confuse the men and women who join." At the same time, he believed that the men who sat across from the recruiters were duped far more than the women who enlist. Women, he found, "don't just do this on a whim. They are much more informed. And they have something to prove."

After word came through to his unit that they should prepare for deployment to Iraq, Chris and the other Marines in his unit asked their sergeant, who had already toured through Iraq, what it had really been like. "I'll tell you about it tomorrow," the sergeant responded. The next day, "He came back with a photograph of this charred body in the fetal position, still with a little bit of flame, and him bent over, attempting to light a cigarette off this body. It was the most horrible thing I've ever seen. I was in shock. I looked at this man as a leader. I knew his wife. He had always seemed very honorable. But the disgrace he wanted to make out of someone's death was beyond my understanding. I lost all respect for the man and all respect for the mission and all respect for the Marines that were there."

Chris was also told that if an Iraqi gets got close to you and your unit, you should shoot him in the head, drop an AK-47 beside him, and put some metal in a plastic bag and leave it around the body, and the fire team would be covered. You could say, "He was a bomb maker. He's got scrap metal. He was out there collecting, setting up an IED." Chris began to think that the slogan about killing babies and raping the elderly—in other words, authorization and injunction to commit war crimes—was not just an extreme part of training but something Marines might actually be expected to do in combat. "I'm starting to grasp that this is something real, this is something that really happens." There were two Marine Corps: "Staff Sergeant Duncan and everyone else taught me the right thing. And now these people are telling me to do the wrong thing, and they're telling me that they're right and everyone else was wrong." It wasn't that going to war was simply wrong, in Chris's view, but this way was wrong, or at least it raised the question of what was right and wrong about war: "You're not supposed to take pictures in combat. You're a warrior. It's not your job to flaunt around what you do. You fight, you come home, and you forget about the things you've done, 'cause you have to do bad things, and you're not supposed to be proud of the bad things you did. He was obviously proud of the bad things he'd done."

Chris needed some time to think, to work out what was happening, and to make some decisions. In early March, he made a desperate move to get out of predeployment training: "I tried to get my wife to break my leg with a baseball bat." When Rea Rose tried and failed to do this, Chris thought of another way: "There was a barbeque brush down on the ground and I was like, 'Screw this, I can't have you break my leg.' So I stomped down on the brush. It sliced through the cartilage of my heel. I had to go to the hospital to get stitched up." Given his injury, Chris was put on light-duty assignments.

Before long, Chris came to the conclusion that he didn't want to be in a situation where he would be expected to kill civilians or acquiesce to war crimes committed by other troops. "I thought it would be an honorable career to protect and defend the Constitution. That was my thing. I was there to do honorable service. I was an American who didn't just kill for his country but really fights deep down in his heart for his country and won't do anything wrong." "I don't want to be here," he told his wife, adding that he was not even going to train for, much less go and do, something he did not believe in.

"I broke. I lost my belief in everything. I had taken an oath to be a Marine, and no one is going to take that title away from me. I'm proud that I went through the training that many people could never do. I'm proud of the oath I took and that I was ready to give my life up for my country. But the mission they put me on was wrong. I believe I didn't betray the Marine Corps. The Marine Corps betrayed me as a Marine, and betrayed the American people.

"Leaving the Marine Corps wasn't a choice. It was my responsibility not to be involved in any part of it. Guilty by association. Literally. I know what's happening there and I can't keep my mouth shut. As a Marine it's my responsibility to say something about it. So, to be a good Marine, I could not be involved with the war. To be a good person, I could not be involved with the war. I could not be involved with taking people's lives for oil, covering up collateral damage or intentional killing of civilians. I could not. No."

On March 5, 2006, he began a drive across country to Canada. "I said, Forget it. I'm done." Three days later, he arrived with Rea Rose in the town of Fort Erie, Canada. "I used my military ID to cross. I said I was transferring over to the U.S. Embassy." He joined the 24,088 soldiers and roughly 6,700 Marines who, by official figures, deserted from 2001 through 2007.[6]

Meanwhile our other five veterans were doing their best to prepare mentally and physically for what seemed like the inevitable. To different extents, they too were full of doubts about the war, though not yet in a frame of mind where they would refuse deployment to the war. Several had mulled over the possibility of filing for CO status. More than one besides Chris thought seriously about heading across the northern border. Their anguish over what they were doing in the military and the duties they knew they would be called on to perform in combat grew daily. And then, in a matter of hours on a transport plane, they were thrown into the war in the deserts and streets of Iraq.

PART TWO War's Crucible

FOUR

Inside Iraq, on the Outskirts of Reality

While family and friends back home in the United States were walking the dog, cursing the boss, studying for exams, or out looking for work, Charlie, Ricky, Tina, Chris, Demond, and Garett were otherwise occupied. From the moment five of them disembarked in the war zones of Iraq, the normal disappeared and fear became the normal. Suddenly and irreversibly life was 24/7 vigilance about the risk posed by IEDs (improvised explosive devices) and suggested by Iraqi civilians who were peering at them from doorways, unknown and often unfriendly. Now when they heard the word *mission* all they could think of was the muddle that had triumphed over whatever clarity they had arrived with. This muddle and fear were what passed for normal now.

MISSION ACCOMPLISHED

On a refueling stop at a U.S. base in Italy on the way to Iraq, Charlie Anderson got a pre–hero's welcome and a goodie bag from the local wives' club and a photo op with a three-star general, with copies for Charlie and the others to send back to their families. Even on the flight from Italy to Kuwait, "I felt like we were being fattened up for the slaughter. Every half hour or so they came by with something to eat, fruit, jumbo-sized chocolate bars, fresh vegetables," Charlie recalled, shaking his head at what he saw as the absurdity of it.

When they arrived in Kuwait on February 2 after traveling for over twenty-four hours, some of them were disappointed to find no hot meals, showers, or even electricity. They slept on the floor in tents. "It was very austere conditions when we got there," he said, but it wasn't really so bad, in his view, because "I realized this is how a lot of the world lives. In fact it's better than how a lot of the world lives." During the next few weeks in Kuwait, he remembered, "I started becoming more religious. Praying a lot. Reading my Bible. I'd been going to a Lutheran church for two years, back in the U.S., going pretty much every Sunday. I had a *Devotional Field Book* that I had picked up from a chaplain. My pastor had given me this *Daily Devotional Guide* and I was also reading that." Charlie put these in zip-lock bags and kept them in a cargo pocket of his BDUs (battle dress uniform). "I looked at the *Devotional Guide* every day, particularly each night when I would go to sleep. I would go to bed with the prayer of St. Francis, and just about every day I would also read the Apostles Creed."[1]

He had been conflicted about the war before he left for the Middle East. "I had questions, which was not unusual. We were split in the unit. Not everybody went for Bush. We did generally think that they had some kind of WMDs, but we didn't know exactly what that meant. I was very uneasy about going." Not filing for conscientious objector status, and thereby agreeing to go to war, "was one of the hardest decisions I ever made. One of the biggest mistakes I ever made as well. Could I have known? The answer to that changes day to day. Some days I think, 'Well, you know, I did the best with what I had.' Other days I want to torture myself more than others."

Then, on March 19, 2003, President George W. Bush appeared on worldwide television to announce that the invasion of Iraq was under way: "My fellow citizens, at this hour, American and coalition forces are in the early stages of military operations to disarm Iraq, to free its people and to defend the world from grave danger. . . . My fellow citizens, the dangers to our country and the world will be overcome. We will pass through this time of peril and carry on the work of peace. We will defend our freedom. We will bring freedom to others and we will prevail. May God bless our country and all who defend her."[2]

Along with 293,000 U.S. and British troops, Charlie crossed into Iraq with the 2nd Tank Battalion attached to the 5th Regimental Combat Team, attached to the 1st Marine Division. When asked if he was with the first soldiers and Marines to cross the line into Iraq on the 19th of March, he simply responded, "Everyone says that they were the tip of the spear, you know, all open road ahead and a stream of vehicles behind me. Honestly, what difference does it make? Who cares if you were the tip of the damned spear?" He did remember that it had been the day after his mother's birthday, which was the 18th of March. "My mom always said when I asked her what she wanted for her birthday, 'Give me something expensive that I don't need.' So I gave her a war.

"We went from the outskirts of Basra to the outskirts of Nasiriyah, then ran straight up the center of the country to come through what was then Saddam City. Now it's Sadr City, famous for the Al Sadr uprising and where Casey Sheehan [the son of Cindy Sheehan, the peace activist], Mike Mitchell, and well over a hundred other people have been killed. And, again, I was feeling, this whole time, a lot like I was a spectator.

"We weren't taking a whole lot of wounded people. My company only had two, total. The battalion had five killed and a handful of wounded. I wasn't involved in most of that. And I didn't want it to be happening, but if it was happening, I wanted to be involved with it. I still largely do feel like there wasn't a whole lot of a point to my being there—that, you know, I got ripped out of my life, shoved into this place where my day starts by drinking a cup of coffee, getting in the Humvee, we drive somewhere, we have another cup of coffee, we chat for a while, we go somewhere else. Eventually they tell us that we're done for the day, and I pull out my poncho liner and I go to sleep. And that's my day and that's my contribution to the war effort."

In the first days and months after the initial offensive to occupy Iraq, the conditions were tough but morale among the troops was fairly high, especially compared with what was to come in the second year and beyond. At first there was the adrenaline rush of being part of a seemingly unstoppable military force, as well as the still pervasive sentiment that this was a dignified assignment, one that was not only supported by the American people back home but, more importantly, welcomed by the majority of Iraqis in palpable ways every day.

On May 1, 2003, thirty miles off the San Diego coast, George Bush pronounced "Mission Accomplished" aboard the aircraft carrier *USS Abraham Lincoln* and boasted to applause, "Major combat operations in Iraq have ended. In the battle of Iraq, the United States and our allies have prevailed. And now our coalition is engaged in securing and reconstructing that country." As erroneous as that statement would prove only a year later, to many soldiers and Marines in May 2003 the claim that major combat was over seemed plausible, and they intensely wanted to believe that they had accomplished something good. Charlie left Iraq and then Kuwait in late May 2003, some four months after he had arrived there with the Marines. "First in, first out."

WAITING TO GET BLOWN UP

Demond Mullins, the onetime dancer and model from the Bronx and Virginia Beach, laughed as he told a story about speaking to an old girlfriend right before he went to Iraq. "I hadn't talked to her in a few years. She told me she hoped I died in Iraq. I told her, 'I'm really glad you said that. Now I know that I won't die, because there's no way in hell I will die. I will make it back, tooth and nail, I will make it back.'"

He arrived in Kuwait in September of 2004. The next month he moved into Iraq and stayed there for a year. In the second and third years of the Iraq War, the conflict had evolved from an invasion and illusory sense of "mission accomplished" to a violent and always dangerous military occupation. Demond was sent with his New York State National Guard unit to Baghdad, where they began running missions in the city itself and some of the surrounding towns. Before long, "We were going out on missions just to say that we're in the area of operations for fifteen hours, just so we can write that on a piece of paper. Meanwhile we lose a guy for that piece of paper," Demond recounted with an appalled edge to his voice.

From the beginning, the area seemed very hostile, with many people, including twenty-five from his unit, eventually killed in the eleven months he was in Iraq. The sense of being on the defensive in a hopeless situation was overwhelming. "Most of the people were blown up. And because they were blown up, and the way that they were blown up—the way that the bombs are placed—there's really nothing that you can do about it, you know? You're just a target, and if your number's up then your number's up, you know? There were no straightforward kills. There were no 'Oh, my buddy got shot and he died.' It was, 'Ten people got blown up today because they couldn't see the bomb under the road and they just rolled right over it.' The most frustrating thing about it, and I carry that frustration with me now, was just the powerlessness that you feel."

Grumbling about lousy living conditions, bad assignments, and inadequate equipment became constant.[3] And other guys in his unit talked shit about "sand niggers" and "camel jockeys" and "towelheads" and "hajjis" and "dune coons." A favorite was "fucking *hajjis*," and just as *gooks* had been used in Viet Nam to dehumanize the enemy, anyone who was Muslim and Arab was a fair target.[4] But, Demond recounts, "I never heard a black guy say any of those things." For the first few months he thought *hajji* meant something positive. "I thought it was actually a term to describe a devoted male follower of Mohammed. But then I realized that it was kind of a racist thing. That turned me off.

"In my platoon they used to call me Mr. Mullins because I was always lecturing people about shit. Telling them about something I was reading while we were on a mission, in a truck. Like some historical event. Nobody would use language like *sand nigger* in front of me, because I would definitely approach them about it. I actually had a couple of fights when I was in Iraq." In fact, he said he initiated both the fights and both times he beat another soldier, not for anything explicitly racist, but because the other soldier had pulled a prank on him. In other circumstances, he might not have responded violently, but, he said, "I was really belligerent because I felt like I was in jail."

Demond worked out every day—as we talked to him years later in a cafeteria at his university in New York City, he said he still could not get near exercise equipment—and stuffed himself at meals. He chatted on the Internet with a new girlfriend as often as he could. The National Guard had bought a satellite dish from some company, and this allowed the soldiers to get Internet in the trailers they shared, six to a unit. After he came back from a mission he would send his girlfriend an e-mail message or sit and wait on an instant messenger service, hoping she would log on.[5]

His colleagues sometimes asked him to lead dance workshops. When they returned from a mission and didn't have anything to do, "guys were like, 'Yo, you should do a dance class.'" It was evident he was proud that his accomplishments in dance were recognized, but he never felt up to giving lessons. Oddly enough, the more living conditions for the troops improved, the lower morale seemed to fall. In Demond's mind, no amount of improved infrastructure could disguise the fact that the occupation had become a losing proposition.

Some of Demond's buddies got a hold of Michael Moore's antiwar video *Fahrenheit 9/11*. But he refused to watch it. "Why watch that when you're here? So I can be more depressed about what I have to do, you know? I already have trouble performing my duties." He didn't feel like writing about what he was going through as some other soldiers did, or even surfing antiwar Web sites and news sources that provided alternatives to the military environment. "You know you're in prison, but you're in denial, so to have freedom thrown in your face? I couldn't. I couldn't think about what I was doing while I was doing it, or else I wouldn't be able to do it."

At the same time, many of the troops were getting all sorts of books and movies through what some called the University of Barnes & Noble and Amazon. For him and others, the books and Internet connections were a life preserver tossed into the insanity of what they were experiencing each day. The first freedom, in a sense, that they were relying on was freedom of information. Demond read voraciously. And some of what he was reading was feeding his anger and frustration about the war. The best thing that he read during his entire time in Iraq was a speech from another century, and one that a lot of officers might have found seditious: Frederick Douglass's 1852 address, "What to the Slave Is the Fourth of July?"

In it, Douglass said that for the slave, the Fourth of July was "a day that reveals to him, more than all other days in the year, the gross injustice and cruelty to which he is the constant victim. To him, your celebration is a sham; your boasted liberty, an unholy license; your national greatness, swelling vanity; your sound of rejoicing are empty and heartless; your denunciation of tyrants brass fronted impudence; your shout of liberty and equality, hollow mockery; your prayers and hymns, your sermons and thanks-givings, with all your religious parade and solemnity, are to him, mere bombast, fraud, deception, impiety, and hypocrisy—a thin veil to cover up crimes which would disgrace a nation of savages. There is not a nation on the earth guilty of practices more shocking and bloody than are the people of the United States, at this very hour." Demond admired both that Douglass had taught himself to read and, more importantly, that he was standing up and saying, "I don't have anything to celebrate. People my shade don't have anything to celebrate."

For Demond and his fellow soldiers, as for many other generations of soldiers, gallows humor both hinted at and repressed the ugliness of their situation. "One of the common things that you would hear us say, daily, is we'd ask each other—kind of saying that this was prison, 'What are you in for? What crime did you commit that got you here?' Me and a group of my buddies, we would say that God gave us a deal, and the deal was that instead of being punished for eternity in hell for the bad things that we've done, He cut us a deal and gave us a year in Iraq. So we'd made out pretty good."

In 2004 and 2005, when Demond was in Iraq, most of the troops didn't know how much the situation had changed from the initial invasion in March 2003, though many undoubtedly sensed that Iraq was more of a mess when they left than when they had arrived there.

QUEST FOR TRUTH

Although he'd been trained by the military to speak French in preparation for a posting to North Africa with the 82nd Airborne out of Fort Bragg, North Carolina, the exigencies of military life instead sent Ricky Clousing into the furnaces of the Middle East. Despite his disappointment at not being able to utilize his training to full effect, Ricky, at that point twenty-two years old, was still excited about his deployment to Iraq in December 2004. "I kind of wanted to formulate my own idea about what was going on," rather than have to rely on the perceptions of returning soldiers and officers or U.S. journalists.

"The biggest reason I was excited was that finally, for once, I felt like I was going to be able to figure out what was happening. I'd spent a whole year with my unit," the 313th Military Intelligence Battalion, "and I was the only guy that hadn't deployed," Ricky reported, disappointment evident in his face. What was more, Ricky was excited to go to the Middle East and especially Iraq for other reasons. "I mean, it's the cradle of civilization! I really wanted to go to Babylon, but we weren't allowed to."

Earlier that year the Abu Ghraib scandal had broken and was already being framed, not as a war crimes story that implicated the Bush White House and the whole set of political decisions that individuals there made, but as a story either about the personal failings of individual low-level reservists like Lynndie England or about what legal or illegal procedures were used by higher-ups.[6] And later this same year, the related stand-out violence of the Fallujah assaults also took place. Ricky followed the battles (in which 1,874 civilians were killed—one out of every 137 people in the city), which he characterized as "the big race for Fallujah, where all the Marines and insurgents were battling over the city. It was a really intense time."[7]

After arriving in Baghdad, Ricky and his unit were assigned to Highway 8, the "Highway to Hell" running between the airport and downtown, and "the deadliest stretch of road in Iraq, as far as the number of IEDs that were set off there." He worked with a Navy SEAL special operations team for about a month, setting up sniper teams to stop people from planting the roadside bombs.

As a specialist (E-4), soon to be a sergeant (E-5) in military intelligence, before long Ricky was sent into the prisons, where suspects were being sent by the thousands.[8] During his time in Iraq, until he shipped back to the United States in April 2005, his assignment was to question Iraqis who'd been captured and arrested in IED attacks, or attempted IED attacks, in the area. "We were trying to find out where they were placing them, what intervals, what time of the day they were doing it, where they were getting their supplies from, who was in charge. Different areas of Iraq had different cells, different insurgent groups assigned to different towns." Since he was not able to speak Arabic, all his conversations with prisoners would be in English, through interpreters, most often Iraqi Americans working in and with the U.S. military.

The prisoners were kept "maybe five, six, sometimes even ten Iraqis depending on how many are brought in, sitting in a six-foot by eight-foot cell. Sitting on concrete floors, with slippers, no cots or pillows or blankets." And the abuse became more brutal from there, eventually including beatings, waterboarding, and even murder.[9]

Ricky would take prisoners from their cells into a small office area where they did the questioning. "Three chairs, myself, the interpreter, the guy. You'd always situate the detainee on the other side of the room, your back to the door so they can't escape. And there would be guards posted outside the door. I would sit there with my weapon right behind me, talking to the guy, trying to get information out of him: who else is he working with and his cell, what other operations are they planning, where did they get weapons and IEDs from, who's the coordinator, who's financing all this."

But these interrogations provided what Ricky referred to as "a lower level of information from guys that are taken off the street." When they got "high-value targets," within two or three days those individuals would be passed on to OGAs, Other Government Agencies, the euphemism CIA operatives commonly use within the military to identify themselves without identifying themselves. In the early years of the war, the groups involved in prison interrogations included the CIA, Special Forces, and even CIA-sponsored Iraqi paramilitaries, all of whom were working closely together. These agencies, Ricky adds, "would come and steal all the people that were real pertinent." Even for the lower-level prisoners, however, interrogations were not always conducted as conversations. He remembered one tactic that interrogators talked about, though one that he never personally carried out, involved blasting music "like Rob Zombie or Metallica for thirty-six hours straight."[10]

In these detention facilities, he would prepare for the interrogations by reading over reports on the people he was to interview. Those reports were far from documenting a set of people captured from the ranks of criminals, fighters, or terrorists: Ricky quickly came to the conclusion that something was very wrong. "Over 80 percent of the people who were brought in there were released because they were innocent." It seemed the military was "going through the motions" with Iraqis who had done nothing more than getting caught in the wrong place at the wrong time. But there was more to the pattern of arrests than cases of mistaken identities and overzealous or careless sweeps of innocent people. There was neglect that appeared indistinguishable from abuse and harassment.

"I was there after the Abu Ghraib scandal happened. The intelligence community, they really tried to tighten up their methods of interrogation, what was allowed and what was not allowed." But abuses continued. "I never really saw any physical abuse to the detainees, but the problem was that, if troops were out in the city and they were fired upon, Iraqis would, you know, naturally turn and run away in the other direction. Well, these soldiers just rounded up people like this from the streets, brought them in and dropped them off to be interrogated," he said in a sickened tone.

The soldiers thought Iraqis who fled were terrorists and kept many of them longer than the authorized seventy-two hours. Some Iraqis were brought in and imprisoned for weeks. Their families were not notified, and since the prisoners were not allowed to contact anyone on the outside, their relatives would not know if they were dead or alive. "That kind of psychological and emotional harassment was everywhere—in all the detention facilities. There seemed to be a real backlog with people being released—but I knew that the process really only involved the commander signing a piece of paper and releasing them."

Meanwhile he heard detention center commanders report up the chain of command that they had, say, "sixty-seven insurgents in our facility, when in fact maybe five of the people that we had were guilty of anything." And as infamously had happened with body counts in Viet Nam, the large numbers of innocent prisoners in Iraq were facilitating career advancement for officers above Ricky.[11] The detainees became "a number and a bullet in their PowerPoint presentation to show that they were being productive in their area of operation" and to earn them a "pat on the back for doing a good job."

Their vehicles carried a sign in back reading "STAY 100 METERS BACK OR YOU WILL BE SHOT" in English and Arabic, though Ricky still had drivers who got a kick out of "slamming into cars that are on the side of the road, just driving into them, sideswiping cars that are pulled over, and laughing." One time the soldier in the passenger seat of the vehicle he was driving rolled down his window, "breaks out a baton and is smashing some of the windows of cars we're driving past. I'm like, What the hell is going on? They were bored. Combat and war is really like that. It's a club of bullies, it really is."

When he was riding to and from the prisons or out on any interrogation assignment, the men who drove him around sometimes shot randomly at objects on the side of the road: abandoned cars, trash, sometimes even people's animals, "just popping off rounds at some guy's sheep for fun." The truth of the situation seemed to matter little to those in command. "When I was in Iraq," Ricky reports, "I brought up each individual incident that happened to the respective commander," whether it was about the killing innocent civilians or farm animals or the arbitrary detention of prisoners by U.S. troops. "I went to my chief every single time, which was probably ten or fifteen times, and I said I was not okay with certain things, or asked him about certain things. And then I went to the commander, even the colonel, a few times. Probably three times to Lieutenant Colonel Gibson, commander of the 2nd Brigade of the 82nd Airborne."

Getting no satisfaction from reporting breaches of proper military conduct to his superiors, Ricky took matters into his own hands. It was time for bodily protest. On his arm. To complement the "VI" tattoo that he and his five siblings now shared, Ricky decided to get another one on his right forearm, this one to read "Veritas" (in Latin, the truth), protesting the shortage of honesty he was finding in Iraq. "Vos Liberabit" (will set you free), he later added on his left forearm.

SPINNING IN GEAR

It was a toilet, of all things, that provided Garett Reppenhagen with his first dose of the rules on the ground in Iraq. "I remember going to the bathroom for the first time, right after we got there." On the wooden door was written somebody's idea of a joke, "Why do Iraqis smell so bad?" The supposed punch line was "So blind people can hate them too." Garett instantly realized that this graffiti assumed that all its readers hated Iraqis. "It dawned on me that these guys that had been there for a year are starting to really resent the local population." This had not been his experience in Kosovo, and the same people he had been with there began to change: "I was able to see that quickly take foot in our soldiers, who went from peacekeeping missions in Kosovo to a completely degenerating situation in Iraq."

Iraq presented other challenges that Kosovo did not, including death stalker scorpions and camel spiders that Garett had to shake out of his pant legs while on sniper missions. At the same time, compared to most past wars, this one was cushy in other respects: his home barracks included amenities like air conditioning, a perk that certainly helped beat the unbearable temperatures that could climb above 120 degrees in the summer, fast food, and the latest movies from home.

Before deployment, like other soldiers and Marines, Garett Reppenhagen was taught the proper "rules of engagement" (ROE) for Iraq, and he learned about international agreements like the Geneva Conventions that legally bind all militaries in the world in times of war to a universally agreed-upon code of conduct and discipline concerning the treatment of noncombatants and prisoners of war. Garett still had these rules in his mind when in January 2004 he headed for Iraq, boarding a plane in Germany, itself home to sixty-four thousand U.S. troops regularly stationed at 287 U.S. military base sites in that country, bases that had remained there since the German defeat in World War II.

But somewhere between the blizzard swirling around his plane in Germany and the sandstorm that greeted him in Kuwait many of these rules and regulations got blown away. He had been taught not only these specific rules but also the idea that obedience to high codes of conduct in warfare was a distinguishing feature of the U.S. military, a core value that elevated it above other armed forces. If the United States waged war better than other armies, it was not simply because they were militarily stronger or smarter; they were also morally superior, in fact more civilized, or so the troops were repeatedly reminded throughout their recruitment, training, and deployment. As they acclimatized and prepared at Camp Wolverine in Kuwait, where "it was nothing but dead heat and blistering sun," the righteousness of the cause of bringing "freedom" to the Iraqi people was constantly drilled into their heads by officers, chaplains, and television news broadcasts from the States.

Throughout their monthlong training, they practiced kicking in doors and doing house raids, learning how to avoid roadside bombs, and driving escort convoys. And at least as importantly, they absorbed the lesson that their mission was worthy and their methods were noble.

Garett crossed the border into Iraq in February 2004, as the 2–63rd Armor of the 1st Infantry Division made its way to Baqubah in Diyala province, around thirty-five miles northeast of Baghdad. They were headed for Forward Operating Base Scunion, where his unit would be responsible for patrolling a slice-of-pie on the western edge of Baqubah and surrounding towns like Al Khalis, Hibhib, and Al Hadid. This sector butted up against the enormous Camp Anaconda, a twenty-five-square-kilometer base with a twenty-kilometer security perimeter, which eventually contained a twenty-four-hour Burger King, extensive post exchange shopping, a first-run movie house, a mini-golf course, a combat stress clinic, and one of the world's busiest airports.[12]

Although Garett was supposed to get out of the military in October 2004, he was kept in through the controversial procedure called "stop-loss" that forces soldiers to remain in the service past their scheduled separation date; the Army reports that 58,300 soldiers were stop-lossed between 2002 and the spring of 2008.[13] So Garett remained in Iraq from February 2004 until February 2005, stationed in Baqubah.

Before long, Garett discovered that the rules of engagement, and for that matter most of the other rules he'd been taught, were treated with indifference by many of the soldiers who had been in Iraq for a year. So, despite being impressed before arrival in Iraq with the Geneva Conventions, he said, "Once you get into the situation and you're surrounded by people that have been there for a year, that have been dealing with that for a year, those slip away, you know? You're like—you're like just one gear in this huge, churning machine, and you can't not choose to spin, you know? You just spin with the whole thing."[14]

Even in a war zone, or perhaps especially in a war zone, the local economy adjusted and a contraband market emerged that provided the local townspeople with money and the soldiers with diversions. A boy in town sold the soldiers whiskey, porn, hashish, or "whatever the soldiers want. He could identify people's rank, and knew what weapons were. He called M-4s 'M-4 *hajji* killers.' For a 240 Bravo [machine gun], he'd say, '240 Bravo Motherfucker.' He'd call sergeants privates, just to piss them off. But he knew the difference. When sergeants weren't looking, he'd approach a soldier, 'Like whiskey? Hashish?' And you'd say, 'Yeah,' give him five bucks, and he'd run off. He'd come back by and you'd hang out, kind of near the side. When the sergeants weren't around he'd give you your whiskey and run off again. He was a little business maker. The kid was probably twelve years old, making money off soldiers," Garett recounted with clear amazement and not a little admiration.

The troops also had regular access to television and the Internet, which helped relieve the boredom but also gave them access to more information than their commanders might have wanted. Garett and his comrades listened in horror to replays of George Bush speaking before the White House Correspondents' Dinner on March 24, 2004, just weeks after they had arrived in Iraq to seize and destroy Saddam Hussein's "weapons of mass destruction." There weren't any, of course, and they watched the speech as Bush clowned around "looking" for the WMD under the podium, "You know, 'Ha, ha, no weapons of mass destruction, you got me! Too late, we're in Iraq!' At the time, there was a lot of us pissed off. I couldn't believe what I'd seen. I didn't really like the guy at that point, but that pushed it overboard. I was really upset. There were a lot of guys who were," he recounted in half-belief.[15]

They also watched a lot of movies. From their arrival in Kuwait, Garett and other men from his squad began watching movies by the Japanese director Akira Kurosawa. "We watched *Seven Samurai* and loved it. And because we were looking for a name for our sniper team that could go over the radio, and we thought the samurais were cool and there were seven of us. We wanted to be like them. So we became Shogun. I was Shogun One, that was my actual call sign. If I was talking to someone whose call sign was X-Ray in my battalion, which was the Lion battalion, I'd be like, 'Lion X-Ray, this is Shogun One, over.' We kept getting more Kurosawa movies, *Yojimbo, Hidden Fortress, Rashômon.* We decided that when we got out of Iraq, if we lived, that we would reward ourselves by going to Japan on vacation."

Soldiers who had been in Iraq for longer taught Garett and his unit the same rule Ricky had encountered: "Keep AK-47s, or shovels, that you find in raids in your vehicle so if you accidentally kill someone that was innocent, you can throw down a shovel, or the AK-47, on him, and you call him 'an insurgent.' You say he was 'digging for an IED' or 'He had an AK-47,' you know? So this was kind of the world I entered in."

The seriousness with which the U.S. military took truth was suspect in other ways for Garett as well. His superiors reported that certain Iraqis were "elected" to do different jobs, when in reality there had been no election at all. "So that wasn't really democracy. Just put a pretty dress on things like reconstruction so Americans can feel good about what we were doing in Iraq." While the soldiers were taking almost entire towns into custody and creating identification cards for people, their real mission boiled down to just staying alive. Meanwhile, "My gut feeling was that there were people getting rich off this war. I saw Halliburton's stock rising. I talked to soldiers who joined the military to boost up their resume so later they could come back as contractors and go out and kill people later for some real money." Like Demond, he too was bothered as he heard soldiers call the Iraqis "ragheads" and "camel jockeys." And then, he said, "Everything became *hajji* towards the end. It's both derogatory and decent, I guess, though for most soldiers it's just a curse word. But it's an honorary title for some Iraqi people."

Then he went on strike for three days—over ice cream. For three days, every time he went to lunch, "I walked around the ice cream area and the soda area with this sign, asking people not to eat ice cream or drink the soda because there was another convoy coming into our base that had to be escorted by our soldiers that were risking their lives with IEDs. And the money was going to some corporation that was profiting over the war." Some of his fellow soldiers "told me to shut the hell up and, 'I like my soda and ice cream because I'm here in fucking Iraq and it sucks.' Some of them were like, 'You're right!' But even the guys that thought I was right—I saw them later on back at the soda, back at the ice cream. What're you gonna do, you know? People want ice cream, I guess." But it was more than treats from home. "Every bullet that we fire, every bandage that we use, every bean that we eat is money going to somebody." And precision munitions and armored personnel carriers were the big-ticket items.

As the year wore on for Garett, it was both a question of protecting fellow soldiers from unnecessarily risky missions, like the ice cream convoys, and understanding why U.S. soldiers were being killed. "I was like, Why are we sacrificing? Is it really to bring democracy to Iraq? Is there some ulterior motive?" The books he had brought back from Colorado in his duffle—*Confessions of an Economic Hit Man, A People's History of the United States*—were provoking more questions.

Around the time Abu Ghraib was uncovered in the U.S. media, in April 2004, Garett and his buddies began occasionally giving MREs to a little Iraqi boy with bright blue eyes. "This boy's father was a truck driver before the invasion, and his truck was destroyed by an American bomb. So he was out of a job, basically. He lost his truck because of us, and he sees other trucks driving down every day with American money, but not for the Iraqi people. I felt bad for him. He had three kids. The boy would always come up to us—he spoke broken English from school—and we would give the kid an MRE for him to share with his family. The father was always gracious and the kid would thank us.

"After Abu Ghraib was exposed we came back up to the house. The kid ran out, got an MRE, and ran back in the house. Everything was normal. But his father came out with his kid, with his starving kid, and gave back the MRE." Garett picked up the pace of his story. "He said, 'No GI, no GI, no mister, no mister, thank you mister, no mister.' And he gave back the MRE. I was like, Psssh. I think it had to do with Abu Ghraib. Everybody in Iraq knew about it. Everybody. Al Jazeera [the Arabic satellite television network based in Qatar] did stories on it. We got less cooperation after that from people. We had more insurgents willing to fight to the death because they didn't want to get captured. An Iraqi policeman I knew told me why he was upset. It wasn't because of the nudity. It wasn't because of the torture or abuse. He was pissed that we were defiling the Koran. That was the number one thing that really upset him. He said, 'You didn't have to do that to the Koran because the Koran is for everyone. All of us worship the Koran, and it's our life, our beliefs.'"

In the middle of his year in Iraq, Garett began thinking that the American public were buying the war only as long as the media were hiding the news from them that most Iraqis did not support the occupation: "Unfortunately we had to lie to them to get them involved in it." The public was led to sympathize with the Iraqis because they had been abused by Saddam Hussein. But, he wondered, "Why Iraq? There're plenty of dictators out there." With constant talk of weapons of mass destruction and images of mushroom clouds over New York City, he came to believe, the American public was also made to fear for their own safety.

The big picture, according to Garett? "It takes a lot of different people with a lot of goals to go to war."

BEING A WOMAN OUT THERE

Tina Garnanez became very attached to her partner in the ambulance, a man she nicknamed Newt. They masqueraded as husband and wife, even wearing rings, which were useful in keeping at bay a lot of men who tried to hit on Tina. Newt made sure no one messed with her. "He's a big, big boy. I liked that. He took care of me. He spoiled me rotten and I loved it. He got me food and always kept me warm. He made me feel very safe." When someone would start to harass her, she would look around, find her partner, shout out, "'Where's my husband? There's my husband!' And he'd come over."

Newt was different from the other soldiers in many ways, a big reader, and "very smart." Tina was taken by the fact that one of the first things they ever talked about was Jack Kerouac's *Orpheus Emerged.* "We talked about books and after being through really stressful situations together we really bonded, taking care of each other. He was just so much fun. I just really like being around smart people."

One of their main jobs was to transport Iraqi patients from a hospital to the gate where their families would pick them up. They also loaded and unloaded military helicopters that arrived with badly injured people. Sometimes she felt the Iraqi men interfered with her job as an ambulance worker and wouldn't let her lift the injured, though they had no problem when Newt did this. "He was welcome to work and do it, and I was sort of pushed aside." Though she found this annoying, and doubted it had to do with her build—an athletic five foot four—mostly she assumed it was some kind of problem that Iraqi men had interacting with women under these circumstances and she tried not to take it too personally. But Tina also said she didn't really get a chance to spend time with Iraqi women to find out what they might say about relations between men and women in that country.

Tina and Newt talked about the war, and she could cry and talk about her homesickness with him. But even with her big buddy, she was never able to escape the intensity, stress, and rawness of the war. "It was very, very stressful—it was hot, first and foremost. It was over 120 degrees most of the time. So that didn't make things any easier." Tina shook her head remembering the feeling of life in Iraq. "You're far away, you're lonely, you're afraid, you're missing your family, your wife, your kids, your dog. It's uncomfortable, you don't have all the comforts of home— like good food. And you're getting shot at and mortars are coming in, and you have to work. And some of the soldiers you deal with aren't all that nice. Some went crazy. A couple of people that I know couldn't handle all of that. They just didn't do very well with being so far away, and they did crazy things to cope, but it was how they coped."

As important as friendships among the troops in Iraq could be, for many soldiers in Iraq maintaining regular contact with loved ones at home—now possible through e-mail and phone in a way no other soldiers in history have experienced—was even more a lifeline to sanity. For Tina this meant talking to her mother and a girlfriend at home.

"I was in a relationship back home when I was in Iraq, and it helped me, God it helped me. It was my sanity, you know, to get on the phone and call my girlfriend, and be like, 'Hi, how are you? I'm alive.'" Tina's girlfriend was not a soldier, and this led to more stress, because she couldn't even share photos of her with others, except with a few close friends in Iraq. People would wonder, "Why do you have a picture of a girl on your wall?"

So Tina put up a lot of photographs just to confuse everybody. But she would sit in her room and look at the one photo and feel, "Ah, no one can know." To make matters worse, men were hitting on her all the time. While she tried to politely tell them, "No," Tina said, they thought that meant "Yes." No matter how much she wanted to tell them, "You're barking up the wrong tree," she couldn't, and just had to tell them "No" fifty times before they got the message.

Tina discovered a program on Showtime called *The L Word*. "I ordered Season 1 and it came to me when I was in Iraq. It was just so funny, because I had a little tiny DVD player, and I was sitting there surrounded in the tent by all my tent-mates or whatever, and I'm just sitting there watching this lesbian show. And I'm in the Army. And I'm 'Doo, doo, doo, doo, doo . . .' I was laughing to myself, 'Hee, hee, hee.' I thought it was hilarious. I'm like, 'I'm gay, in the Army.'"

Though she took some pleasure in pulling a fast one on the military and its severe allergy to gays and lesbians in the ranks, she was also nervous. "I hadn't come out to my family, and I thought, 'God, how would I explain that? Getting kicked out of the Army for being gay. 'Mom . . . I'm a lesbian.'" Overall in Iraq and elsewhere in the military, Tina found,

"Women were often seen as either promiscuous or lesbians. I just didn't think it was fair that I had to pretend to be straight. It was very uncomfortable for me. At Fort Hood I had two or three lesbian friends. We were all hanging out one day, and I forget how but it came out, and we went, 'We found each other!' We instantly bonded and after that were always hanging out with each other.

"Just being away from home and discovering. It was sort of like college, I guess. You know, your first year away at college. You go get wild and do crazy things. That's what I did. I discovered I am gay. And once I got to Iraq I was on my final leg and I just didn't care. I didn't care anymore about folks assuming I was gay. No one ever asked me, but I just didn't care. I was done hiding it."

Tina was tormented by how U.S. servicemen treated her as a woman, despite the fact that she was a "fellow" soldier. She was also deeply bothered by how these same troops treated Iraqi civilians.

Across the Tigris River from where she was posted early in her time in Iraq, Tina saw the mud huts where poor Iraqis lived, their barefoot children running through the streets, and weary men going to and from work. On her side of the river in Tikrit, U.S. troops were living in Saddam's palaces, jumping into his swimming pools. She remembered the palaces as gorgeous and huge. How could the locals not react to the contrast between their misery and what must have seemed like the U.S. Army soldiers' comforts? "I never had a one-on-one encounter with the Iraqis outside the base. But they certainly weren't welcoming us with open arms." Maybe some of the Iraqis working on the base were grateful for the jobs, she allowed, because their economy was not doing so well.

For a soldier who cared about what the Iraqi civilians thought of the U.S. troops, it could drive you crazy. Even more motive, then, to stay close to the fellow soldiers who did care about you. Tina said she surrounded herself with kind people during her Iraq tour, like the short Filipina woman, a captain, who was one of her best friends. "She was my sanity," remembered Tina with fondness. "She's just a brilliant, brilliant girl."

But even if you worked and bunked with the greatest comrades, you were still stuck in Iraq. "I did not want to be there," Tina reminded us, emphasizing each word as she spoke. "In Kosovo, when I was watching Iraq in the news, it felt like sitting at the edge of a slide. 'Okay, the war is starting.' And then, kaboom, 'Go! Go! Go!' And then I land in Iraq, and I couldn't get out of it. I didn't want to be there. I was against the war. Stuck there. Everyone is." Tina summed up the widespread sentiment of her fellow soldiers: "We're here for the oil. The president and his wonderful buddies up there making all that money while these poor kids are getting sent off to be cannon fodder. This is bullshit!"

She'd signed up for four years in the Army and, like Garett, got "stop-lossed," with no recourse but more of the same. Mosul, Balad, Kirkuk. Convoys. IEDs. Wounded. One-hour catnaps. MREs. Sand. Heat. "My partner got some pills to keep us awake. Then pills for us to sleep. It was just constant pills. I remember getting really sick from taking too many." Tina was not alone. Even official Army surveys found more than one in ten of the troops regularly taking (in 2006) either antidepressants or sleeping pills to cope with the war. This number no doubt far underestimates the scale of medicating going on, given the stigma still associated with being unable to "hack it."[16] Tina went on to describe the strains of working in Iraq: "We would be driving and you don't stop for anything, ever. If you have to pee, pee in a water bottle. I vomited in a grocery bag and had to sit with it between my legs for a whole drive. I didn't want to litter. That was my big thing, I started a whole campaign, 'Keep Iraq Beautiful!'"[17]

A million stories—quite literally—have been told by soldiers about their experiences entering Iraq. Many of them are about the grinding challenges of walking in full, hot battle gear through the desert and even more of the swirl of fear, anger, and sometimes pride associated with doing the work of war that they were assigned. A few have told the stories that Tina did about the sexual assaults and homophobia by their own colleagues.

All these vets' stories begin to give voice to their growing realizations and reservations about the adage that war is hell. That old saying suggests war is a timeless evil that somehow just happens. These soldiers were starting to realize that the hell they were introduced to in Iraq was very much of some humans' making.

FIVE

Face to Face with Iraqi Civilians

MAKING MONSTERS

For most troops, opportunities to interact with Iraqis were rare. Garett Reppenhagen considered himself lucky to have known a few Iraqi soldiers and police. Because he was a cavalry scout sniper, one of his assignments was to train his Iraqi counterparts in how to use various weapons. This gave him a chance to talk to locals and learn about their lives. As we talked years later over breakfast in a coffee shop in downtown Colorado Springs, Garett remembered, "I befriended a police officer named Maqbad, and then another guy named Ali, who were terrific people, and so I got a chance to really talk to them and try to understand them and work with them. We also had work going on in our base where we'd have civilians come in and do building, and we'd have to guard them, and they would take breaks and stuff, and we'd talk to them while they worked."

But mutual respect and cooperation between the armed forces of the United States and whatever Iraqi troops they could cobble together had its limits. "No matter how much I liked them, I was still one of those gears, you know?" There was only so far you could take a friendship with Iraqis who depended on you for their livelihoods and safety, and who knew you would be gone the instant you could return to the United States.

In addition to training Iraqi soldiers and police, Garett had contact with Iraqi civilians at checkpoints. These were well-established inspection sites or more likely "surprise" checkpoints to catch imprudent Iraqi insurgents carrying explosives and ammunition. If drivers and passengers were lucky they simply got waved through and were allowed to continue on. The less fortunate had their vehicle meticulously examined for hours in the hot sun. Language differences and the inability to communicate except through pantomime compounded problems. At checkpoints throughout Iraq, U.S. soldiers have reported deadly shootings of innocent civilians because their car approached too quickly or because the driver didn't stop in time.[1]

One particular night, Garett found himself once again flagging down a quickly approaching vehicle. They were in the town of Al Khalis, around the end of April 2004. There was going to be a search of some houses in the town, and Garett and about fifteen other soldiers were to provide the outer protection cordon. "We set up a hasty checkpoint—we tried to be unpredictable—with our Humvees blocking the road. Two rolls of concertina wire and traffic cones." It was about midnight and there was little traffic. Garett was in front waving cars down to stop them for searches. "And here came a guy probably driving home in the middle of the night, who drove this way all his life. And normally there were no checkpoints in this spot. Until that day.

"And he saw the checkpoint too late. He was coming up too fast. You're thinking there could be a car bomb. You got your heart pumping and your adrenaline flowing because you think you're just going to get bombed," Garett said, his words coming out faster and faster. "You're thinking about the time when somebody didn't fire and he got in trouble for not firing because they said he was endangering his unit. You're thinking about the guy that did fire another time and killed an innocent, but he didn't get in trouble for firing. A few of us in the middle of the road were trying to wave this guy down and he hit the brakes and the car screeched to a stop. My adrenaline was through the roof. So I rushed this guy. I was on the driver's side. I rushed the car door and I tried to open it. I was yelling at the guy in the car, 'Get the fuck out of the car! Get the fuck out of the car!' Only he didn't speak English, so he was not getting out of his car, you know? His hands were in the air and he was trying to explain something.

"I was trying to open the door, but the door was jammed because his car sucked. It was junk. And I was frustrated because you couldn't open the door. I was embarrassed that I was trying to open a door that didn't open. So I just grabbed the guy by the shirt and kind of under his armpit. I pulled him out the window and I threw him on the ground, rolled him over, and I zip-stripped him.[2] And then I realized, out of the corner of my eye, that his wife and kids were staring at me with this intense hatred in their eyes, like, 'My God, what are you doing to my father?' And it was a look of hatred, is what it was. It was this angry look of 'I do not like you. I don't like Americans. I don't like what you're doing and I'll probably never like you.' I just realized I was part of the problem. And I didn't mean to be, and I didn't want to be, but I was there, you know? And that was the crime. The crime was that I was there.

"I felt like if we weren't there in Iraq, my soldiers and myself would not be in danger, so we felt justified to use oppressive and abusive tactics against Iraqis to ensure that we live. We didn't have to be there. That didn't have to be going on. It just really made me question the whole thing. It made me question myself because I always saw myself as doing the right thing, that would take the proper course of action, that thought about ethics and morality. And here I was, the one with my hands on this dude, feeling justified to rip him out of his car and throw him on the ground and put him in handcuffs."

They searched the car and found nothing. Eventually they cut the zip-strips off the man's wrists and let him and his family go.

"It made me feel like an asshole. It was like, 'Here I am, I'm the guy acting like a Nazi.'" But regardless of how he felt, "I still couldn't help but do my job." What he did, said Garett, was go along with other soldiers

kicking detainees into submission: "We usually zipped their hands behind their back, and sometimes we'd zip their feet together. Sometimes
we'd zip the hands locked to the feet locked, and then they were completely immobile. So that was common practice in house raids. Same
thing. We zip-stripped them and threw the bags over the head, put
empty sandbags over the head, and threw them in the truck and carted
them off.

"So, I don't know. Even though I understood and respected the Iraq
people and the culture, I still couldn't help but do my job. Even if I tried
not to, you know? At one point, we stopped a vehicle that we thought
was involved in an ambush, and we pulled all the guys out and put them
on the ground, and one of them was just yelling and screaming and resisting and I was telling him to shut the hell up, because our colonel
was right there, and the colonel was trying to talk to somebody else, and
having a hard time hearing. And I knew that if this guy didn't shut up,
there'd be repercussions against him. So I'm yelling at him, and he's not
listening, he's not listening. And I'm like, What the hell do I got to do
to this guy? And I ended up having to kick him in his ribs to get him to
shut up.

"And, you know, here I was, like, the least likely person to want to
abuse anyone. I just wanted this guy to be quiet. And here I was kicking
a detained, handcuffed Iraqi person. I was like . . . if you could get me to
do these kinds of things, you can get anybody to do it. It doesn't take a
type of person to be out there and to commit atrocities. It's just circumstance. So, I don't know, I always think back to that and I'm amazed. The
ease at which an individual person can have control and power over
another individual human."

In Garett's view, the problem was not that nasty people go to war in-
tent on doing nasty things but that war, or this war in any case, produced
abuses and atrocities. This crucial distinction allowed him to understand
how good men do bad things and how impossible situations require
changing the whole context, not improving the training of the person in
that impossible situation.

Discomfort at the treatment of civilians by U.S. troops began to develop into Garett's private agony, and it eventually became unbearable.

Still, as long as he was in Iraq, he hesitated to raise his concerns with his superiors or with the lifers and die-hards in his unit. The contradiction between saying you were in Iraq to free the population from a tyrant and the reality of flagrant and widespread mistreatment of Iraqi civilians by the U.S. Armed Forces pounded at him every day. He saw the tacit nods from commanders who promised immunity from prosecution in all but a tiny number of sensational cases like Abu Ghraib and the later massacre at Haditha.[3]

Private contractor Blackwater, whose employees killed seventeen civilians in a fifteen-minute barrage of unreturned gunfire at Baghdad's Diyala Square, continued to make millions in new government contracts to ply their trade in the country.[4] They also enjoyed immunity from Iraqi prosecution because, before the handover of sovereignty, the United States imposed "Order 17" on Iraq, allowing U.S. private contractors to escape prosecution by any branch of the Iraqi legal system. As a result, neither Blackwater (now renamed Xe) nor any other private security contractors have ever been prosecuted for crimes they have committed in Iraq, up to and including multiple murders.[5]

But to the extent that soldiers were bothered by such contradictions, Garett believed, this only made matters worse: "I think a lot of guys recognized it maybe subconsciously, you know? But they never understood why the situation was the way it was, and it only—it only made matters worse, because they understood that they were doing the wrong thing, and so they started to loathe themselves. But instead of changing to make it better, they changed for the worse. They just kind of adopted that way of doing things and dove into it and just became monsters," he said, his voice trailing off.

FINDING A NEW CONSCIENCE

Like the others, Tina Garnanez had some basic preconceptions quickly dispelled after she arrived in Iraq. The idea that the U.S. troops would be met with open arms and greeted as liberators was short-lived. "In

America in general people had this image, 'Yeah! America liberated the Iraqis! They're free now!' American soldiers and civilians thought that we did this great service by invading Iraq. 'We did a wonderful thing. Women have rights now! We liberated them!' But it wasn't like that at all. The image that they were super grateful and happy and, 'Oh, thank you, American, for saving us.' But it wasn't that way." Before she even arrived in Iraq, Tina had the attitude, "We shouldn't have been there. We weren't welcome."

Tina recalled when we spoke in her sunny kitchen in Santa Fe, New Mexico, "We had a couple work with us on base. It felt really bad, you have to guard them. You have your weapon in your arms and you're guarding them as they're working. And then at lunch they all sit down and they invite you to come sit in their circle and share food with them."

Despite her desire to see the Iraqis who worked on base "just as they are, as people, and to talk with them," she found herself both influenced by and going against the tide of anti-Iraqi sentiments among the U.S. soldiers she lived and worked alongside. "I'd always get swayed by the other troops who always insisted on keeping their weapons ready. That would freak me out. Should I have been afraid? Was I supposed to be afraid of them? I didn't feel like I should. They were just people. But then I'd get confused and not so open."

That was why, when the Iraqi workers offered Tina food, she said, "I'd want to take it. I was, like, 'I've never had that. I'll try it!' But then I'd always have a soldier come up and I would be, 'I don't know. It could be poisoned . . .' Then I would sit there thinking, 'Well, they're eating it. Why would they eat their own poisoned food?' I was very go-with-the-flow," she said matter-of-factly. And she gradually came to realize that these same Iraqis who were working on U.S. military bases were putting themselves at great risk. "It was a common fear among these Iraqis who worked on base that if someone knew you were working with the Americans something could happen to your family."

Tina's grueling guard work was the result of the calculation by commanders who felt it wiser not to run the risk that one of the civilians was an insurgent infiltrator. Tina didn't know any Arabic, but she found ways to communicate, with a lot of pantomiming and hand gestures. "I liked the older men, the wise ones. I would just sit there and think, Wow, he looks like my grandpa."

Already in Kosovo, before she had set foot in Iraq, Tina had grave qualms about what the U.S. military was doing to Iraqi civilians. One night in Kosovo she sat in a hospital ward on her shift and watched images on television of the bombing of Baghdad. "I watched that city get destroyed, and I just sat there crying to myself, thinking, Dear God, all those poor innocent victims, all those grandmothers, all those children. This war is not just warriors that get killed. Innocent bystanders and suicide bombs and IEDs and things like that. I just thought it was so sick. I get so caught up in that. I sit there and think, 'We went in there to get weapons of mass destruction, there were none. Okay, we're going to get Saddam, we got him. So why are we still there? They don't want a new government, it's not going to last very long once we leave anyway.'

"And what they've been doing has been happening for well over a thousand years, and we're just meddling in someone else's business. I just couldn't see them as the enemy. It was not just the warriors getting killed from U.S. bombs, either."

These ideas mirror those of the U.S. media, where historically inaccurate views of Iraq and the Middle East as awash in thousand-year-old "ancient tribal hatreds" are common. Therefore the conflict being observed was the fault of the Iraqis alone, and, she feared, any attempt by the U.S. military to "meddle" in Iraqi business was doomed to failure.

In another way, Tina felt not hopeless but anxious about the potential that she would do harm to locals. Even if she believed that Iraqi culture was somehow more warlike, she could not bring herself to see Iraqis as the enemy. "Even if I shot at someone and missed, that stray bullet could kill a child, it could sever the leg of some woman walking down the road."

She could not bear the idea of that kind of accident weighing on her conscience when she returned home. "They're people, men and women with hearts. They know love. They know affection. They know happiness. They're people. They weren't some boogeyman in the middle of the night. They have lives and they've got families." Tina was a woman who, she said later, had always held pacifist beliefs but was only now discovering the words to describe her opposition to warfare.

Recognition of the shared circumstances and humanity of Iraqi civilians and the abuse of them by U.S. troops contributed in infinite ways to disintegrate the warrior spirit for Tina and for other American men and women who had been sent to defeat the enemy in Iraq and now found themselves not only at war within Iraq but expected to wage war on the civilian population at large. So it was no accident that Tina, like other soldiers, rarely felt good about her participation in the invasion and occupation and that she sought solace wherever she could, even in the smallest encounters with Iraqi civilians.

She remembered most of all the shared humanity some Iraqis showed her, such as "the way some of the locals were kind to me. They'd smile and be like, 'Hi!' if I went to the restroom and one of them was cleaning it. I was always very friendly, very civil," Tina recounted cheerfully. "Because they were another person on the planet. It was the little moments like that when, despite everything outside of the restroom, the war, two people, another woman and I smiled at each other and had a connection as people. It wasn't anything big. Just little, tiny moments like that that made me see things the way they are, and as they should be."

"HEY, MISTER, MISTER! LOOK!"

Sometimes contact with civilians could save American lives.

After running missions in one particular town for a couple of months, soldiers sometimes came to recognize children in the area. Often they would build up a rapport with them, especially if the soldiers made a regular habit of handing out candy. Demond Mullins remembered some of them running alongside his vehicle shouting, "Mister, Mister, Mister! Chakalaka?!" So he'd throw out bars of chocolate or potato chips or whatever the U.S. soldiers had. And the kids asked for money, too.

"As a matter of fact," Demond said, "giving kids money saved our life one time." They were escorting two large fuel trucks into a town. The assignment was to accompany the trucks in and then cordon off a surrounding area out to a perimeter of a couple hundred meters. The soldiers had to make sure no one could get close enough to blow up the trucks.

The fuel trucks were brought there to distribute their cargo to the Iraqis. As they passed out the fuel, two platoons of soldiers mounted guard, and another platoon patrolled the area watching for anything suspicious. On the route into town, the vehicles had to cross a small bridge. While Demond and his fellow soldiers cleared the bridge, a small boy, maybe seven or eight years old, ran up holding a small fin from a rocket. "We had an incentive for the kids: show us anything that has to do with bombs or anything like that and we'll give you some money. We gave them a dollar." All the children in the neighborhood knew about this deal.

So the boy came running to the platoon sergeant with the fin of the rocket, shouting, "Hey, Mister, Mister! Look!"

The sergeant either didn't see what the boy held or didn't understand its significance, so he pushed him aside. Then he paused, reconsidered, decided to hand the boy a dollar. It was as if he was thinking to himself, "Well, even if this fin is useless, just for your integrity, I am going to give you something." In response to getting the money, Demond related, the boy did the math and realized if he earned a dollar just for a stray rocket fin, "I wonder what he's going to give me for *this*." And so the child showed the sergeant a couple of tank rounds that were strapped together as a bomb. It was an IED that had been placed on the bridge that the platoon would have crossed over to return to base. If someone had detonated this bomb under one of the fuel trucks, that would have blown up the next fuel truck and in turn the entire convoy. "So that pretty much saved our life."

And for that child, it was just another day at work in a war zone.

Then again, most of the contact that Demond observed between Iraqi civilians and U.S. personnel was not in any way positive. "I definitely had my share of witnessing just egregious things happening to civilians, by accident and on purpose. Casualties inflicted by U.S. troops. The ones that troubled me the most were the ones inflicted by my buddies.

"I was out there chasing vehicles one time and a kid just shot through the checkpoint and then got out of his car and started running into a building. A guy in my unit shot the kid in the back before he got to the house. And he's like, 'If the kid gets to the house he can have anything in there, and then we're shit out of luck.' Later there was an after-action review, we got debriefed, and we were told the kid was only fourteen. But honestly, at first I was just like, 'Shit, goes with the territory.'"

When roadside bombs went off, Demond said, try as you might to figure out who did it, that was mostly impossible. "We wound up arresting people who had absolutely nothing to do with it, but they knew who did. The guys who were blowing us up were like the warriors, and they were supported by the people in these neighborhoods. We were getting absolutely no help. The worst thing that was happening in Iraq was that the civilian community could not be coerced into joining the side of the occupiers." Then, when the insurgency took off, "Everybody was a 'Tango,' everybody was a target. When the sectarian violence first started, I was in Iraq, that's when they started blowing each other up. And the other U.S. soldiers would be, 'Well, at least no Americans got hurt.' But I'm like, 'Yeah, but you got women and children and old men blown to pieces for nothing.'" As the insurgency grew, Demond recalled, "In my group of friends we developed a lot of respect for Iraqis. A lot of respect for them. Because in a combat patrol we had four Humvees with at least two 50-caliber machine guns, 240 Bravos [machine guns], and at least sixteen personnel, all with M-4s or M-249s. We got armor and all this stuff. Then you get ambushed by a group of Iraqi insurgents who have a bomb, a makeshift bomb. I mean they put it on the side of the road. Maybe they have an RPK and a couple of AK-47s. And they're willing to go head to head. You got to respect it. You got to respect it."[6]

THREATS TO FREEDOM

As will be remembered, after wavering about filing for conscientious objector status before deploying to Iraq, Charlie Anderson decided to "go with the flow" and quietly shelved the CO papers he had filled out and copied at Kinko's. He was sent to Kosovo, sort of a war zone, or at least the aftermath of one, and he found plenty not to like in this tour, including popular resentment of the U.S. military presence in the Balkans. But Charlie soldiered on and kept going with the flow, even if it was pulling him now toward Baghdad. Even so, at least to himself, Charlie continued to question the advisability, efficacy, and morality of sending U.S. troops abroad.

Shuddering a little as we spoke, he remembered thinking about 9/11 as he landed in Iraq. "Most of us did not see firsthand the carnage of September 11th. We saw it on the news. We saw it on TV. But it wasn't among us." In Iraq, they did see butchery and violent explosions in all sorts of personal and immediate ways. "In Iraq, the occupation is there. In Iraq, civilians see the soldiers walking down the streets every day. They see them kicking in the doors." Said Charlie, "They might even be kicking in yours."

You couldn't tell who was a friendly Iraqi and who was the enemy. This was "a war in which the enemy is seldom seen, in which the person working on your base during the day may be the guerilla who's attacking you at night." This was a war that caused U.S. soldiers to do things they would never do at home, "holding a weapon on children, or separating children from the parents, or kicking down a door and waking a family in the middle of the night, throwing a bag on somebody's head and marching them out in the presence of their family."

He remembered one humiliating incident early on when he accidentally hit a small child. "We were on a road march back to Kuwait. We had stopped and were supposed to have security set. I was eating an MRE real quick. We only had ten minutes. I was just finishing up when I heard this really strange grunting noise, so I looked to my left and there was somebody standing there. I unholstered my pistol and I swung it as I was stepping back. I smacked a kid in the head. And I realized just as I hit him and drew down on him that it was a small child. He's rubbing his face." Charlie then realized the boy was hungry and trying to get some of his MRE.

While this kind of episode caused many men like Charlie Anderson to question the war effort, others reacted differently. Most soldiers and Marines were convinced that the U.S. military would invariably prevail in warfare, especially with an ill-equipped enemy that lacked a coherent command structure. In what has been called a "technocentric" military, the assumption is that bigger and better weapons invariably make for quicker and more decisive war fighting. So Charlie and his buddies remained secure in the superiority of their arms and organization, even when they witnessed the Iraqi resistance and insurgency grow. Not for the first time, a militarized masculinity helped to explain away what should have been obvious to everyone. When neighborhoods and whole cities like Fallujah proved difficult to bring under U.S. military control, there were always U.S. troops who concluded that this just proved Iraqis didn't know how to be free. Like the public at large in the United States, they also ignored every public opinion survey among Iraqis that showed widespread opposition to the U.S. occupation and the desire for the U.S. military to withdraw from their country. These U.S. troops were amazed that not all Iraqis were entirely grateful for their help.

Charlie found it increasingly difficult to go with the flow. He felt "kind of schizophrenic": he wanted to believe in the mission and the idea that U.S. troops were there to help the Iraqi people, but at the same time he experienced a gnawing distrust because there was so much risk all around him. At one point, he encountered thousands of Iraqi refugees walking along the road, without water. He and some of his buddies approached, trying to offer them water that they had decanted into the plastic sleeves that packaged their MREs. In a halting voice, Charlie continued, "I saw this guy walking, and he's got his kid sleeping on his shoulder. He's plodding along. I approached him and he put his hand up to stop me. I said, 'No, no, no. Water.' And he still kind of waves me off, and we're doing this dance almost. I point to his kid and he just stared at me and in broken English said, 'You done enough.' He turned and I could see that she had a huge shrapnel wound in her head. Obviously she was dead. She's not sleeping.

"I was just so upset. You know, my kid is about the same size. And I can't imagine. . . . We're here to help these people. Whatever that means. It was the first time I started to think that 'help' is defined by the person that receives it, not the person that gives it. I went to pull out my Bible and I just sat there and looked at the cover for a while and then I just tossed it. I didn't want to read my Bible. This was the moment I decided that if the Judeo-Christian God that the chaplains had been talking about since we got there, if that God existed, he had a hell of a lot more to answer for than George Bush ever did. That kid didn't do anything. That kid wasn't a threat to freedom."

IDENTIFYING THE TERRORISTS

The U.S. troops who had been there from the initial invasion were received much differently by the Iraqis, but by the time Ricky Clousing arrived in the country at the end of 2004, well over a year into the occupation, Ricky recalled, "I think the Iraqis started to realize, 'This isn't right.' Talking to Iraqis, I mean that's what I did all day every day for the whole time I was there. So when I'm talking to Iraqis at this point they're telling me that they had been detained because they'd been in the wrong place at the wrong time. At first they thought it was great that the Americans were coming, they were hoping for the best, that Saddam would leave. After a year of lack of accountability and abuses, that's when people started building this resentment, and then resentment grew into resistance, and then resistance grew into just not tolerating things, and from there to sacrificing your life to blowing up this or that or driving your vehicle into a U.S. convoy, or whatever."

"I talked to Iraqis who told me that 'we didn't hate you when you first came here.'" Unfortunately, although he tried talking with buddies in his unit about the problems he saw in Baghdad, Ricky found that "the guys in the rest of my unit didn't really want to talk about it, they weren't really open." But he continued to try to understand what was happening by talking to both Americans and Iraqis—anyone who could shed light on the war.

Several encounters with civilians stood out in his memory.

Talking one morning in his apartment in Las Vegas in the winter of 2008, he told the story of four brothers, ranging in age from twelve to twenty-three, whom he had to question after they were arrested and thrown into the U.S. military prison compound where he worked as an interrogator. "A lot of the insurgents fled Fallujah after the Marines bombed the city with white phosphorus.[7] This was around November 2004. The big fight for Fallujah. So a lot of the insurgents fled to Mosul, and we were sent there to do interrogations. These four brothers were walking in their neighborhood in Mosul, and shots were fired from one side of the street. The four brothers ran inside this old building.

"Later they told me they were walking home, two of the younger ones were coming from school, and the older ones from the store. I can't even tell you how many situations where this was people's story. Of course, especially kids are going to run in the opposite direction of gunshots. So these kids took cover inside a building. U.S. soldiers chased them down, didn't find any weapons, didn't find any ammunition, and didn't find any reason to suspect that the brothers were the ones who'd fired at them. Sometimes there was even celebratory fire, because Iraqis at weddings and stuff like to fire their AKs up in the sky, so soldiers might think they've been fired at and arrest somebody. So what happened to these brothers is that they got arrested and then dropped off at our facility. We were told they had been shooting at a U.S. convoy and that they were insurgents and we needed to find out more. They were in our facility for over three weeks."

There was another interrogator Ricky had to work with, "really on a power trip, really egotistical, wanting to throw his weight around all the time. My tactic wasn't screaming at people. I didn't need to yell and freak out and kick tables. I thought that I could get information out of people in a calm, collected state. Just by talking to people, even though this usually meant going through the interpreters. So the brothers looked at me like the good cop. I was like their friend. Every time I saw them they would call me over, ask me if they were going to get released, what was going on, if they could call their mom, if they could write a letter. Their parents had no idea what had happened to them." When prisoners like these were finally released, Ricky believes, "now they were a threat, because now they were pissed off."

Not all Ricky's time was spent in prison facilities. Other experiences "that really kind of made me question my involvement over there were a couple different times of going from base to base, being escorted by the infantry guys. One time we got out of our vehicles to secure a road, and a car turned onto our road going about five miles an hour. I was closest to the vehicle. It was a young man driving, and when he saw U.S. troops in the road, with weapons drawn, he immediately braked his car, grabbed the steering wheel to turn around. And when he was turning around the soldier in the turret behind me just opened up fire on the car.

"I ran over there with a medic and another soldier, pulled him out of the vehicle, and looked down at his face as his stomach was falling out into his hands and his eyes were rolling around. I found out en route to the hospital that he had died. I was just really disturbed. I went to talk to the command and told them that their soldier had ignored the rules of engagement that are outlined when you get in the country and say what kind of force is authorized. And that soldier had completely ignored them.

"I was really disturbed that an innocent Iraqi had just died, and when I brought it up I was kind of brushed off and even yelled at. I was 'an inexperienced soldier.' I 'didn't know how infantry operations worked.' 'This is the reality of Iraq and what's going on.' Basically, that 'the safety of American troops is number one, even if that means accidental happenings like this situation.'" On the Summary Intelligence Board in the Operations Command room, he saw that the number of civilian Iraqis killed was increasing during his time there. They were dying at the hands of U.S. troops who were, in Ricky's words, "inexperienced, young, emotional, adrenaline-driven soldiers that are trigger-happy, that just pop off rounds and don't think, don't abide by the rules that we're supposed to abide by." And there were few if any repercussions. The pervasive attitude was, "At least no American died." Among the troops, as in the media at home, some congratulated the military for the cultural sensitivity of giving the families of the deceased a small amount of money as compensation, $2,500 at the time per death (although a car run over by a U.S. tank would be compensated at full market value, often exceeding the amount paid parents for a child killed by U.S. troops).[8]

And the checkpoint episode that so disturbed him was not the first or the last. On another occasion in Mosul, Ricky was posted to a traffic circle when a car began coming at him going slow, "maybe ten miles an hour." When the car got closer, maybe thirty yards away, Ricky could see through the windshield. The driver was a young man who wasn't paying attention. "Before I even realize what's going on, the guy looks up and sees us and freaks out and goes to turn his steering wheel. Just then I hear right above my head in the Humvee the 240-Bravo machine gun in the turret, 'pa-pa-pa-pop,' right inside the car. Then the guy slouches over. So we run over, pulled him out of the car and he's like this seventeen-year-old kid, a real young kid, superthin, really young.

"He's shot a few times in his stomach and his chest. I see blood pouring out. And he kneels down, rips his shirt open. And I'm just standing over the guy with my weapon in my hand, looking down, totally freaking out in the moment because this was the first time I watched someone die." Ricky paused, remembering the image before continuing his account. "But I am standing over this kid, and he just looks up at me and he just looked up at me and it was the craziest look in his face. His mouth was starting to fumble a little bit and he was shaking and scared. He just looked up at me. And it was just taking the covers off the situation of Iraq, Americans, the war, looking at another human and the questions and knowing that he was going to die.

"All these things are just so intense. I am looking down at him, just frozen, probably for about twenty, thirty seconds, just lost in the moment. And then I get yelled at to snap out of it and provide cover. Ten minutes later he had died.

"This is the side I'm on?"

Ricky reported the incident to his command, but nothing happened to the soldier involved. The only superior who consistently listened to Ricky's concerns was his chief, Chief Warrant Officer Brian Kirby. "He was great, really had a lot of support for me. All those concerns I ever had, I always went to him and talked to him about mistreatment and some of the things that were going on. He knew firsthand." Ricky continued to tell his command about incidents of abuse against Iraqi civilians and property. One of those times his colonel was upset about soldiers

Ricky was riding with who shot at livestock from their vehicles. The colonel put those soldiers on house arrest, though Ricky concluded that was not much punishment, since they were confined to base and got to sit in their bunk areas and play Game Boy.

Especially infuriating to Ricky was the fact that the U.S. media continued to portray Iraq as the front for the war on terror in general and to claim that Al-Qaeda in Iraq and other groups were coming to Iraq to fight the American soldiers. But Ricky insisted that, at least when he was there, "that wasn't the case. The reality was that people who were fighting against us were normal people that live in their community. They were tired of American soldiers kicking down their doors, breaking stuff, going in, beating their dads up, taking their cousins off to jail for weeks on end and not really knowing what was happening to them. They were tired of the neighboring town getting phosphorus bombs dropped on them without accountability. People were just tired of it all, and especially tired of the United States occupying their country."[9]

Thus, when Ricky came to the conclusion that the U.S. military was actually creating the resistance as much as anything else, he did what any conscientious soldier was supposed to do, or so he thought: he reported to his command that the insurgency they thought they were fighting was the same insurgency that they were helping to create as a result of the behavior of the American troops. Ricky saw this as "the cycle of violence and the hypocrisy of it all." But no one seemed to be listening.

"I mean, the thing now is that the type of war we're fighting isn't conventional, and that front line really is just anywhere in the city. So it's not that only the infantry guys are out on the front line fighting. I was exposed just like a lot of truck drivers and medics and cooks that are traveling back and forth from the secured bases are exposed to the front lines of events. There were times when we drove around the city where I was really kind of anticipating a bomb to go off and just didn't know when—you never know when or where it's going to happen. So that was kind of scary. We also had incoming mortar rounds fired on our base a number of times, but I was never actually in a firefight. Thankfully I was never in the middle of that kind of situation."

Ricky continued his interrogations of prisoners brought into the U.S. military prison facilities on any number of pretexts. There were many types of prisoners. "Sometimes you get these guys in there that were terrified because they had heard stories about being under U.S. capture. Then you would get some guys that were just cocky, arrogant, and knew how the system worked." Sometimes he realized that people were being held captive because some neighbor had informed on them, and sometimes that involved more what he called "a Sunni/Shia revenge thing." Not that he'd been taught anything about differences between Sunni and Shia branches of Islam. "I didn't even know, to be honest, before I went over there. And I was in intelligence."

The people Ricky was interrogating "weren't Al-Qaeda, they weren't bin Laden's counterparts or their team members. These weren't the same people. These were people that confessed to hating Americans, said they wanted to kill us, didn't want us to be there. But they were not Al-Qaeda. They were just tired of Americans being in their country, occupying them, oppressing their people. So they were resisting our occupation. The bottom line was that their actions didn't fall under the blanket category of terrorist, like the media and the president talk about." As his months in Iraq dragged on, Ricky said, "I'm just thinking to myself, Oh my gosh. This is really the side that I'm on? This is really happening? We're the good guys? Are you kidding me?"

Ricky's stories, like the others', illustrate that troop morale is dependent on soldiers believing in the righteousness of their mission. If their leadership tells them they are being sent to liberate another country, they ought to be sure that's what the troops find themselves doing. Otherwise they begin to question the whole shooting match.

six. Awakenings

Ricky Clousing got into a little trouble during one of his interrogations. Instead of controlling the situation, he began to let his prisoner ask the questions.

"You're supposed to direct the conversation, you're not supposed to give up that control. This guy wasn't just some broke, dumb Iraqi with a gun firing at people. He was somewhat of an idealist, which is why I looked at him differently and respected him more than some of the other guys that I talked to. He wasn't just some punk that was wanting to kill Americans. Naturally, I was curious to get inside this guy's brain. How does he think and feel?"

Through an interpreter, Ricky delved into a much more complicated back-and-forth with this prisoner than usual. "So he was telling me a lot of the stories that I heard repeatedly over there: his cousin or his neighbor was shot by Americans walking home from school or at a checkpoint, like all the incidents that happen every day. The media in the U.S. doesn't report those, so they have no idea why all these frustrated Iraqis are dueling us up when their daughters are raped and their daughters are killed." Ricky ended up talking with the Iraqi prisoner for almost an hour. The man kept asking Ricky why he was being held and what they were going to do with him. Ricky asked the man why he thought he was being held. Did the man consider himself a terrorist?

"And he asked me, do I think that *I* am a terrorist. I kind of looked at him funny, like, 'Okay, um.' And then he asked me what the definition of a terrorist was. And again, mind you, this is during the latter part of my deployment, after seeing some things, seeing firsthand U.S. soldiers shooting civilians, killing civilians, seeing guys in the turret shooting people's livestock for fun, seeing emotional and physical harassment. I mean, after four months of seeing this kind of stuff I am having the conversation with this guy, and he asks me what the definition of terrorist is," Ricky explained.

"Technically, from my MOS, from the perspective of my job, I shouldn't have even answered. But as Ricky Clousing, not as Sergeant Clousing, but as Ricky Clousing, I went with that. I humored him. I said, 'Well, I don't know the Webster Dictionary definition for a terrorist, but I know that it's somebody who uses terror to achieve whatever goal they're trying to get. It is someone or some group that inflicts terror, scare tactics or violence, on a person or a group of people for some sort of political agenda.' And he looked at me and he smiled. And he said, 'What do you think the American soldiers are doing in my country? What are they doing here?'

"And he had caught me off guard. It was just like a one-two punch. Because he had caught me, and for just that one moment I didn't feel like I was even wearing an Army uniform. I just stopped and I was, 'Oh, my gosh. All these things I've seen and felt and that I know are going on. This is why.' And now I'm seeing why people are responding to our actions, and that whole cycle was really clear to me. I was taken aback. I mean, I got chills on my body. And we just stopped talking. I obviously didn't tell him, 'Yeah, I agree with you.' But I think he could probably tell. So for the rest of my deployment I had that on my mind. He'd planted that seed of doubt and of confusion and even more doubt."

Ricky returned to his prisoner's words as he continued to hear stories about U.S. soldiers returning from patrols with televisions, jewelry, American money, video games, all of which they had pillaged on searches and raids of private homes. Then he heard about an even more horrific incident. Sitting around the barracks, some soldiers "were joking that they had been on patrol and their staff sergeant, a guy who was actually a higher rank than me, had put two of his soldiers on guard at one of the homes they were inspecting while he went inside and raped an Iraqi girl who was fourteen or fifteen years old. The soldiers were blocking the door so no one would go in. When I saw them they were laughing about it, saying that they'd heard noises from inside. I didn't know what to say. I was just disgusted. It's crazy. I can't imagine being in the moment. It's just appalling that someone could actually not just witness that but contribute in a way."

These incidents and the fact that command seemed unwilling or unable to stop or punish the U.S. troops who were committing them made Ricky further question his ability to continue with his tour. Not only were innocent people dying all the time, not only was there an abuse of power without accountability, but the insurgents that they were trying to fight, those the media and the U.S. government labeled terrorists, were just, he was convinced, "a normal population of people."

BIBLE READINGS

Frustrated at every turn with his attempt to understand why the United States was in Iraq, thwarted by chaplains and counselors who seemed more interested in stifling his misgivings than considering them, Ricky said, "I just kind of hit a brick wall and didn't know where to go." He began expressing his doubts to other members of his unit, and he told them his feelings were intensifying with each passing day.

When Ricky told his command that he was having serious issues with the Army and with the war, they told him to speak with counselors and chaplains. He did so on several occasions but was disappointed. Somewhat sympathetically, Ricky noted, "I mean, I guess I was asking pretty big questions. But I was just wanting to find some answers." His commanders asked Ricky if he was trying to get out of the Army. "But I wasn't. There's ways to do that, such as saying you're gay or saying you have mental problems. I was insulted, to tell you the truth. I wasn't trying to play that card to get a ticket out of the military." More problematic was the fact that the officers Ricky talked to had no explanations for him. Instead, they tried to reassure him about God's will and urged him to focus on his work.

"I went and talked with the chaplains and told them about the spiritual basis for my conflict of conscience. They came back with all these cliché statements, and even Bible verses taken out of context, justifying war and saying God is favoring us, and that I should just trust in his plan. Just surfacey, watered-down statements that didn't answer anything that I was really feeling."

"I was reading the Bible and finding a lot of scriptures that were showing me a different side of Christianity, primarily about being peacemakers. The verses about love your neighbor as thyself, those who live by the sword die by the sword. I was going to Bible study for a while, but I stopped going because I didn't feel like I fit in, it wasn't comfortable. The chaplain was praying before missions that we would be God's hand of justice, and all the guys around me were bowing their heads and praying for this when forty minutes before they were watching porno on their computers and laughing about shooting animals. I was like, 'You guys are praying, you're Christians, are you kidding me?' I just came from being a missionary and this is not right. It didn't feel normal to me at all."

Ricky also started reading more literature about the run-up to the war in Iraq, and from there he sought out books on U.S. foreign policy around the world. While on leave, he had gone to a local Borders bookstore and picked up as much as he could find about "real history and basically what had happened with the First Gulf War." The first book he read was *Confessions of an Economic Hit Man*, by John Perkins. He could relate to what Perkins was saying because the author too had worked in the intelligence field, through a private company tied to the CIA. "That book catapulted me into reading a lot about even deeper history." He read some Howard Zinn, including *Declarations of Independence: Cross-Examining American Ideology*. Through his readings, Ricky encountered the idea that the United States had long engaged in proxy wars with puppet governments put in place by CIA interventions. He went online, looking for progressive Web sites, and found Noam Chomsky's writings as well.

Henry David Thoreau's essay *On Civil Disobedience* stunned him. Parallels were clear to him between the Iraq War and the situation Thoreau had found himself in 150 years earlier. "It blew me away. Just the idea that we as a people have responsibility not only to be aware but to be involved and to know. That we have to demand a better government. So many times we just roll over. Because our lifestyle now is so convenient and it's so leisurely that it's hard for people to care about issues. And so me being directly affected because I'm in the military kind of forced me to be concerned and care about stuff.

"And I started really being disillusioned. My reality was shattered. My whole perception of America, and the U.S. Army, and what I was doing in the Army, was really broken up." He sat quietly for a moment and then noted that he had not known what to do with all this new knowledge or with the feeling that his involvement in the U.S. military was morally wrong. But not only was he still in the military; he was still in Iraq.

During Ricky's time in the Army people teased him for being what they called a tree-hugging hippie from Seattle. He had never wanted to get his head shaved. "I didn't really adapt well like a lot of other people do," Ricky said, echoing the language the Army itself employs to distinguish between good soldiers and bad. Some soldiers called him Sergeant Flower, probably, he said, "because a lot of times I would question things, be like, 'Why is this?' or 'Why do we have to do this or that?'" Ricky ultimately saw his enlistment and trip to Iraq as a path that had been laid before him: "I was just stumbling upon things that were put there for me to discover." And he saw being in the military as having forced him to care about problems that he suspected most Americans never wanted to learn about, much less resolve.

OUT OF THE MILITARY BUBBLE
THROUGH A CHAT ROOM DOOR

Demond Mullins's epiphany happened in a most unexpected way: instant-messaging while surfing the Web after returning from a mission. Chatting online with a stranger that day would change his life forever.

Between moments of high anxiety and frustration out on patrol in villages or running missions in the cities, when they were not trying to catch a few hours' sleep or wolf down food that didn't come out of a plastic bag, U.S. troops at established military facilities had access to the Internet on their downtime. In this way, the war in Iraq was like no other before it. Soldiers could call or write home through their computers, surf the Web for information and diversion, and even order things online that would be delivered within two or three weeks to their temporary homes in Iraq. When he was especially bored, Demond Mullins liked to enter a chat room to see if he could strike up a virtual conversation.

"I remember I was in a chat room, I don't know if it was AOL or what service it was. I just needed some kind of stimulation from someone who wasn't in Iraq right then. So I'm trying to talk to people in the chat room, and I wind up saying, 'Hey, I'm in Iraq right now. I'm a U.S. soldier, an infantryman,' whatever. And some dude in the chat room was an Iraqi in Iraq. And we started IM-ing one another. The guy was a professor; his English was so-so. We wound up talking for maybe half an hour through IM.

"He explained to me why U.S. soldiers needed to leave, and I wasn't putting up a fight about it. I was, 'You're right, you know we don't want to be here either.' And then he was saying that he was afraid of U.S. soldiers, like at traffic control points. We started to have a conversation about that. He said that every time he sees one he's so afraid of U.S. soldiers because they kill so many civilians, so he tries to turn around and drive the other way. I explained to him that if he did that we were going to shoot him or chase him because we were going to think he was trying to get away from us.

"And explaining all this in that exchange, I realized how we were destroying people's lives. This guy was trying to go to work, but he can't even go to work to provide for his family without thinking, 'I'm leaving my house and I'm going to get shot by a U.S. soldier because they think I'm suspicious.' He was talking about how obnoxious the U.S. soldiers were and their temperament, how unnecessarily violent and authoritative they were. I was, 'Look, dude, every day when I leave this fence, this barbed wire, I'm scared for my life. And I'm looking at you and anyone else like you and thinking you could possibly kill me. All the other U.S. soldiers are looking at you like that. So when we treat people rough it's not a personal thing. I'm not even this type of person. You would be surprised to know certain things about me. This is not who I am. I'm just stuck here.'

"So at that moment, when I realized that you can't even be a professor in Iraq and keep your standard of living and just live without being fearful, that's when I realized that we were really messing people up in Iraq, the civilians in Iraq. After that, I started to be a lot more empathetic to people when I was on missions."

War has a funny way of bringing together people who would never otherwise connect. "My best buddy when I was in Iraq," recounts Demond, "was this really country-type white guy from northern New York State. He used to go hunting all the time, played Metallica, stuff like that. But I loved this guy to death. And he really felt like, 'Hey we're going to save people.' He was a great guy. I loved this guy. I'd give him the shirt off my back. But the thing was that he was so sold on this story he couldn't think outside it."

Demond, on the other hand, was still angry about what he saw as the tricks and lies spread by Washington after the Twin Towers were attacked. "Bush played on the country's emotions after 9/11. You know, 'Yeah, we want to fight someone, because we're pissed off that happened.'" It didn't seem to matter that the attack was not connected to

Iraq; someone had to pay. "There were so many people who supported the war before we went," said Demond. "But then after you go through all the situations and combat, and then you think about what we were doing, there was no reason for it. And then you had to find that reason. And all you could come up with was ugly."

The way Demond saw it, the deceptions had only multiplied in Iraq, and his roommate was too susceptible to them.[1] "He couldn't think, like, 'Damn, we're actually really fucking these people up rather than helping them.' It was difficult for him to accept that. And I spent all my time with him, showered, shat, and shaved with him every day, and we'd talk about it all the time, to the point he would just be like, 'I can't talk about this anymore because it's difficult.'"

Demond's peers were not unusual. Polls of soldiers in Iraq in 2006 found that almost 90 percent believed that the U.S. invasion was retaliation for a Saddam Hussein role in the 9/11 attacks, and 77 percent erroneously believed that Saddam was protecting Al-Qaeda inside his country and that this justified the invasion. Nonetheless, 72 percent thought the United States should leave the country within the year, with only 23 percent agreeing with the Bush administration at the time that U.S. troops should stay "as long as they are needed." Morale was low enough that the Mental Health Advisory Teams, which have surveyed thousands of soldiers each year of the war, stopped reporting levels of "low" and "very low" morale after 2003, when those numbers were 57 percent of junior enlisteds, 49 percent of NCOs, and 25 percent of officers.[2]

By the end of his time in Iraq, Demond felt he had changed as a person. "I never went there with the mentality of 'I want to own kills and go home and say that I killed some people.' For me, just seeing people get hurt was really humbling. It kind of made me a nihilist. I think I became kind of a nihilist because of the war. I just don't see the point in a lot of shit. Everything's kind of just futile."

On the other hand, Demond talks about a professor he had at CUNY before he went to war, whose values and ideas were still inspiring in retrospect. Teaching about the history of different racial and ethnic groups in the United States, the professor made an analogy to trees. Native

Americans, he said, were eradicated by European settlers because they were like oak trees and couldn't sway in the wind but stayed strong until they were torn down. African Americans on the other hand, according to this teacher, were more like willow trees that swayed in the wind and compromised themselves. "He said that it's not necessarily a bad thing," comments Demond, "but I think that's a terrible thing."

In the course of his time in Iraq, Demond began to think, "I was an oak tree, regardless how hard the wind blows. The wind could tear me down, pick up my roots, destroy my whole bloodline. I could give a flying fuck because I was standing for something, living for something, and dying for something. And there was something I honestly admired about the people we fought and killed in Iraq. A lot of people were saying, 'Allāhu Akbar' [Arabic for "God is great"] at the time they expired. I admired that because they believed in something so much that they were an oak tree. They were an oak tree, and they were willing to die for it. I was not willing to die for what I was doing in Iraq." When he finished his comment, Demond stared off at no one and nothing in particular.

CROSSING THE RUBICON
OF EMPATHY FOR THE ENEMY

Even before he was stationed in Kosovo or Iraq, Charlie Anderson wrestled with the idea that war invariably brings destruction to entire populations of people. He remembered having felt sick to his stomach after 9/11 when he listened to pious and confrontational pronouncements from U.S. government officials. "Do you remember the Bush speech from the memorial service for the victims of 9/11? He talked about the innocents struck down by cowards, and then he said we have a duty from God to smite down the people that did this."[3] Later, in Iraq, Charlie heard more talk about cowardice, especially "this concept of Iraqis being cowards because they were using roadside bombs. What's the difference between an IED and a claymore mine? What's the difference between an IED and an armed aerial drone? Not that much except that one is much more technologically advanced than the other."[4]

After President Bush gave his speech about innocents and cowards, the Navy Choir came out and sang the "Battle Hymn of the Republic":

Mine eyes have seen the glory of the coming of the Lord:
He is trampling out the vintage where the grapes of wrath are stored;
He hath loosed the fateful lightning of His terrible swift sword:
His truth is marching on.

"The only way they would have gotten this any more holy war–invoking is if they had done a rousing chorus of 'Onward Christian Soldiers,' but I think that would have been too obvious. And I saw that and I saw footage of bin Laden's *fatwās* and I couldn't tell the fricking difference."[5] Later, watching the news of Afghanistan, Charlie recalled, "I felt heartsick, watching the people, primarily poor people in Kabul, digging bomb shelters in their front yards."

Being able to see the suffering of civilians, according to Charlie, was not in itself exceptional for a soldier, Marine, or sailor. Most of the troops in Iraq were entirely aware of the problems the U.S. military was inflicting on people there. What for Charlie became unbearable was that he began "to acknowledge and own" what he saw and did. "Even if you say, 'I really couldn't do anything different at the time,' there was still a sense of responsibility and the sense of empathizing. I don't think anyone ever goes straight to it, to empathizing, from one pole to another. I think you go back and forth for a while. But the ability to empathize is important. That's crossing the Rubicon once you make that determination. Once you come to that conclusion, it's a willful act of disobedience. It's really not easy. It's not something that most people are able to do."

For Charlie, thinking about how to reconcile responsibility and God became a source of torment. He continued to read his Bible and to talk with others about what he thought the teachings of Christ said to this question. And he continued in Iraq to seek out the guidance and counsel of chaplains. Theological questions plagued him throughout his military service. Back at Camp Lejeune, he got to know one chaplain very well. "Sometimes I just dropped in to see him. No appointments. I asked him about the ethics of carpet bombing, basically, 'Who would Jesus bomb?' though I don't think I worded it that way. We talked about moral justification. His whole argument was, 'The Ten Commandments really meant 'Thou shalt not *murder*,' not 'Thou shalt not *kill*.' At the time, that was sort of what I was looking for: 'Tell me I'm okay.' My chaplain, who was kind of fruit loops, actually yelled at me for saying that I hoped George Bush really gave thought to what he was doing to our families."

Then, in Iraq, there was a confrontation with another chaplain. A friend had told Charlie, "'Hey, the chaplain's down here from 7th Marines.' And so we went to church, and the chaplain's whole sermon was about how we are here to go to war with Islam, in the land where Jesus walked. He was using the word *hajji* in the sermon, by the way: 'When the *hajjis* come to put in the electricity on base, did you think of offering them food, offering them water? Because those *hajjis* should see that we are Christians, that we are good men. And that they don't mean to be evil, but that they don't know any better and you have to show them.' And I'm thinking to myself, Are you out of your fucking mind? When I stopped by later and asked him not to use racial slurs as part of his sermon, he didn't know what I was talking about. He was actually offended by the idea that I thought he was using racial slurs."

Wanting to be accepted by the Iraqi people and at the same time sensing that his life was at risk from these same people who did not want him in their country, Charlie developed what he later called a "schizophrenic feeling." Coupled with his frustration at not getting good answers to his religious questions, Charlie said it was at this point he decided to stop "dating" his current religion: "That's when I decided that I was pissed off at the Christian God. And I told Yahweh that we should start seeing other Gods."

WHERE FEAR COMES FROM

There were, of course, real limits to what soldiers in Iraq who began to question and oppose the war could do. As long as they remained isolated one from another, they could not, one by one, change military operations in any significant fashion. But they sometimes found ways to communicate their fear and anger about the war to others in their unit. Tina

Garnanez continued a tradition she had started in Kosovo, where she began making art and postering her walls. In Iraq, her "Bush comedy," as she called it, consisted of newspaper and magazine clippings that, collaged together, poked fun at the president, Dick Cheney, and Donald Rumsfeld. She also put up peace quotes and photos of the Dalai Lama, Gandhi, and Mother Teresa, her heroes: "They've got a very powerful message of compassion and love."

Tina occasionally talked with other medics about the war. Some ignored her political views, others dismissed them: "Oh, crazy hippie flower child, she's at it again." Neither she nor anyone who agreed with her "would do anything, though. I guess we just saw it was a lost cause. We were here already, what could we do?" Through peace posters, artwork, and photos Tina kept herself halfway sane in Iraq. But the fear and anxiety were always there, below the surface.

Fear for Tina came daily from the threat that Iraqis who opposed the U.S. occupation might attack her, on base, on convoys, in public spaces and private. In this respect, her experiences as an American soldier were typical. In addition, however, Tina faced a whole different kind of fear that most of her comrades did not. As a woman, as one of the 15 percent of the U.S. Armed Forces in and out of Iraq that were female, Tina and her women comrades had to confront the daily threat of sexual assault from other soldiers.

"It's very sad, just being a woman out there." Tina knew what the surveys and investigatory records show, which is that sexual assault is endemic among the troops in Iraq. The Department of Defense's own numbers show 2,212 sexual assaults in 2007, with only 181 of them even brought to trial. Some female soldiers who report rape say they have been threatened with punishment as a result.[6] Tina was one of many women soldiers who developed ways to protect themselves from constant harassment and the threat of rape.

On her base in Iraq, the Morale, Welfare, Recreation (MWR) shack was a good half-mile away from Tina's sleeping area. If she wanted to check her e-mail or call home, she had to make her way there. If she got back from a convoy at two in the morning, she would figure that, given the time difference, it might be a good hour to call home to her mother in New Mexico. "I would call her and then I'd have to walk all the way back in the dark. I was always ready with my knife. I'd sort of have it open, have it tucked away a little. Just ready, so I could pull it out. I was listening constantly." Although she had her rifle strung across her back, "if someone had their arms around me I couldn't lock and load it. So I kept my knife handy at all times.

"The road was gravel and so I'd walk in the grass next to the road, and if someone was behind me, I could hear them on the gravel." Tina's voice got quieter. "Like with my brothers at home, I always had to be smart. I couldn't overpower them, so I just had to be smarter. I was always very careful. I'd use the moonlight, look for shadows. Anything to be ready.

"I was so angry at the fact that not only did I have to worry about dying on these convoys, but I'd worry about coming back to the base, about my fellow soldiers doing something to me. That really, really bothered me. Before the military, my father abused me, so I've always had an attitude of, 'Hey, men are dangerous.' And then I was attacked when I was sixteen, though I was able to fight the guy off and nothing happened.

"I didn't really trust men too much. And then to be in the military and have all the unwanted advances by older men. That just rubbed me the wrong way and scared me. I certainly didn't want anything to happen. But that fear of sexual harassment or rape was further instilled in me when I had friends come forward and tell me stories about their drill sergeants or people they worked for. In Iraq the fear was always there."

And how did the officers around her respond to this situation? "I don't think they thought about that too much. You know, 'They're all soldiers, they're all green. They'll behave. You can trust each other.' I think that's maybe what they thought. But I certainly didn't trust everybody I was working with."

One important part of Tina's growing awareness about what the problems were with the war and occupation had little to do with Iraq itself. It was grounded in the realization that sharing that green uniform changed little in terms of the abuse, harassment, rape, and other violence women suffered.

Danger came from the world outside her base as well. As required, she carried her rifle everywhere. "It was kind of surreal. I had a bicycle to get around the base, because it was huge. I had a bike, and would get my bike helmet on and my gloves, and get ready to sit on my bike, and I'd go, 'Oh, yeah. My gun.' I'd just strap it across my back and ride down the road. We named our weapons just to remember them." Tina named hers Juan, after a friend.

The constant threat of death wore on Tina, perhaps more than most soldiers. The extent of its impact became clear to her in the middle of her Iraq tour, when she was allowed a two-week home leave. On one of those nights in New Mexico, she was asleep on the couch in her mother's living room when her brother's girlfriend loudly dropped a frying pan on the floor in the kitchen. Tina bolted awake, thinking, "'It's a mortar.'

"So I jump up, and I'm getting ready to put on all my gear—my helmet, and my vest, and get my M-16. . . . It took me a minute to figure out where I was, and it took a long time to calm down. It was emotionally overwhelming because I was still all pumped up, the adrenaline was still going.

"So I walked down the hall to my mom's room, and I woke her up and I crawled into bed with her. I said, 'Mom, will you hold me?' I just lay there and I started crying, because I was home, I was safe." As she told us this story, Tina cried again for her lost security and her gratitude that her mother was there for her. In Iraq, "I was always afraid. There were times when I would beg, 'God, kill me. Just kill me. Because I don't want to live with this stress. I'm tired of being afraid all the time, of dying.' Or, you know, 'Just let me make it home safe and sound, just get me home.'"

FROM QUESTIONS TO ACTIONS

Before he was deployed to Iraq, Garett Reppenhagen was sent home from Kosovo for a two-week leave to visit his family in Colorado Springs. It was April 2003 and the U.S. invasion of Iraq had just begun. On a layover in the Dallas–Fort Worth airport, trying to get home, he was still wearing his battle dress uniform. The forty-eight hours had elapsed for Saddam Hussein to give himself up.

"The forty-eight-hour ultimatum ran out, and we started bombing Baghdad. On the television in the airport I saw Bradleys crossing the line. Here I was, in my uniform and surrounded by all these Americans that were cheering and hollering like the Dallas Cowboys just won the Super Bowl. I was just shrinking in my seat going, Who *are* these people? And I realized that since I'd left for basic training I hadn't much been part of America at all. So I was really alienated by society and I realized these people had no idea what they were cheering for. They didn't know what these bombs were doing and what these Bradley gunners had in store for them and who was going to be at the other end of those bullets and bombs."

Such nationalist displays were almost enough to persuade Garett that he should apply for CO status before deploying to Iraq, but as we know, he just could not bring himself to take that step, so he reported for war duty as ordered. And when he was in Iraq, he insists he saw "no real criminal activity against Iraqi people, no rape or murdering civilians that are known to be innocent," though to be sure there were many situations "where Iraqis got beat up and punched and kicked. But they were always people we suspected of doing something, not just a random guy, 'Let's just beat the shit out of him.'"

When doubts continued to arise for him in country, not so much about abuse but about the overall mission, the whole purpose of the U.S. invasion and occupation, chaplains were usually present to bolster his and other soldiers' morale. They were the front lines of mental well-being of the soldiers. "I talked to one, my battalion chaplain in Iraq, and he wasn't helpful. He was, 'It's for God and country, and if you have any other doubts, then you're wrong.'"

Some soldiers no doubt appreciated the chaplains' counsel as a kind of psychological service or cushion for their anxiety and stress. And service chaplains in Iraq have had their hands full, having to advise many enlisted personnel grappling with psychological trauma and guilt about what some see as sin. When "I shot my first civilian in Iraq," recalled Garett, "I came back to my hooch and I destroyed it. I just tore everything down. I pushed my bunk over, I threw all my gear around." Garett's staff sergeant told him to go see the chaplain.

Even though he was an atheist, Garett did as he was advised. He told the chaplain, "'This is what happened. I'm pissed off, you know—a citizen, a person died, blah blah blah.' And he comes back to me that I did it for God and country, that I'm in God's hands, I'm a tool of God, you know? 'Get out there and, you know, get back to work.' 'Okay. Thanks! You know? That's not helping me at all.' I was like, 'What? What is this guy doing?'" Garett later concluded the chaplain was trying to "manufacture meaning" for him. "I realized the meaning was fundamental to my psychological well-being. If the war doesn't have any meaning, what is the sacrifice for? Why are we here at all? That's what soldiers are trying to grasp," he explained, patient as a teacher. For some, achieving this understanding was a lot harder than for others. The chaplains were there to encourage religiously grounded reduction of doubts and fears and to validate the U.S. military mission, Garett and other dissenting soldiers reasoned: by portraying the purpose and actions of the U.S. military in Iraq as righteous and religiously sanctioned, military chaplains were meant to keep as many soldiers on the front lines as possible.

Although it was not any one thing that turned Garett decisively against the war he was charged with fighting, he was deeply struck by the Iraqi soldiers who were supposed to fight alongside the U.S. troops. "We would be getting ready to go on a house raid and they would hide themselves because they were afraid to be identified, because they were traitors. They were afraid of being found out. I would say that 90 percent of them were just in it for the money. And a lot of them switch-hit. During the day they ran around in the army, and at night they were insurgents." It was hard to sustain faith in the mission when the Iraqis themselves seemed at best ambivalent and far more often in outright opposition to the U.S. military presence.

Garett was still in Iraq when he began writing antiwar blogs with some of his friends there. "We were getting picked up by various antiwar organizations that were reproducing our stuff." He developed close e-mail correspondence with several U.S. Viet Nam antiwar veterans and from them learned that at the Veterans for Peace annual meeting in Boston in the summer of 2004 seven or eight Iraq and Afghanistan veterans had come together and decided to form a new organization, the Iraq Veterans Against the War (IVAW).[7]

"I was still in Iraq. It was about halfway through my tour. The IVAW had just formed in Boston, and by this time I was already speaking out against the war through the Internet. I was blogging, writing people. They were posting stuff. A band called the Bouncing Souls, a punk band that I met in Germany, had an entire page up on their Web site called 'Letters from Iraq' that me and my buddies were writing to. And they were posting them. I wrote a poem called 'Letters from Iraq,' and they made it into a song."

As for IVAW, "They gave me four or five of their e-mail addresses and I e-mailed all of them. I was, 'I'm in Iraq right now, I'm a sniper. I am very against the war. I am not a veteran yet. But can I be part of your organization?' They said, 'Hell, yeah!' I was the first active-duty member of IVAW."

Now the personal mission of Garett and so many other GIs was simply to return home in one piece and to inflict as little additional damage on the Iraqi people as possible before they left the war zone. If they could just make it home alive, they hoped, they could find ways to make things right.

PART THREE Aftermath and Activism

SEVEN Homecoming Traumas

"YOU'RE A MAN NOW!"

Demond Mullins vividly remembered the last days and hours of his tour of Iraq, when he began to realize that the worst was over and that he was actually going to make it home, and in one piece. This definitely was not a moment he or any of his buddies took for granted. They may not have known the exact numbers—around the time we spoke with them, thirty-five thousand official casualties among their U.S. forces and twelve thousand dead and wounded private contractors in Iraq and Afghanistan wars—but they knew what might have been.[1] They had all seen the deaths and injuries to others in their units, including those who had returned home with grotesque burn injuries and mangled or missing limbs, and who sometimes faced dozens of surgeries and months or years of painful rehab.

137

Demond was among those who had made it through the carnage seemingly intact: "When I came in from my last mission in Iraq, as we drove into the camp, there were all these people from my company to greet us. And we were all shouting, 'Wow, this is our last mission! We made it! We're going home alive!' My executive officer walked up to me and said, 'You're a man now!' That's what he said to me. And I thought about that, and I still think about that now. Daily. Because is it violence, is it acts of violence that make me a man? Or is it my potential for violence that makes me manly or masculine? You know what I mean?"

Demond's commanding officer's comment did not sit well with him. "I think that the military really plays on that. From childhood, you're socialized into your ideology of what masculinity is or what manhood is. And pop culture plays on that well. When you're too young to get into the military, you're fed these images. Then, just joining the military, it's like you're trying to prove that you are a man. And to say you're a man because 'I experienced combat.' Well, how did that make me a man?

"I was twenty-two when I first went to Iraq. I was already a man. Do my violent acts make me an alpha male among civilians now? It's messed up, because even though I know all this, I internalized what I learned. All those things that I learned, those negative things about masculinity and violence. I internalized that even though I know consciously that it's wrong. In some ways I exert myself in a violent way to show that I'm a man. I was really aggressive when I first came home.

"When I was in Iraq, I had a lot of stomachaches. I had to go to the clinic a lot and speak to the medic about them. There were even times when I had to miss missions because of them. They started to give me all sorts of crazy things for my stomach. The final diagnosis the doctor gave me was 'You just need to go home.' It was coming to the end of our tour and I had an incredible relationship with the man because I'd seen him so much about my problem. He was, 'Everyone's tired. This is probably a nervous condition. You need to just go home. When you go home you'll be better.' And my stomach has been a lot better since I've been home. I still get stomachaches, though a lot less frequently."

After he returned to the United States, Demond was told by some-one at the Veterans Administration (VA) clinic that he suffered from post-traumatic stress disorder (PTSD). Consistent with this diagnosis,

Demond noted, "My eyes are really sensitive to the light. I get a head-ache if I don't wear sunglasses. So I constantly wear them. Sometimes when I wake up in the morning, the first thing that I do is put on my sunglasses."[2]

For some time after he got back, Demond's girlfriend refused to be with him, she said, "until you get help." Though he never verbalized it, she could tell something was wrong, and Demond later admitted that he was having suicidal feelings. "I went to ballet school with this girl. She'd known me since we were really young. Her mom has a video of us together from when we were just six years old." And she insisted he go talk to someone at the VA.

After admitting himself to the VA hospital and getting diagnosed with PTSD, "I saw a psychologist at the VA for a while, and I really had prob-lems talking to her because I felt like she was patronizing me. When I came home I always had this feeling that I was going to die, just sud-denly. Like I'd be hit by a bus, or fucking I don't know, someone would just come on me and stab me. Or shoot me. One of the counselors I saw at the VA told me that people who suffer from trauma generally feel like they're going to die at any moment."

In some ways, this was merely a continuation of what it was like to walk around inside Demond Mullin's skin in Iraq. "When I was over there, we were on the truck doing missions. You'd be out there for four-teen hours, because we got some order about a fragmentation device. Or whatever. And I would just be, like, 'Dude, I wish somebody would blow this fucking truck up right now and just fucking kill me. Because I can't take this shit anymore.' Just mentally, it was so difficult."

The feeling that death was imminent was so strong that, on a leave home, he'd quickly blown seven thousand dollars, figuring that he might as well spend his money if he wasn't going to make it home again. "I stayed in a hotel on Park Avenue. Got room service the whole time. Took my girlfriend clothes shopping. She didn't even want to buy anything. I was just buying her everything. I didn't care. She couldn't stop me either, because I was trying to live.

"When we got back, a lot of guys that I knew were having trouble with their marriages. One guy was so in love with his wife, when we were in Iraq all he used to talk about was his wife. And his wife was beautiful. When he got back they just couldn't hold it together because he had changed. He wasn't the same. She couldn't take it, and she left him. And then right after she left him, he killed himself. Shot himself."

And there were others who had no such clear trigger to self-destruction. "Another buddy of mine went really crazy. He drove his car into a wall in the Bronx."

One way Demond found to escape the pain and suicidal feelings was through what he called "nihility." As he put it, "It makes me feel comfortable. I'm like, You don't have a pot to piss in. Everybody's in pretty bad shape because we're all just trying to make it. Some people are really well off, and some people are not. This actually comforts me. There's some people that it scares, that life has no point, no structure. To me, I'm comforted by it."

His war experiences also left him deeply alienated from the religion that once meant so much to him. "I used to be a very religious person before I went to Iraq. There was a time when I was so devout. And then I traveled away from it, slowly. Certain experiences that I had started to change me. This experience is defining for me because I cannot see myself ever practicing any type of organized religion again, and I can't now see why other people do. When I was a kid, I grew up in a Baptist church. Even when I was a teenager and could decide for myself, I was really active in church. Now religion kind of turns my stomach. When females send winks to me on a Web site, because they want to meet me, I look at their profile. If it says that they practice any type of religion, unless it's Buddhism, I don't respond to any of that."

On return to civilian life, Demond struggled to regain his prewar sense of self and identity, and especially his earlier interests. "I come from being this warrior, and now I'm trying to go back into my artistic self. I can't find it. It's somewhere in there, but I can't access it any more. And the reason why is because I put this hard shell over myself to perform my duties when I was in Iraq. I definitely projected a more violent self-image so I could find my comfortable place in that hierarchy.

"I realize that being a vet there are so many expectations of you. On so many different levels. You're expected to be some kind of hypermasculine person, especially being an infantryman. You know, you were in combat. You're expected to be so many different things to the guys you served with, your family when you get back home, your superiors, people that you don't even know. What I have found, and what has made me happy since I've come home, is that I'm learning what it's like to just redefine myself. I think that a lot of vets need to know that, need to hear that. They need to hear that it's okay to redefine themselves. Because they're kind of trapped with the perception that an individual in the military must be hypermasculine. It's from the movies but it's also the way the military advertises itself. Look at those commercials."

NIGHTMARES, SUICIDE, AND SEEKING HELP

Soldiers, sailors, and Marines brought back a lot more than memories of the war in Iraq. Many who return home have or will develop crippling psychological problems—by one Veterans Affairs estimate, 30 to 40 percent of combat veterans, and 19 percent according to calculations of a RAND study in 2008.[3] Even this smaller percentage means three hundred thousand young men and women have already come back from Iraq and Afghanistan suffering from PTSD and depression.

After returning to the United States, Charlie Anderson was given an honorable discharge from the Navy after being diagnosed with PTSD. "I got put out of the military for PTSD. People usually think PTSD means diving for cover when a car backfires, and that's certainly part of it and certainly happens. One of my triggers is noises, or situational triggers like heavy traffic. Helicopters. But those exterior symptoms are the tip of the iceberg. When I was still active duty, I went through group therapy, and it worked very well, helped me get some tools for dealing with my overt symptoms. We talked through some of our feelings and we identified our trauma scenes. But eventually I just kind of quit going, which happens a lot."

When he got out, though, Charlie said he did not have good luck at the VA seeking further treatment. He found an excellent counselor, but when that therapist quit, he was faced with a choice of starting over with another one or quitting himself. "It takes a lot out of me to start a relationship with a new provider, because I have to go through the whole damned thing again."

"I have to tell all about the story, about what happened in Sadr City. I have to talk about having two different calibers of bullet going past my head at the same time. I have to relive all that. It's not just telling a story. I have to relive it. After another interview I had nightmares for most of the week. Very vivid nightmares about a variety of things. And there's another, additional burden: I have to prove again that I have the PTSD in the first place.

"I did go through one support group meeting at the VA, and I didn't find any support. I spent most of the night talking about why it was okay for me to be a veteran against the war, and listening to some of the other members of this group talk about how we should just have a policy of genocide because if we don't kill everybody in Iraq, then they're going to come over here and kill our kids. It didn't even make sense."

Despite feeling like an alien in this group of vets, he nonetheless felt much in common with them. Like the others, Charlie had to cope with what he called "survivor's guilt" and the feeling that he was personally responsible for helping other returning vets with their own cycles of depression.

On Friday, December 16, 2005, one Iraq vet, a member of IVAW named Douglas Barber, put a shotgun under his chin and pulled the trigger. Barber's suicide had an immediate and profound impact on Charlie. "They had to identify him with his tattoos. I had just talked to him the week before. I called my Vet Center counselor because I decided I needed help. I was in a very bad state of depression. I was struggling with suicidal ideation myself.

"I had a lot of overt symptoms. I ended up in a neighborhood that I should have known pretty well but couldn't figure out where I was. And the more I didn't know where I was, the more hyped up I got. The more I started feeling very vulnerable. The more I started going back to that thing of looking at the kids on the side of the road and looking at the windows and the doorways and the rooftops.

"I was in a really bad state when I finally got to my counselor. He sent me over to the VA hospital. He wanted to get me some medication, something to help me sleep, something to kind of knock me down a little bit. I get there and I had to register. It's three o'clock when they finally finish registering me. An hour later the triage nurse gets to me. I tell her I'm there because a friend of mine committed suicide and my VA counselor told me I should see someone because I got PTSD. She tells me the psychiatrist went home an hour ago, that I should come back to the walk-in PTSD clinic the next week.

"And essentially what she's saying is, 'Please get out of my emergency room. You're not a real patient.' Whether she was actually trying to say that or not, that's what she said to me. That's what I heard her say. And I walked out, pissed off, feeling completely disrespected. And the headline actually flies to my brain, 'Iraq Veterans Commits Suicide in VA Parking Lot.' Had I been just a little worse off, if I had been somebody else . . . I very well could have put a gun in my mouth in the parking lot of the VA." Having been through this, Charlie said, he would never judge others in a similar circumstance: "I will never tell anyone they can't commit suicide."

It was several years after this episode that we had met to talk, sitting huddled around a space heater in a chilly room in Charlie's Boone, North Carolina, home. GI benefits were limited, so Charlie kept the thermostat low and his other expenses down. And he was still trying to come to grips with his tour of duty in Iraq, his divorce and child custody battle being the two major aftershocks from his time there. While he had gone from a daily existence of surviving under mortal threat to the routines of a college student, all was definitely not right or at peace for Charlie or the world in general.

"HERE'S A PILL. DON'T BE SO PISSED OFF."

Over the years, the military has called soldiers' traumatic response to war shell shock, combat neurosis, battle fatigue, war-zone stress reaction, or, now, PTSD. This is all an improvement over calling the response to combat malingering or cowardice or, in more contemporary language, "anger dysregulation."

So what does Garett Reppenhagen think medical practitioners should do for individual veterans with PTSD? What response can they offer that takes into account the real traumas soldiers went through and the fact that what caused the traumas of war can hardly be traced simply to individual soldiers' vulnerabilities? Garett answered us in a patient though emphatic tone, punctuating key words with broad gestures.

"If you're a clinical doctor, you cannot fix a problem that's social and political. Let's say you sit down with a counselor and say, 'I've been betrayed by my government and I'm fucking pissed off, and this is debilitating. I am unable to fit into society. And it's directly because of the war.' Well, they're gonna be like, 'Here's a pill. Don't be so pissed off.' They try to make it your problem. And it's not your problem. It's society's problem. You don't have to readjust to society; society's going to have to readjust to you."

While many returning vets reject treatment because of the stigma attached to it or find it inaccessible, some antiwar vets accept treatment and medications but reject how the VA understands their diagnosis. Some refuse standard treatment and argue that other methods will help them move beyond their suffering. These antiwar vets all agree with VA doctors that they have received a traumatic injury to the self, but they see the injury as an assault not simply on their mind but on their whole person. What the medical establishment calls the disorder of PTSD they call a form of dehumanization.

Although some troops and veterans have sought relief from their post-traumatic nightmares by popping what some medics in Iraq sarcastically call "happy pills," Garett is staunchly opposed. "I'm certainly not going to take any medication. I am flat against that. Personally, I don't want to separate myself from my war experience. I think my war experience is part of who I am now, and I've got to learn to carry that. My healing comes through helping other veterans, being part of the movement. IVAW is redeeming me.

"I'm not necessarily the victim in this scenario. And I think that's where a lot of the people who envision PTSD get a little sidetracked. There's plenty of people that have experienced individual trauma, they've seen their buddy blown up in front of them, they couldn't help their buddy from getting shot. Or they saw innocent people get waxed, whatever.

There's plenty of scenarios where there is legitimate trauma, and that's going to be scarring."

But, Garett insists, for the most part, the average American soldier is not the victim. "He's the victimizer. And I think he feels like a criminal, honestly. He feels like the killer and the rapist and the thief, and he comes back to America and it's 'Thank you for your service.' But we're, like, 'You have no idea what you're thanking me for. You don't know what I did.'"

Like many vets, dissenting and otherwise, Garett is focused on what civilians do not understand, their sometimes deep ignorance of the most basic aspects of war and of this war in particular. Those veterans see civilians spitting on the soldier, but not in contempt for his war work. They see congratulatory civilians spitting, in a sense, on their experience, making them out to be someone other than who they are.

"And they're not being punished like a criminal would. If we did the things that we did in Iraq, in the streets of D.C., you would go to prison, and sometimes you'd just be executed. These guys aren't being punished. Society's not saying, 'Okay, you did a bad thing and here's your punishment and when you're done, you know, you did your time? And now you can go, you know?' So they feel like, 'Okay, I did it, I'm punished, now I can start over again.' These guys are coming back and, since they don't receive that punishment from society, they punish themselves, and they start drinking themselves to death and doing drugs and being abusive to their family and committing suicide because they can't find that redemption."

Garett knows some vets take other routes besides self-punishment. "Especially these kids in Walter Reed that are holding onto a noble cause for dear life because it's the only thread of sanity they have left. You tell them the war was a bunch of shit and they're like, 'Fuck you! I'm not here in this hospital missing my legs because of a lie. I did a good thing and I did the right thing and I did the honorable thing. And that's why I'm here.' They can't come to grips with the idea that they did it for nothing and are feeling like criminals."

Ultimately veterans like Garett who reject the definition of PTSD as a disorder are making a political statement more than a medical or personal psychological diagnosis. The point, both for antiwar veterans who seek counseling and medication for post-traumatic stress, and for those who prefer to avoid such treatment even though they may suffer from the same symptoms, is that regardless of medicalized analysis the fundamental cause of their affliction, in their minds, is that they have witnessed and participated in dehumanizing crimes against people in Iraq and Afghanistan. How soldiers react to civilian war injuries and death is clearly decisive, as we have seen, for their emerging critique of the war and their understanding of the injuries of war to themselves and others.

READJUSTMENTS AFTER THE WAR

Most soldiers arrive at what Garett calls "that polarized line" well before they get to Iraq: they see no middle ground and realize in a profound sense they have to be for or against the war. For obvious reasons, at least as long as they are busy dodging bullets and explosives and focused on working within the tight and generally positive bonds within their units, few come to openly oppose the war, even if they are skeptical about the larger justification for the mission: often feeling they have no choice, they stay on the prowar side of the line. Later on, when they return home, especially if they have been wounded, the motivation to believe that their tour or tours in Iraq were for some greater good is strong.

In Iraq itself, however, soldiers who believe the rationale for the war is primarily to spread democracy can quickly become resentful of the Iraqi people. "Guys go quickly to hate, just because in Iraq they're being hated on. You're being told, 'All right, soldier, you're going to Iraq and you're freeing those Iraqi people. You're giving them democracy, you're giving them safety.' And here they are, the Iraqis, trying to kill you! You're pissed off. 'If George Bush is right, I'm here helping you. And you hate me and want to kill me?! I'm risking my life, and I'm out here, away from my family, to help you, and all you do is resent me?' A lot of soldiers, it pisses them off. What they don't see is that maybe George Bush isn't telling them the truth. And that maybe that's not why they are in Iraq.

"A lot of guys don't see it until they get back. It takes other stuff to realize that maybe your government is lying to you. Maybe you're not getting the VA help that you want, and you're injured. And they realize, 'Wow, they're lying about the medical care that I'm going to get as a soldier. Maybe they also lied about the war.' That pisses people off. Maybe it's the nightmares. Maybe it's finally that they can release that shield around them. Before it was, 'Okay, I'm in combat, I have to believe this. I have to do my job, roll out the gate every day and do my job. I have to just accept that it's for the right reason.' And when they get home, they don't need that any more, other than to protect their sanity."

For Garett, hearing jackhammers can trigger an attack. "I just feel it in my spine. I don't feel like I'm being shot at. I feel like we are shooting out, and I'm like, Oh, contact! Where is it?! Where are they firing at so I can orient? I feel it in my gut and my spine." When we talked in February 2008, Garett still was most comfortable in a restaurant if he was facing the exits. "If I'm in a crowded restaurant, if my back's to the door, I feel a little crazy, especially if I am sitting at a bar. I feel very uneasy, so I often sit sideways." He remembers one time when he was living in Washington, D.C., after being discharged on May 31, 2005:

"I was just walking through kind of a hairy alley, just cutting through some buildings. I was already tense and a dump truck dropped a huge garbage bin. Caught me way off guard. I jumped. And I backed up to the side of the alley. I took a knee. And then I started moving again. For the rest of the walk home I was scanning buildings, looking in windows, looking on roofs. I got to my house, checked behind me, got inside and locked the door.

"Everybody talks about the desert in Iraq, how it was in the desert. But most of the time we were in a city in a desert. So it was very urban. We did missions out in fields and in rural areas trying to catch mortars and IED guys. But most of the action was all in the city."

He has seen some of the steadiest of his buddies collapse under the weight of what they saw and did in Iraq. One of them, a guy who "was all military, loved the military. He hated his family, so it was like the first real family he had was soldiers, so he loved it. He loved taking care of soldiers, so he made sergeant. He comes back, having some PTSD problems, and he can't get help for it. This kid is true blue American, never did a drug in his life." Then he came back, still in the military, got caught smoking pot, and got kicked out. "Lost all his benefits. When he came back he just felt the Iraq situation was so bad, and he couldn't get help."

"Then there's my buddy Zug. Zug was hit by seven IEDs and a vehicle car bomb in Iraq. He's got post-traumatic stress disorder and traumatic brain injury. He's still got shrapnel all throughout his body. He's, well, he's not as sharp as he was. He's forgetful. And he's got a very bad temper. When we got back to Germany he bit a kid's finger off in a bar fight. So, he's not okay. We lost track of him after he got a divorce."

That friend is one of approximately 320,000 veterans of the wars in Iraq and Afghanistan likely to have returned with a traumatic brain injury. Of these, only 43 percent told RAND researchers they had ever even been evaluated for their head injuries, and a significant number suffer from both brain and emotional injuries.

Watching those Kurosawa movies with his buddies back in Iraq, Garett and the others imagined how they would go to Japan if they survived the war. "It was our motivation for a while, a way to keep our spirits up. We didn't talk about having so many days until we got out of Iraq. We talked about having so many days until we were going to Japan. We started doing research and studying. I even got a language CD to learn how to speak Japanese. We kept that trip as our motivation.

"Also, one of my goals after experiencing war was to go to Auschwitz and Hiroshima. I wanted to see two monuments to the apexes of war, how destructive war can be. I wanted to see some history of what humans have done to each other in the history of time and through warfare. I wanted to look at the darkest moments. I have a lot of guilt about some of my stuff that I did in Iraq. I wanted to see how dark it was compared to other things that have been done."

The group got a thirty-day leave, and they used it to go to Hiroshima. "I found a little separation from what I was doing in Iraq and what those were. They were all just different situations, but there were elements of both. In the Peace Park in Hiroshima, there's a whole full-scale model of what Hiroshima looked like before and then what it looked like after, side by side, with the epicenter marked on where the bomb exploded, and the description of what all the buildings are. We were using this bridge as a landmark to drop the bomb, and on one side of the bridge there was a elementary school." As he might have expected, "It was hard being there and being American."

Ricky Clousing's "search for answers" continued when he returned home in April 2005. But he found little support among others in his unit. When they talked up details of what they had seen and done, no one seemed to be distressed in the same way as Ricky. "I wasn't well received when I came home. I was talking about things that bothered me. I was talking about some of the things I witnessed, and how they affected me. I was a sergeant now, and I guess I was always well liked by people. But I didn't blend into the Fort Bragg soldierization process as well as some people do. I had my hair on the verge of regulation all the time."

He was lucky in one respect, though. His immediate commander in Iraq, Chief Warrant Officer Kirby, was always there to listen.

"I went to my chief and was really candid with him. I told him I was wrestling with ideas. He's a Mormon, a spiritual person, and open to the spiritual side of things. He told me to go talk to the mental health people. I went down and chatted with them. I dumped more information on them than I think they were prepared to deal with. Because I wasn't just going in because I didn't know how to talk to my wife. I was having a meltdown. Iraq had shattered my worldview and the way that I perceived myself and my own identity."

Despite talking with his chief and mental health personnel, overall Ricky describes this period after his return from Iraq in spring 2005 as one in which "I really kind of closed up to everybody." As soon as he would get off work he would retreat to his room. He went online and began his reading of books critical of U.S. military interventions abroad. "It showed me what was happening in Iraq by giving me perspective on all these other times in history with the same kinds of events. It was nothing new, the business of war, the contracts, the organizations that rebuild countries.

"Then I went to the psychologist's office, the counselor's office. And I'm throwing out stuff that they didn't even know how to chew on. I'm ranting and raving. I was in a very different emotional state. I was talking about the Iraq War and history and U.S. foreign policy and that people don't even care. So I went in there and just dropped a bomb. And they didn't even know how to respond to me.

"And on top of all the new information that I was reading and taking in, I was coming at it all from a spiritual perspective. So from there the counselors just pawned me off to go talk to the chaplain because I was talking about religion. And I went to talk to the chaplain. I told him what I was feeling. Now, I went to a Bible school, so I'm not just some Sunday school kid that went to church. I had a pretty good understanding of the Bible and Christ's teachings.

"So I was talking to him about how I felt and that I didn't think the war in Iraq was right, and that we were not doing good over there, and that as a soldier I didn't know how I was supposed to be part of that and a Christian. I told him I didn't understand what all this meant.

"He just kept going and referring me to Old Testament scriptures about God blessing nations and about God ordaining war. All kinds of scriptures that were completely out of context. I knew this. I was like, How can he pull out this old, outdated stuff? He talked about Saul and the kingdom and God sending him to war to wipe out different tribes and blessing them. He also went into Romans 13, which I've had a huge issue with ever since I was in Iraq. It talks about how the government is established by God and that we're supposed to follow it."

The first two verses of Romans 13 that the chaplain was referring to read: "Let every soul be subject unto the higher powers. For there is no power but of God: the powers that be are ordained of God. Whosoever therefore resisteth the power, resisteth the ordinance of God: and they that resist shall receive to themselves damnation."

Ricky responded to the chaplain, "'So what about these governments established by God in other parts of the world? But our government all of a sudden doesn't agree with theirs so we kill them, and they're abiding by their government and honoring God?' He didn't answer any of my questions. He started getting really frustrated with me. I was, 'I'm not trying to call you out or catch you in something. I just don't understand things.'"

The chaplain, Ricky points out, had not even been in Iraq. "He was so disconnected from that war. He was following orders and throwing free Bibles out to people. He'd never been over there to see what I was talking about. Once I started talking about the political side of things, he just starting going off, really got frustrated, mad at me. He talked about the military level of not questioning our leaders. He directed me to start thinking about applying for CO. I didn't even know what CO was at this point."

After he found out what it meant to be a conscientious objector and began to get an idea of what might be involved in applying for CO status after having served in Iraq, Ricky told the chaplain and his command, "'I'm not trying to get out. I just got promoted to sergeant. I'm trying to find out what the hell's going on and what is expected of me.' Now that I was promoted I was in charge of people. And I didn't feel comfortable training them to go to war." They told Ricky that he wouldn't be deployed overseas again, that he could stay stateside. He considered this promise for a few weeks and came to the realization that "whether I was in uniform or not, whether I was in Iraq or not, I was still part of this machine of war." For two and a half months, as he later describes it, Ricky could not decide what to do, what he was supposed to do.

"I felt like I was being ripped. I felt like my identity was gone. I was being ripped from two different sides. The logical side of me was saying that I was a sergeant, in charge of a team, that I had been promoted and had a year and some to finish my contract, get my school, to suck it up and deal with it, go on financially. My logical side was telling me to come to grips.

"Then my emotional side and spiritual side inside of me was really at war with feeling that every day I was in uniform I would break down and feel trapped. What was I supposed to do? What was I going to do if I got deployed back to Iraq? I didn't know if I should apply for CO. I was trying to research it. I was really having a hard time.

"And I was having dreams of really nasty, really vulgar, violent stuff. People being decapitated, Iraqis. I kept seeing Iraqi people getting injured. I had one dream where I was standing by as this was happening and not doing anything.

"My mom was really supportive. I talked to her all the time. I would wake up in the middle of the night and call her."

DISORDER?

The mental health people wanted to put Ricky on antidepressants. But, he protested, "I am reluctant to say I have PTSD." Although he recognized that some soldiers came back pretty messed up mentally, he thought that for the Army PTSD was often used as "a patch" to conceal deeper problems. "I mean, really. Post-traumatic stress disorder? It's not a disorder. It's a natural reaction of culture shock, of being in a combat zone, and the realities and expectations of fighting, and being expected to kill people, and then coming back home to what we have here." Far from representing an abnormal adaptation to civilian life, Ricky added, traumatized soldiers were the norm: "They're actually tapped into their human and spiritual and emotional side enough to feel the effects of the war. They're not numb enough to just blow it off like it doesn't matter." He got frustrated when the media called PTSD a disorder, "because it's not really a 'dis.' It's not like people that have it are failing to adapt."

He was sent to classes on transitioning back from the war zone. "But I didn't need to be transitioned back into reality. I saw what reality with the U.S. in Iraq was now, and I was not okay with it." The only options he saw were applying for CO status or staying in the Army and dealing with it until his contract was up.

He started the paperwork for CO. In drafting his statement, he came to a point in the form where he had to explain his reasoning for opposing war, why he could no longer fight. Religious conviction had to be at the root of it, according to his military commanders. But this presented Ricky with a fundamental dilemma: "I didn't necessarily think that 100 percent of the time war was wrong."

He was definitely against the war in Iraq. He didn't even agree with what was going on in Afghanistan. But "everybody throws out the golden icon of World War II, and if we were in some World War II situation, naaaaah." The way he saw it, if there were some terrible tyrant taking over the world, he would probably enter the fight. "And I was, You know what? I can't say that if I was in World War II that I wouldn't fight. I know I wouldn't want to. I wouldn't want to be in war. All I can tell you is that I don't want to fight in this Iraq war right now." The commanders told Ricky that he couldn't be particular about conflicts and wars. It had to be every one and all the time.

"I went and told my commander, 'I don't think that CO status is for me.'"

While all the discussions about CO were occurring, Ricky had found a Web site for the GI Rights Hotline, a coalition of activist groups dedicated to providing GIs information on their rights within the military, including navigating the system of filing grievances and complaints, as well as the regulations concerning discharge, and he called them.[4] Like many people in the military, Ricky did not have someone he could talk with who was both outside the Army and knowledgeable about it. He spoke with Chuck Fager, a GI Rights counselor in Fayetteville, North Carolina, who, he said, "didn't have any influence on me, but just let me know all the different options of what I could do, and what might happen if you took any of those options—if you stayed in or whatever."

On the night of June 22, 2005, Ricky telephoned the woman he was seeing. "I was just super-restless, had another crazy night and dream. I woke up and called my girlfriend, who was actually still in the Army herself. I was freaking out and crying. She didn't want to talk in the middle of the night. So I got off the phone. What do I do? I just didn't feel like I could be there. Ahhh! Every day I was having anxiety attacks. In the mornings I'd be putting on my uniform and I was like, Oh, my God. I'm an agent of empire. This is crazy to me. I don't want to be here.

"My mom was very supportive. She just said, 'You know what? You need to be emotionally stable and emotionally happy and mentally happy. Those two parts of your health are very important. And if you have to leave to make yourself okay, then you need to do that. I'll support you if you do that.'"

At three o'clock in the morning Ricky looked around his barracks room and said to himself, "I'm leaving." He gathered his clothes, carrying them and other personal belongings down to his car in repeated trips. All his books, his TV, his computer. For three hours he made the circuit from barracks to car, hoping no one would see him. He had to be done by 6:00 when the duty day started. If it got to 6:30 a.m. and he was supposed to be at formation he would be sunk. The last thing he brought down was a snowboard that he strapped onto the roof of his car.

Before he left, however, Ricky taped a note to his door, with a quote from Martin Luther King, which he roughly remembered as follows: "Cowardice asks the question, 'Is it safe?' Expediency asks the question, 'Is it politic?' Vanity asks the question, 'Is it popular?' But conscience asks the question, 'Is it right?' And there comes a time when one must take a position that is neither safe, nor politic, nor popular, but one must take it because one's conscience tells one that it is right."[5]

Ricky knew what he was about to do would be unpopular with some people, perhaps even his friends. He knew deserting was the most dangerous decision of his life. But he'd reached a point where he had to do what his conscience demanded. Taping the quote to his door, he stepped away, went down the stairs one last time, and did what he knew was right.

"I was driving out of my barracks area and my platoon sergeant was walking across the street. He stopped and looked at me, with my car full of stuff and my snowboard on the top. I didn't even look at him. Just drove away. It was intense."

He turned his cell phone off and later, when he stopped at a rest area, called Sprint to have them shut off his phone for good. No one was going to find him or try to talk him out of his decision. From North Carolina he continued driving all the way across country, stopping to visit a couple of people along the way, finally arriving back in Seattle a little over a week after fleeing Fort Bragg, right before his birthday, the Fourth of July. Independence Day.

TO LEAVE THE NATION

You may be wondering what happened to Chris Magaoay, the Filipino American Marine from Hawai'i. He took on a mission other than a tour of Iraq. After months of doubts during basic and advanced training, he finally decided he'd had enough and headed for Canada, arriving there on March 7, 2006.

One day he was a lance corporal in Delta Company, 3rd Amphibious Assault Battalion, 1st Marine Division, in Twentynine Palms, California. Three days later, after a nonstop sprint across most of the continental United States with his wife in their 2004 light blue Nissan Sentra, he was just Chris Magaoay, a young guy on the run from the U.S. Armed Forces, hiding in Canada and just starting to realize he could never go home again. "My staff sergeant called me up and he said, 'Where the fuck are you?!' I told him, 'I'm in Canada!' What's he going to do, come and get me? There's no extradition—I looked it up."

Chris was not in hiding for long. The War Resisters Support Campaign that he had found online and contacted to find out how to flee to Canada had other plans for Chris. The day after he arrived he learned that there was something called International Women's Day that leftists around the world had been commemorating for most of the last hundred years on the 8th of March. People from the War Resisters Support Campaign asked Chris to speak at a rally they were organizing that day and he felt obliged. It was the beginning of many talks he was to give at rallies, meetings, and high schools all over the Toronto area and sometimes as far away as the small towns in northern Ontario. "I've done counter-recruitment here in Canada, which has 2,500 troops in Afghanistan."

For a guy who had been a "card-holding Republican" and a JROTC cadet in high school, Chris had been going through a lot of changes in just a few years. As we sat in a Korean restaurant in Toronto, Chris laughed when he casually mentioned, "I was pretty right-wing in high school. The only thing that I didn't believe for the right wing was same-sex rights. I believe you have the right to marry. Prochoice things are still iffy with me. I was baptized Mormon when I was around five. My grandmother at the same time took me to Catholic services. In high school I attended the Assemblies of God services, as right-wing, gung-ho as you can get."

Among the key people who helped Chris and his wife get settled in the Toronto area, he singled out the Religious Society of Friends, the

Quakers, and the Mennonite community. "They gave us housing for the first month. Where I come from, churches don't get along with each other. But the Quakers and the Mennonites seem to get along. They donate money, offer housing and shelter. They were great people."

When we spoke in May 2008, Chris added, "I have some spiritual feeling, and I believe there's some kind of higher power. Sometimes I catch myself reaching out for a higher power, for logic in everything that's going on. But I also believe that organized religion is the cause for a lot of the struggles throughout the world and throughout our history." His disdain for military recruiters based on his experience in the Marines doubled when he talked about military chaplains. "First you get recruited by the military, then inside they have chaplains, religious recruiters trying to pick your brain and steer you away if you are searching for some compassion in the world." If you are having thoughts about deserting, Chris said, "you go talk to the chaplain and he tries to talk you out of it."

Given his religious upbringing combined with his searching for some empathy while in the Marines, Chris faced daily moral challenges as his deployment to Iraq grew closer. Ultimately, as we know, he chose desertion over deployment. "For me it took more courage to resist against the government, and resist against your friends, your family, and the political beliefs of your entire nation. Well, at least what they portray as the political beliefs of the entire nation." But in Chris's view, "A coward is the one who just follows direction and gets pushed around. It takes courage to make your own decisions and say, 'No, forget it.' That's my personal opinion."

One reason he thought it was difficult for many Americans to understand how much courage it took to desert was the lack of information about the Iraq War and the actual nature of combat. "The U.S. government has learned a big lesson from the Viet Nam era. You don't let reporters show live coverage of Americans shooting up Viet Cong and civilians and napalm. I've seen video clips where you have these piles of Vietnamese bodies on NBC live. You're never going to see that about Iraq. The military has learned how to cram down on the media and how to clamp down on public education so they can't teach these things." In this kind of context, Chris felt that he was always going against the opinions of others, even if these opinions were often based more on ignorance than knowledge about the war and military service.

According to Chris, his wife, Rea Rose, supported him when he joined the Marines, joined him near Twentynine Palms when he was based there, and agreed to accompany him to Canada when he fled the Marines in March 2006. She was a Canadian citizen, and Chris counted on this to establish himself legally in Toronto. But "as my politics and feelings towards the war started to shift, our relationship strained a lot. I was different. She was different. She didn't agree with a lot of the antiwar stuff. When I came home we'd have huge fights over why I was not out looking for work, why I was organizing. She wanted me to stay as far away from activism as possible." In July 2006, barely four months after Chris had arrived in Canada as a Marine on "unauthorized absence," he and Rea Rose broke up and began filing for divorce.

In some ways, as hurtful as the divorce proved, the most distressing consequence of Chris's flight to Canada was his father's reaction. "When I deserted, at first he was pretty embarrassed. He didn't understand what was going on. He just thought that I was a coward because I was a deserter. He thought I left because I was afraid to fight.

"I called him a few months after getting to Canada and told him how I felt, explained the political situation. I told him I couldn't fight because of what I believe in, that what we were doing was wrong. My dad could have done a lot of wrong things, but he understood the idea behind fighting for what is right and what is wrong. When he started to understand that civilians were dying and what my sergeant showed me about lighting a cigarette off a charred body in Iraq, he started to understand. In turn, he's been telling all his friends what's going on there. But he still wants me to come home."

SITTING WITH YOUR BACK TO THE WALL

When Tina Garnanez returned to New Mexico, she was one of many who came back home with memories that tormented her, recollections of all these things she had seen and done. A lot of people self-medicate with drugs and alcohol, and Tina did drink too much, she said, at the beginning. Some veterans of the Iraq War have committed suicide, others have thought about it when they find themselves unable to hold down jobs because, as Tina put it, they no longer have "customer service skills." Even people once tolerant and outgoing, like herself, develop "a very short fuse, so short it's almost nonexistent." She added, I don't think I could tolerate dealing with a customer who rubs me the wrong way and having to smile nicely and be like 'You're right . . . here ya go, I'm sorry I screwed that up.'" If you can't interact with customers, it's often hard to keep a regular job, even to sit at a desk and be friendly to co-workers. This sad reality for many Iraq veterans, she said, is similar to what happened to Viet Nam veterans as well. They came back and they were never the same again.[6]

After we spoke with Tina one evening in Santa Fe, New Mexico, in June 2008, we returned the next day to pick up our conversation across her kitchen table. She said she'd had a bad night, tormented by what our questions and her answers had provoked. "I didn't sleep much," she confessed. She tried to explain to us "what it's like when I speak about all this. I get all nervous. It feels like going downstairs into this really creepy basement, and finding all these creepy things that you've avoided or tried to put away, and then bringing them upstairs and putting them out in the front yard and letting everyone on the street walk by and look at them." At four in the morning her girlfriend was soothing her and whispering, "'Just think of all the kids who will read this and think of all the people you'll be helping by reading this.' And I was, 'Okay, yeah, I'll do it.'"

Northern New Mexico looks like parts of Iraq, and when Tina first returned from the war and saw a dead prairie dog or a dead skunk while driving with her family, "I'd freak out. The Iraqis would put bombs in anything, you know, cans, dead animals, mounds of dirt in the road." Her family saw her reaction out on the roads around Farmington and they thought, "Oh, my, something's not right with her."

The first thing Tina's family noticed was that she was "skittish, very jumpy. I had been the happiest little girl in the world, and then I came home and, 'Grrrrrr!' Angry rage. Sleepless nights—I just didn't want to have nightmares and I'd stay awake or read or go to IHOP and drink iced tea, write in my journal. But I wasn't feeling safe in a crowd either, really." The night we met in 2008, Tina sat with her back to the rest of the customers in the restaurant we were in and used reflections on the top of the salt shaker to check behind her.

"When I'm driving in the middle of nowhere," she said, "it's not so bad. Just keep an eye on the road, hilltops, ridges, whatever. But when I'm back in town I'm watching the windows, the people, their hands, the little kids across the street, what's in the road. If I don't know where I'm going, it's too hard for me, too much to take in." Running was still one of her enduring releases, and she jogged with her dog Calamity Jane and her headphones almost every day.

The Army's response to soldiers who experienced such anguish, at least initially, Tina said, was "'You're okay, got all your limbs. Be grateful.' But a few soldiers don't seek treatment for PTSD because they're afraid of losing their benefits. They'd ask to go to the Army doctors to get help, and sometimes they would give them a diagnosis other than PTSD so when they go to get medically discharged, they don't receive their benefits. Yeah, I've heard that happen to someone I know, and I'm just thinking, God that's terrible." This is in fact a very real risk. To growing controversy, the military has been discharging troops with PTSD and other mental health issues by asserting that their symptoms are the result of a "preexisting condition," that is, a condition that predates their recruitment. Such a discharge makes them ineligible for medical care for their combat injuries. Over the six-year period up to 2007, 22,500 individuals were so discharged.[7]

Other stories that Tina had heard were cautionary tales as well. There was the story of a man whose "son came back with PTSD and depression, and he was committed to a hospital, and as soon as he got out and was well enough to leave, they sent him back to Iraq. They were like, 'Hey, we need more soldiers,' and they sent him back."

Tina herself became aware of her diagnosis only after she had been home for some time. She was at a conference with other vets when PTSD was discussed. They were "listing all the symptoms, and I'm just like, 'Oh my gosh, I've got that and that and that and that.' And I'm like, 'Oh my God, I've got PTSD.' It didn't really click until I was there. Because I just wondered what was wrong with me. I was like, 'God, I was never like this before. What am I doing?' Anger, and crazy behavior, not normal, but I would always put it off on something else" like being stressed or tired.

It took Tina three years to prepare her case for disability status with the VA. It was clearly upsetting to her to share this history with us. Frustration and anger seemed to go against her deep desire to make peace with the world and all those with whom she interacted. The forms required her to list stressful incidents, with dates and details about her unit and where they were deployed. "I'd start trying to think about one and then it would turn into a big long thing and then I'd get pissed off and, 'Just screw this!' And I'd have to start again a month or two later. To go back and relive it all and bring it all back brings up so many emotions."

It had also taken Tina several years to be able to hear her mother comment to someone else, "This is my daughter, Tina. She was in Iraq." For a long time, Tina would interject, "Mom! Stop!" wanting to hide this from others at home. "I was so ashamed of it. I didn't want to be in Iraq, and I totally disagreed with the war. It wasn't something I was proud of until I went to Wounded Warrior, a four-day retreat that was all Native American healing techniques. Before that I was very ashamed of being a vet, and I didn't want anyone to know."

After attending Wounded Warrior in Oregon in the winter of 2008, Tina had a change of heart. At least in part. After this experience, "it wasn't so much being proud of being a vet, but no longer being ashamed of it. Accepting it as part of who I was now. It wasn't, 'Woo, hoo, I'm a vet!' It was a part of me. So when my mom did it after that, I was, 'Ah, shucks, Mom,' though it's not something I go around advertising."

Accepting that she was suffering from PTSD and that being a veteran was not something she had to hide, Tina began to help others in her family, among them her great-uncle Willis, the one who had been a gunner in Korea and whom they called Crash Willis because he'd been in so many car crashes: "He had so many vehicles, and they're all held together with duct tape and bailing wire, and ya know, just so many accidents."

"That man is crazy," she relates with a laugh. "He's not *crazy*, but, well, no one understood him until I came home with PTSD. Now we're making the link, 'Oh, that's what's going on!' And he understands me. Sometimes we go off by ourselves and just talk about everything. He's my buddy."

Such bonds between veterans, kin or not, have been lifesaving for many. They are used to navigate the return home, through the maze of injuries and the even more stressful obstacles of care.

EIGHT Speaking Out

A W O L   I N   S E A T T L E

The path back to Seattle for Ricky Clousing was almost like a road to anywhere in Iraq during the war: traveling across the country at a frightening clip, his way scattered with unknown debris and the metaphoric threat of explosions by the wayside that could stop him dead in his tracks. Sensibly enough, Ricky described the decision to go AWOL as both sudden and not impulsive at all. His was a decision a long time in coming, no matter how impetuous it might appear to outsiders. This was the culmination of all Ricky had been living, thinking, feeling, reading, and coming to realize. Even though he had left his post in the middle of the night, "There wasn't a defining moment of just deciding I was fed up." It had been a long transition to the point where he was able to return to his sense of living as a young man with an ethical center.

For thirteen months from mid-2005 to mid-2006, Ricky was AWOL in the Seattle area. "I wasn't trying to desert or disappear forever. But at the same time, I didn't know what to do. So I was kind of waiting." On arriving in the Northwest, he got more information from the GI Rights Hotline and their "Help for Unauthorized Absence (AWOL) Members of the Military" Web site. He learned that after he had been gone for thirty days he was dropped from the military's rolls ("DFR," in the language of the armed forces). After that, if and when he returned to the military, he would be discharged, punished, or both.

But the reception at home was not as positive as he had expected and hoped it would be. When he arrived in Seattle a little more than two years after the initial U.S. invasion, the war "was still a sour topic, it wasn't something that people were open and willing to talk about. At that point, I felt like nobody in the country even knew what was going on, so they didn't want to talk about it. It was like one of those weird dinner conversations where you just don't want to bring it up because nobody wants to talk about, but everybody has their own feelings about it, but nobody knows what's happening, or what's going on." All the more reason for him not to tell anyone but his closest family and friends that he was on an "unauthorized absence" from the military. Even among the few who did learn about his situation, there was too little support for him and what had been a terribly difficult decision.

"When I finally decided to go AWOL, I really thought I would be well received by my friends and family that were still active in the church, that were Christians. When people in church disagreed with my decision, it really made me step back even more and realize how the church was so intertwined with the government's idea of war and how we fight."

His disappointment with church members' response was a further challenge to his previous religious beliefs. When we first spoke in September 2006, Ricky still considered himself a Christian, and his dissent was very much couched in biblical language and belief. By February 2008, however, when asked if he still saw himself as a Christian, Ricky replied, "I don't identify myself as a Christian except the way Gandhi said, 'I'm a Christian, a Muslim, a Hindu. I'm everything.' In that sense, it's not that I am *not* a Christian anymore. My friends are still involved in the church, and I'm still that person in the foundation.

"A part of my quest of finding truth and trying to find out what it means is on a spiritual level, not just a political or historical one. When I was in Iraq, one of the translators I worked with was a Sufi, and I really started reading some of the Sufi writings. When I came back I was really in this conundrum of not knowing if my traditional view of God and my framework of spirituality was accurate or right, or at least right for me. I stepped back and found a lot of inspiration from Gandhi." It was at this time that Ricky added another tattoo to his "VI" that stood for the six siblings in his family. The new one had the Hindu sign for the sound used in some forms of meditation, *Om*.

Now with a lawyer and the continued help of the GI Rights Hotline, Ricky continued to explore his options. His lawyer contacted his Army unit to find out where he should go, but the military stonewalled, refusing to inform Ricky where his unit was then stationed or what he was supposed to do. He told himself that if a whole year had gone by from the date of his initial departure from Fort Bragg and his situation was not resolved, he would simply turn himself in to the Army. If he was going to bring his year as a fugitive to an end, he now had to decide if he would do this quietly or if he wanted to go public. "I never had the intention of wanting to go to the news and talk to everybody, but after stepping back and realizing that it's something that I felt people deserved to hear about and a perspective that people needed to hear about," he decided, "I did want to go public."

In the meantime, in June 2006, Lieutenant Ehren Watada had become the first officer to publicly refuse to deploy to Iraq, arguing that the war violated the Constitution and the War Powers Act, as well as the UN Charter, Geneva Conventions, and Nuremburg Principles, all of which make "wars of aggression" illegal. He was charged not only with "missing movement" but with "conduct unbecoming" for making public statements against the war.[1] For war dissenters within the military, this created an even chillier climate than the one Ricky already faced.

As it happened, the Veterans for Peace organization was going to hold their annual conference in Seattle in August 2006. Ricky wanted to coordinate his public return to the Army with that event by holding a press conference at the same time. "In my backyard, all these antiwar people were gathering. I contacted the director of the conference, told him about my situation, what I wanted to do, to add momentum to the cause, and proposed that we plan a press conference on the day of the conference. The morning of my press conference, Friday, the 11th of August 2006, I had an exclusive interview with Amy Goodman on *Democracy Now.*"

Later in the day, he went to the campus of the University of Washington to read a statement to reporters from Canada, Germany, France, New Zealand, and the United States:

"First, to my family, friends, brothers and sisters of the religious community, members of the press, and fellow citizens of this nation we are grateful to call home, thank you for your support here today before I turn myself over to military custody.

"My name is Ricky Clousing. I am a sergeant in the United States Army, and I have served for three years and have been absent from my unit since June 2005. Like many in uniform today, I enlisted after the events of September 11th, wanting to defend the freedoms and privileges we enjoy here. After eighteen months of instruction I completed my necessary training as an interrogator and was assigned to the 82nd Airborne Division. As the invasion of Iraq unfolded I felt confused about the premise behind such an attack. But in November of 2004, I deployed to Iraq in support of the first stage of elections to be held.

"In Iraq I operated as an interrogator and was attached to tactical infantry units during daily patrol operations. As an interrogator I spoke to Iraqis each day. This gave me an idea of what local civilians thought of coalition forces. Throughout my training very appropriate guidelines for the treatment of prisoners were set. However, I witnessed our baseless incarceration of civilians. I saw civilians physically harassed. I saw an innocent Iraqi killed before me by U.S. troops. I saw the abuse of power that goes without accountability.

"Being attached to a tactical infantry unit and being exposed to the brutalities of war, I began to second-guess my beliefs. I thought about these experiences and what they meant each day I was deployed and until I was back in garrison in April of 2005. Upon my return I started to ask my unit the same questions I had been asking myself.

"Wearing the uniform demands subordination to your superiors and the orders passed down. But what if orders given violate morality, ethics, and even legality? If those orders go unquestioned down my chain of command, am I exempt from reevaluating them? My convictions, spiritually and politically, began to second-guess my ability to perform day-to-day functions as a soldier. I could not train or be trained under a false pretense of fighting for freedom.

"Under the recommendation of my unit, I sought counsel from military chaplains and counselors, and as my feelings crystallized I realized that I could not fulfill the duties expected of me. After months of questioning, I began considering the possibility of leaving. Each day I felt haunted by my conscience that my association in uniform at this time was wrong, and my involvement directly or indirectly in this organization at this time was a contradiction to my beliefs.

"I stand here before you today about to surrender myself, which was always my intention. I do not know what to expect, or the course of my future. We have found ourselves in a pivotal era where we have traded humanity for patriotism. Where we have traded our civil liberties for a sense of security. I stand here before you sharing the same idea as Henry David Thoreau: as a soldier, as an American, and as a human being, we must not lend ourselves to that same evil which we condemn.

"Thank you."

Looking back on that eventful day, Ricky says he has few regrets. At the time, "I could honestly say that I felt at total peace about my decision. I knew I was doing the right thing, I knew that the journey I was on and the path I was on was laid out before I could even know that it was there. I was a stronger person because of the decision. Whatever would happen, I knew that there was a long list of people who had suffered and been sent to prison for resisting the government in one way or another, or for speaking out for one thing or another. If that happened, I would join the ranks of people that had suffered for doing the right thing."

After talking with the national and international press for over four hours, Ricky went to have a last meal with his family. Then they drove him down to Fort Lewis, near Tacoma, down the interstate from Seattle.

"I walked up to the gates. They already knew who I was. I think they saw it on TV. When I got to the gate the MPs bum-rushed our car. So they arrested me right then and I went into Fort Lewis. I was there around three days until they processed me. I was kept on house arrest, in one room the whole time. They organized my return to my unit and shipped me out Monday morning. But of course this is the government, so they're going to give me the cheapest, most undesirable way back. They bought me a bus ticket."

The MPs dropped Ricky off at the bus station and told him his bus left in six hours and he had better be on it. This was on Monday the 14th of August, and if he wasn't at Fort Bragg in North Carolina the following Friday the 18th, he would have added charges against him.

Instead of taking the bus, Ricky once again came up with an alternative solution. "I stayed at home for a few more days with my family and friends, and I flew out on Thursday, arrived at the airport on Friday, and turned myself in at Fort Bragg."

THE BRIG

The court-martial was not for two more months. During the wait, Ricky mowed grass and did other odd chores on post. The Army wanted to charge him with desertion, but he had turned himself in, and by doing so he felt he had negated that charge. In addition, he remained committed to the idea of having been, and continuing to be, a good soldier, which is to say, one who does the right thing and follows orders. "I said I would take responsibility for going AWOL. I would plead guilty. But I wasn't a deserter. I didn't desert because that means I had the intention to never return. I had been promoted to sergeant as fast as you can be promoted. I'd never got in any trouble before."

There were at least twenty others in his platoon of DFRs at Fort Bragg, men who had been apprehended or had turned themselves in. "I don't think any of their decisions were rooted as much in the politics and philosophical reasons that I was dealing with, but I think that, if not all of them, at least 90 percent of them felt the same way I did about things."

Partially as a result of the media attention to his case, Ricky believes, the military treated him in unusual ways. "Before I got there the other guys that were in the AWOL unit had no privileges. They had to sign in on the hour, every hour. They weren't allowed to go on and off post.

They weren't allowed to even talk to lawyers. They hadn't been getting paid. When I arrived, partly because I'm a NCO and I was the highest-ranking guy in the group, I was given my own room with a bathroom. I was told I didn't have to sign in. I was able to go on and off post. I was set up with a lawyer right away. Then all their restrictions were lifted. So they jokingly called me 'the Savior.' I think because of the media attention the Army was aware that people were watching how they were treating soldiers that went AWOL."

Ricky was facing a maximum sentence of one year in military prison, and in a pretrial agreement his lawyer was able to reduce the sentence to three months' "capped time" in the brig. In October 2006, Ricky was driven to the Marine Corps base at Camp Lejeune to begin serving his time.

From October until his release a week early for good behavior, on Christmas Eve 2006, Ricky Clousing spent all day in the Camp Lejeune brig reading. The great thing, as far as he was concerned, was that they allowed him to read anything he wanted. "I couldn't bring anything. I had to get books sent to me that were from the publisher or Barnes & Noble. Something sealed. But, yeah, I got a lot of great literature when I was there. People were sending me books all the time."

Not until he began receiving mail from people all around the world, from New Zealand, Great Britain, other parts of Europe, Africa, and more, did he tell other people in the brig about his situation. With the Internet and networks of antiwar activists, word had gone out that he was in jail, and he began receiving as many as ten or fifteen letters each day, which made his buddies in the brig ask, "Who the hell are you?!"

Other than a couple of soldiers who, like him, were serving their sentence for having gone AWOL, most of the other forty men in the brig were there for drug offenses, insubordination, assault, and other crimes. He wasn't called "the Savior" here, but all his fan mail did earn him the nickname Hollywood. As at Fort Bragg, conditions here generally improved with Ricky's arrival. Yet they remained austere, even cruel and unusual. "It's so unlike normal jail, not that I've been before, but just from talking to other people, that when you're in a county jail or a normal jail you can play cards, sleep all day, watch TV, whatever. We weren't—we had to get up at five in the morning, make our hospital bunk beds, clean up, do our personal hygiene, sit on the side of our beds in these little chairs, we weren't allowed back on our beds until ten o'clock that night. We had to sit in our chairs, not falling asleep, just sitting there, all day until we got called to do details. Some days you just sit there all day."

After he was released on Christmas Eve, 2006, Ricky flew to New York City, where he met and fell in love with a woman named Kristy. When we talked in February 2008, Ricky and Kristy had moved to Las Vegas, where she had a job in a school and Ricky was taking classes to be a casino dealer, naturally one of the main jobs with good pay available in the area. To make ends meet before receiving his license, Ricky was working in a hotel gift shop on the Strip, where he even got to use some of the training he'd received care of the U.S. Armed Forces with French-speaking tourists. He was also hoping to become more active in the future in Iraq Veterans Against the War.

THE IMPACT OF ONE'S OWN WORDS

After she returned to Farmington, New Mexico, in April 2005, Tina Garnanez gradually became active in the antiwar movement. She taught herself to speak at rallies and other public events. At first she hung out with small groups in the northwest corner of the state when they held vigils or other protests. Often someone would say, "Hey, we have an Iraq veteran here," and then she would get asked to say a few words. Fairly soon, after moving to Silver City in southwestern New Mexico, she found herself at a meeting of the Grant County Peace Coalition.

Though not wanting to make a big deal out of her combat veteran status, she did mention it to a couple of people she met, and "They just thought that was the greatest thing ever." Members of the Green County Peace Coalition were headed for Crawford, Texas, to join Cindy Sheehan, the mother of Casey Sheehan, who had been killed in Iraq on April 4, 2004, at her protest encampment outside George Bush's ranch. Tina decided to join the caravan and stayed at Crawford for ten days. After only a day there, word spread as if "I had it tattooed on my forehead that I was an Iraq vet. Everybody wanted my attention."

She was soon in demand as a speaker at antiwar events around the country. From Crawford she headed for Virginia, then Washington, D.C., and various college campuses and town hall meetings.

"The support was overwhelming. There were a lot of people who opposed this war, and I thought that was very powerful. I talked to a lot of protesters," she says. "It was the protesters who brought me home. They were the one thing that inspired me, saved me.

"I had sat there feeling betrayed by my government as I watched the news, 'One hundred protesters rallied today to stop the war in Iraq.' That made me happy. I would think, Wow, they want us home as much as we want to be home. I was very grateful. Some people were saying, 'You're lowering morale. You're sending the troops the wrong message.' But I knew there was a huge difference in supporting the troops and not the war, because that's what I was doing. We felt so isolated, so abandoned. To see some of the American people opposed to this war made us very happy. We felt very loved.

"I was interviewed constantly. I had no idea that there was such a need for veterans to speak. It was very hard at first. When I first started I didn't realize the impact of my own words, my experience. I kept it light; I kept it simple. I was in Iraq and it was bad and that was it. But as I started thinking about it more and hearing other people's stories, I realized I needed to go deeper. I needed to go to the dark scary places inside and use those memories.

"The first time I spoke about something like that was in Virginia. I stood on the stage crying, trying to talk. When I finished, the positive response was overwhelming. Later, I didn't prepare anything when I talked, because I couldn't read when I was crying. I just talked from whatever came out. I taught some people a thing or two about what was happening. And they said I should share my story with their kids."

She became increasingly comfortable speaking in public against the war. Tina jumped with enthusiasm into high school visits, trying to dissuade other young people from joining the military. "When I go into a school, a teacher sets up the whole thing, clears it with the principal, and then just brings their class. Teachers would do this awesome thing, ask the kids before we spoke, 'How many of you have considered joining?' All these hands fly up in the air. Then we would speak and at the end of the session and ask again, 'Who wants to join the military?' And maybe one kid kind of timidly raises his hand. Mostly they are, 'Thank you. I thought of going but now I don't want to.' I'm like, 'Good, good, another kid is not going to come home messed up and in pain, or addicted to drugs or alcohol.'"

When she talked with high school students, Tina made a point to explain the options to pay for college besides the military. "Don't forget there are scholarships, grants, AmeriCorps, many different ways to pay for school," she told them. And as for travel to exotic lands, "If you want to go into the service because you want to see the world, it's not going to be to the places you'd pick to travel. They're going to send you where they want, which is Iraq."

Having been in JROTC herself in school, she felt she was able to connect with the aspirations and uncertainties facing high school students. "I went into the high schools and I saw all these young seventeen-, eighteen-year-olds. I'm like, Oh, look at the babies. They look so cute! They're not much younger than me, but God, they look so young. Some walk in to my talks curious and wide-eyed, 'Who's this girl?' Some walk in sort of angry, 'Oh, God, another boring public speaker.' And I sit there and I'm like, Okay, I've got to talk to these kids. I've got to tell them something that's real.

"Just to see them at the beginning, talking to their friends, playing with their cell phones, or whatever. Then, in the middle and at the end, they're all sitting there, just riveted, completely captivated. They pay attention. They're listening. And they're crying. They're all sitting there, like, 'Oh, my God. I don't want to go to war.' And afterwards they come and they thank me. I love it when a boy or girl comes up and says, 'I was thinking about joining, and what you have said changed my mind. Or it made up my mind that I don't want to go.'

"I touch on a lot of subjects: You have a future, there are other options. I tell them this war is illegal, immoral, and what it does to you when you come home. I talk about protesting. I don't want them going uninformed.

"I hate that I have to hurt them by sharing the brutal, honest truth. They're scared and they're crying. This little girl had signed up for the Air Force. She was saying, 'I'm going into the Air Force and this is going to happen to me!' She was crying and I felt terrible afterwards. I just hugged her and said, 'Oh, honey, I'm sorry.' I had no idea. Or they have family members who are there, and they are thinking about my stories happening to their family. But they need to know.

"I usually try to include a Dalai Lama or a Gandhi quote, because those are my heroes. Nonviolence and compassion, that's all we need really. There's no need for weapons and fighting and anger and all that. I could easily, easily be this bitter, hardened woman. But my little heart's too happy, doesn't know how not to love. So she got me through it, and she just loves everybody. You know, it's a good little heart."

BURNING MEMORIES

Military recruiters can be especially poisonous, Tina believed. "Some of them will be honest but others will sugarcoat a lot of things. I don't want kids having only one side of the picture. I want them to see the whole truth. You *can* come home missing an arm, missing a leg, paralyzed for the rest of your life. Or you can come home with all your limbs and have PTSD, or come home after being raped. That's reality. I don't think recruiters sit them down and tell them that these things are possible. It's just, 'Oh, go serve your country. Go join the military and see great things and go to school and all is well.'

"I tell the kids, 'You can look at me and I look okay, I pass as normal. But there's so much inside, so much pain and anger and suffering. It never goes away. Most of my day is spent just dealing with myself. If you've ever noticed all the homeless people on the street, notice they're all wearing camo jackets. You go, you come home, and you don't come back normal. You don't just come back, get a job, all is well. I was very confused and didn't know I had PTSD. I didn't know why I wanted to jump across the table and smash someone in the head for saying something I didn't agree with.'"

At one high school event, a couple of kids had made antirecruitment posters, and they were standing next to a recruiter at the high school. The recruiter stood in the auditorium sneering while Tina was thinking to herself, "Oh, my God, that's wonderful. These high school kids are taking their future into their hands and saying, 'You're not getting me!'" She also challenged school principals to not allow recruiters on their campuses, reasoning that no groups that discriminate are permitted so why were they giving the military access? "I told the kids they discriminate against gays. Ask your principal why discriminatory groups are allowed on campus."

One of the nicest things that happened to Tina after she left the military was coming out to her family and friends. After this, "There was nothing to hide, and I love that. Everybody knows I am gay. It was the biggest secret I held on to, and I freaked myself out for nothing." She was especially nervous about how her mom would react. "I thought for sure she'd say, 'You're going to hell. The Bible says . . .' My wonderful mom just said, 'I know, I know.'" She also found groups of veterans like Vets4Vets, which runs special weekend workshops, some of which are designed for gay or female veterans. Soon after we talked in June 2008, following a week helping out with the family's sheep and goats, Tina was headed to San Francisco to participate in the Gay Pride events on a float just for gay and lesbian veterans.

Tina met members of the Iraq Veterans Against the War early on, in Crawford in 2005. "I had no idea there were so many of them. I thought I was this lone Iraq veteran who was doing this stuff. I was like, Wow, there's more than one! Wow, there's a group!" She signed up on the spot. "Whenever I ran into a veteran we immediately bonded," she said, and with IVAW she found an outlet: "people I can talk with instead of being home by myself." Not that everyone responded well to her antiwar message. "When I was protesting in Crawford and D.C., people would drive by and flip us off or yell things out the window, calling us 'un-American' and 'unpatriotic,' calling me a 'traitor' and saying I loved Saddam and bin Laden. Oh, my God! They have no idea what they're talking about."

The friendships she formed with other antiwar veterans were vital to Tina's mental health. In addition to activism, meditation, and jogging, she also participated for two months on The Longest Walk, an environmental awareness trek across California and Arizona in the winter of 2008. In the solitude of her marches each day, she said, "all the things that I had been avoiding about the war just kept coming up. I had to face them and walk with them for twenty miles." After leaving the Army in spring 2005, Tina continued to work on her beading and collage projects, to write in her journal, and to spend as much time as she could outdoors. She even got a job with the Forest Service for a while.

Her family was very proud of her activism. "Well, my mother. My brothers really don't know what I'm doing. My brother Miles told me, 'Well, you did sign up.' And I said, 'Well, yeah, I did.' But I was stop-lossed an additional year and sent to Iraq. I told him if the war were really truly for terrorism I wouldn't be protesting. I would just shut my little mouth and go about my life. But it wasn't about terrorism. It was about one man's agenda and his greed. He and his wonderful buddies, just making money while poor kids are sent off to be cannon fodder. I disagreed with that, so I spoke out when I got home. It's very sad. He told me, 'You do have a point. You didn't volunteer for *this* cause.'"

Tina knew she had been an Army volunteer. And she did not regret everything about her decision to enlist. "At times I am really grateful for the experience of being in Iraq, because it opened my eyes to so much. Not only are we all connected, but we *have* to work together. We have to love one another. There's no way one of us or a small group of us is going to make it alone. It's just not possible. Compassion and love were things I learned in Iraq. Because of the war. Without the war I don't think I would feel it so much. I mean, I always thought we should work together, but not until that experience did it really fully hit me."

Through much of her five years in the U.S. military, Tina kept journals where she documented her ideas, fears, dreams, and anything important that was happening in her life. "I would write, fill them up, put them away." One day a year or two after she returned from Iraq, she was at her grandmother's in Oakspring, Arizona. She was feeling "this growing anger towards the war, towards the government. It was a building thing for me. I didn't want to have ever been there." She felt she had to do something dramatic to put all that behind her. So what did she do? "I just burned a lot of stuff."

She gathered many of the journals and some photographs and pictures she'd made, found a big trash barrel, and "I just threw it all in there and watched it burn. I just needed to do a big cleansing. I didn't want those memories, any of those reminders." Did that get rid of the memories and reminders? "No," Tina laughed, "but if felt really good."

BRINGING THE WAR HOME

As the first active-duty soldier to join the Iraq Veterans Against the War, Garett Reppenhagen had no trouble hitting the ground running when he returned to the United States. Discharged from the Army at the end of May 2005, Garett began attending meetings in Colorado Springs with Vets4Vets, an organization started by a Marine veteran of the Vietnam War to provide opportunities for veterans of Iraq and Afghanistan to talk with each other about the challenges of coming home from war. He was later offered a job in Washington, D.C., working with the Vietnam Veterans of America Foundation (VVAF), which later changed its name to Veterans for America.

While still in the Army, back in Iraq, around the same time he established contact with and joined the IVAW, Garett and other active-duty enlisted soldiers were blogging on the Fight to Survive Web site, which became one of the central sites for GI resistance on the Internet. The blogs continued after they arrived in Germany for three months to "stabilize" after combat duty. A woman who called herself Newt contacted Garett and asked him to write for her blog, "This Is Rumor Control." Bobby Muller, the director of the VVAF and the co-founder of the International Campaign to Ban Landmines, read Garett's blogs and contacted him on a visit to Germany. Muller was paralyzed in Viet Nam in 1969 and had built the VVAF and been working on vets' issues for more than thirty years.

"He wanted to meet me, so I jumped on the train and met him in Frankfurt. We sat down to breakfast and were supposed to just do that, but we ended up sitting at the same table until lunchtime. We were still arguing, talking about the war, and what we wanted to do. I saw anger and a despair in him that I couldn't get past. It was like he saw everything in full circle happen over again. It was as if by sitting down and talking to me about my war experience I finally drove the last nail in him that made his war experience, his injury, everything he did in Viet Nam completely useless. Not only did he fight a war that was unneeded, unwanted, and at the end of the day wrong. We didn't learn from the lesson.

"We didn't learn and we were repeating it. I was terribly upset. And I began working as hard as I could so that in thirty more years I would not be sitting at a breakfast with another generation of war veterans across from me. Hopefully, I can prevent that from happening. Just because we're out of the war doesn't mean we're going to stop fighting. I'm still wearing my dog tags. I probably will for the rest of my life because it's an ongoing struggle. Until we can stop that repetition." Garett eventually joined Bobby Muller in Washington, D.C., and starting in September 2005, worked on a veterans' advocacy project for some two years.

Before he began working with Muller, while attending the Veterans for Peace convention in Dallas in August 2005, Garett met "a nice mother, Cindy, who'd lost her son." In talking to her, Garett learned that she had "hatched this crazy idea to go out to the Bush ranch near Crawford and talk to him." Cindy approached Garett and others and asked them, "Would you represent my son? Will you stand by me and be Iraq veterans in the place of my son?" Garett didn't have to think twice and told her, "Hell, yeah, we will! Let's go. Let's do it!" After gathering camping supplies, "I pitched Cindy Sheehan's tent, at Camp Casey. I helped pitch the first tent." He had a flight the next day and said he had to return to Dallas. In the airport, "probably on the same televisions where I saw the start of the war, I saw Cindy Sheehan on CNN, and I was like, 'There she is! Look at that!'"

In early 2006, he also was involved in organizing the Veterans and Survivors March, in which Iraq War veterans and Hurricane Katrina survivors joined forces to march from Mobile, Alabama, to New Orleans, Louisiana. Organized by some of the major military antiwar groups—Veterans for Peace, Iraq Veterans Against the War, Vietnam Veterans Against the War, Military Families Speak Out, Gold Star Families for Peace, and hurricane survivors' organizations—protesters marched the

130 miles to New Orleans, where they arrived on the 19th of March, the third anniversary of the U.S. invasion of Iraq.[2] As they advanced down Gulf Coast Highway 90, the protesters demanded an end to the war and the immediate restoration of the areas destroyed by Hurricane Katrina in August 2005. Looking at the devastation along the Gulf Coast, Garett thought about how "damage to buildings because of bombs and bullets is different from flood and wind damage. But it's destruction nonetheless. The unfortunate thing about the war is that it's a manmade disaster: we chose to put that upon somebody. When you're walking so far every day, you have nothing to do but just think about it and compare and contrast it and evaluate it.

"I would say that 90 percent of the people we encountered on the march were supportive. People came out of the middle of nowhere and chose to march with us. We got new Iraq Veterans Against the War members out of the march that just showed up and said, 'Hey, I'm an Iraq veteran. I want to join this march.' We definitely also had people that heckled us and were against us.

"At one point, in Slidell, Louisiana, we passed a Stryker vehicle plant.[3] We didn't realize we were going to encounter it. And here we are on one side of the barbed wire fence, waving to these people inside that are working on these vehicles and giving them peace signs. And there they are, waving at us and giving us peace signs. I just found it ironic that the guys that were making the vehicles and that were using the vehicles both wanted peace. But we all went to war and they're still building the vehicles. Who's the middle man with the dollar bill that's pushing to continue to do this?"

Some of the political challenges Garett experienced after he returned from Iraq did not have to do with the war in particular, one of which had to do with sexist language. He had never thought of himself as "the typical jingoistic machoistic dude, even in the military." But, as he put it, even if they were just regular guys trying to do the right thing, guys who would never mistreat a woman, there was still the language: girls were still bitches and sluts, and *faggot* was the number one insult. His experiences in the antiwar movement had a profound impact on the words he used even in casual conversations.

"I know that I've tried to cut a lot of that language out of my system, even though I didn't mean it when I said it, I didn't look down on women in any way. But I was still using the language, so I would tell somebody if he didn't want to do something that he was 'bitchin' out.' I don't say that anymore because I realized that I'm assuming that women are cowards because you won't do something that a woman wouldn't do. Being in the movement's helped me, and being in IVAW has helped me a lot in that regard. Because I'm around women and I don't need to use that language. I don't have anything to prove to anybody else about how much of a man I am.

"I do what I can to protect my friends, and a lot of my friends are women, so I'm going to protect them as well. I'm not going to tolerate anybody talking down to them. A lot of it has also to do with the fact that I have a daughter. I don't want people talking like that around my daughter. So maybe it's not fair to say that it's the movement that helped me along. Could be the fact that I do have a daughter."

When we talked in February 2008, in his spare time Garett was living again around Colorado Springs, organizing with IVAW, and working on contract with Veterans for America. His daughter and her mother had moved several hours away, but he was paying child support and visiting Isabella as often as he could. Mainly he was attending Pike's Peak Community College, living on around $1,200 a month from the GI Bill. "If I went to Yale I'd still get twelve hundred dollars a month on the GI Bill, so I'm pretty much pigeonholed into going to a very inexpensive school."

Colorado Springs, near where Garett grew up, is as military as a military town can get. Nearby are Fort Carson (the Mountain Post), home to some fourteen thousand soldiers and three thousand civilian military employees, the Air Force Academy, Peterson Air Force Base, and Cheyenne Mountain Air Station. Despite this militarized context, as the war in Iraq dragged on, there were changes in how the war was seen and GIs were treated. "The troops used to be the sacred cow that nobody could talk about or touch." In years before, rowdiness and disciplinary problems were more or less tolerated by local business people. Now, "there's definitely a sobering as far as the blind patriotism, prowar kind of sentiment connecting with the troop support. I've noticed more local

businesses around have become a little bit more hesitant in allowing soldiers to come in and really mess the places up." By 2008, Garett noted, "it
was, 'I'm just sick of these troops coming in here and screwing things up,
and I'm sick of the war and tired of what it's doing to this country. And
I'm tired of what it's doing to my military and I've really had enough.'"

ANTIWAR THERAPY

When he was first diagnosed with PTSD, Demond Mullins was seeing
a therapist at the VA. The treatment was getting him nowhere, he felt,
because his counselor was patronizing. Around the same time he began
working with IVAW, however, and he found that "the most therapeu-
tic for me. Any type of antiwar activism, counter-recruitment, talking
to other vets who can understand." He quickly became very active, giving counter-recruitment lectures, antiwar lectures, and press conferences
and making appearances in documentaries like *The Ground Truth*. This
became his passion for a while, especially, as with Tina, doing antiwar
work in high schools.

"I would make a connection with somebody in the school, like a
teacher, and then they would try to get a time set aside for me to talk.
My brother goes to school in Queens. I went to the awards ceremony for
his football team. I identified one of the principals of his school and gave
him my card. I said, 'Look, I'm in Iraq Veterans Against the War. We do
counter-recruitment. Your school is 95 percent African American. I know
that the recruiters are having a field day with it.'

"My brother told me how the recruiters walked around the school
freely. They stood in the restrooms and talked to the kids when they went
in there. They went to the football practices and praised the guys when
they were doing well on the football team, and tried to talk to them and
recruit them afterwards. They had all their information—their names,
addresses, phone numbers. They were calling my brother's house. So I
told the principal, I really want to set up a counter-recruitment lecture
in your school, especially for these seniors and juniors." In this school,
though, the principal "was totally in opposition to it. Totally. I mean, she
didn't even give me the time of day."

Demond went to Washington, D.C., with the writer and director of *The Ground Truth*, Patricia Foulkrod, and met with people from the Congressional Progressive Caucus. An aide to the junior senator from Illinois was there, and after listening to Demond say "something punchy," shook his hand and offered him an internship. Demond declined the offer, explaining that he lived in New York. But with a little arm-twisting, he soon took the job in Washington, D.C., working as a consultant on veterans' issues in the office of Barack Obama. It didn't last long, though, as he soon began feeling burned out: "I was dealing with it every day, with guys who come back who are really fucked up, at Walter Reed. I was, like, God damn, dude." After just three months he quit, for the sake of his own mental health. "I just told them at the end, you know, I never applied for this job. My parents were surprised I didn't want to stay in Obama's office. I mean, the guy is very charismatic. And that's an understatement."

Moving back to New York, Demond was able to finish his undergraduate degree at Lehman College in the spring of 2007 and start in a doctoral program in sociology at the City University of New York the following fall. When we talked in January 2008, he was still living in a studio apartment in the Bronx, studying full time, and teaching some dance workshops on the side at a community center called The Door that was geared toward gay and lesbian youth from the city. He said he was feeling pretty good about himself and life at that point, finally able to contend with the expectations of others. "As a vet, I completely felt that on all sides, no matter where I turned, people were expecting me to be something, something that I'm really not. And I wasn't happy until I realized that I have to accept myself the way I am. That's basically where I am now, redefining myself."

"THE DISEASE OF DISSENT"

From the second day he woke up a deserter in Canada in 2006, Chris Magaoay leapt into activism, speaking to journalists from Europe, Canada, and as far as his home state, Hawai'i, and to groups around Ontario.

He was convinced that "people don't understand why the United States is in Iraq. All these people in the United States are against Bush, but young men and women are going to die unless something is done. It might not be a big number of Americans, like Viet Nam, but even if it's three a day, that's three families that were crushed by a death. Three military families. Somebody saying that your son died, and handing you a flag and telling you it is from a grateful nation. How grateful is it for you to give me a twenty-dollar flag and say 'From a grateful nation,' and put my son in a pine box and lower him? How grateful is the nation if most people don't approve of this war? Not a very grateful nation."

The parallels between Viet Nam and Iraq for Chris are many. "The Viet Nam War was the most controversial military action in history. Look at Iraq. This isn't what people enlist for. Young men and women of America do not join the military voluntarily to go out and invade another defenseless country. You fuel us with pride and patriotism to defend our country, and instead you're using us as a weapon of aggression for your own economical gain. What if the president gives us an order that doesn't abide by the Constitution? Do you do it? The Constitution's the supreme law in the United States. Nothing comes above the Constitution, except apparently," he added defiantly, "the Patriot Act."

More than two years after deserting the Marines, Chris continued to feel strongly about abiding by the Constitution—and, indeed, serving the aims of the Constitution as he saw them through service to the Marines. "I am always contradicting myself," he confessed in May 2008. "I contradict myself every day. There are days I wake up in the morning and I'm like, 'Why am I not still in the military?' Up until about two months ago, when no one was looking, I would march in step and sing cadence in the hallway in my apartment. Sometimes in my head when I walk down the street, I still sing cadence to myself. It's in me."

Before long, talk of the Constitution—and maybe the Marine cadence in his step—led to problems with the War Resisters Support Campaign. "I didn't realize when I started getting into activism the political infighting and the division of the Left. They were kind of using me as a counter-recruitment tool at some of the high schools. I was happy to do it. But the second you stop speaking the party line, you're out. The resisters are treated more as a commodity than an organizing tool. When I started using the Constitution as an example, or the United Nations, well, they don't recognize these things and they had issues with me talking about them in the meetings they sent me to."

One of the reasons, Chris said, that he contradicted himself was that no matter what his political beliefs were, "I did have responsibility as part of a smaller unit, my core of friends, twelve other people that I worked with every day, to be there and fight by their side. So, I feel that being a deserter should not sound distasteful, but, yes, I deserted my unit." His unit went over to Iraq in September of 2006 and stayed for fifteen months, until December of the next year. Out of his sense of responsibility to his unit came his anxious statement, "There were injuries but no deaths, from what I understand."

Chris wondered if he could have somehow managed to stay in the Marines and stir up dissent inside. "Sometimes I think I could have done more staying in the military, with my ideals, preaching my ideals to these active-duty soldiers. I could've spread what the military would call this 'disease of dissent.' I've thought about doing some jail time for the military. But I don't want to spend a single day in prison for something I didn't do wrong. I don't think I should be the one in prison. I think the guy who ordered me over there should be in prison.[4] I think soldiers who are going over and killing civilians should be the ones in prison, not the guy who said he won't be part of it."

No matter what people in the United States think about the deserters who fled to Canada, the response of family back home in the States runs the gamut. Initially, Chris's dad was disappointed. "After explaining to him what was really going on he became supportive. My grandmother, my mom's mom, doesn't support me at all. She stopped communication. My brother and sister are both supportive. They think it's cool, 'Yeah, my brother's on TV!'" His mother was another problem. "She's in and out of prison, the Maui Community Correctional Center. She works in cycles, one year she's either in jail or in rehab, then she spends a year clean, then the next year is the demise back to rehab, the Sand Island State Rehabilitation Center, or prison." When we spoke to Chris in 2008 his mom was living in a shelter; he had just called her and talked to her there, and she told her son she agreed with his beliefs, too.

There was no doubt in his mind that he would like to be able to return, especially to visit family in Hawai'i, but even more he wanted to be able to stay in Canada. "If Canada decides to deport me, I won't have an opportunity to come back to Canada. I will be barred permanently from reentering Canada." Despite the cold, quite a change in climate from Hawai'i, he said, "I permanently want to live in Canada. But I'm scared of getting deported, because I don't have status. I don't even have a passport."

While awaiting a decision from the Canadian government about his status in 2008, Chris was busy with groups involved in expanding the rights of immigrants of all kinds to that country. As difficult as it was to plan too far into the future, he still dreamed of some day going back to college to get a degree in international relations. In addition, "I want to study the militaries of the world and figure out how they operate in comparison to the U.S." Feeling a bit at a loss as to how antiwar activism could have more impact, he thought it would be good if more people wrote letters to politicians. "Just write all the people in your government. Your senators, your representatives, the president. And don't just have you do it, get everyone around you to."

In August 2008, the most well-known deserter in Canada, Jeremy Hinzman, a conscientious objector whose CO application was rejected, was ordered deported after the Canadian Supreme Court ruled against his application to stay in the country. He will very likely face court-martial and imprisonment when he returns, unlike the great majority of those who desert; of the 4,700 who deserted in 2007, just 108 were convicted.[5] Where Chris will fall among these factors and numbers remained unclear as this book went to press.

OUR VETERANS AND OUR WAR

While still an active-duty hospital corpsman in the Navy in October 2004, Charlie Anderson decided to drive up to Washington, D.C., to participate in an antiwar protest. It started at Arlington National Cemetery and ended at the White House. "It wasn't big, but this was my first protest action." A counterdemonstration by a group calling itself the Free

Republic had assembled as well, and they carried signs and shouted at the protesters about loving your country. "And I'm thinking, 'Well, of course I love my country. Why else would I be here?'"

He went with other vets to talk to people in Congress about not having been properly trained for Iraq and not having the necessary equipment. "I talked about not knowing what the hell we were doing there in the first place, and I talked about the veterans' issues. I talked about the fact that 30 percent of us are coming back and seeking mental health care. I talked about the total skewing of priorities, at a time when we're creating veterans at an exponential rate—combat veterans, veterans that take much more to care for than peacetime veterans—why are we cutting the VA budget? Why, in the name of God, would you be closing mental health care centers? You should be *opening* hospitals, hiring more staff!

"But, in reality, we don't take care of our veterans. As a nation, we look at our veterans the same way that we look at a napkin, a paper towel, or a condom. You use it once and you throw it away and you don't think twice about it."

Veterans' affairs became a central focus of Charlie's life. After leaving the service, in addition to joining the Iraq Veterans Against the War, he also enrolled as a member of the American Legion, the Disabled American Veterans, and the Iraq and Afghanistan Veterans of America.

And he found veterans of all kinds in the most unexpected places. On the way to a Veterans for Peace convention being held in Dallas, Texas in 2005, he hailed a taxi at the airport to take him to his hotel. Charlie thought the driver might be of Arab descent, and, despite his best efforts to feel otherwise, he began to be uncomfortable. "I really hadn't had much exposure to Middle Eastern people since coming back from Iraq. Part of it was I felt uneasy around people who spoke foreign languages. We didn't have enough interpreters in Iraq so we never knew what people were saying." Especially with the announcements broadcast from speakers in the mosques, Charlie and his buddies would sometimes wonder, "Is he calling people to prayers or is he saying, 'Hey, the Americans are at 6th and Main. There's four trucks'?"

As they drove along on the way to the hotel, the driver initiated a conversation. "Why are you in Dallas?" he asked. When Charlie explained about the convention, the driver responded, "You look too young for Viet Nam." Cautiously Charlie told him, "Yeah . . . I was in Iraq."

"So was I," said the driver. That seemed odd, of course, so Charlie asked how that was the case. "I'm from Iran," he said, "and I was in the Iran-Iraq War." As they continued talking about their war experiences, some of Charlie's initial discomfort slipped away. As he was getting ready to pay the fare, the driver looked into the rearview mirror and spoke the simplest truth, "War is bad."

When we talked in January 2008, Charlie was studying at Appalachian State University in Boone, North Carolina. He mentioned with a smile that he was laying low in the local American Legion post in Boone, getting to know the older veterans there, and planning to hold back on his politics for a year more. Then, after the others had come to know him as a person, he hoped, it would be possible to discuss issues like the war and support for the troops. "We live in a society where every day we hear or see somebody say something about supporting the troops. And if you don't support the war, then supposedly you can't support the troops. The idea is that these are somehow separate ideas. They're not. I've been called a traitor. I've been called a terrorist sympathizer. I've been called a terrorist. But I looked up *patriotism* in the dictionary, and the definition of patriotism is to love your country.

"It would have been much easier to not do this antiwar activity at all. This is strictly a mission of conscience. It would actually have been significantly easier to melt into life. I might even still be married if I had. But that was not something that I could do. A lot of people don't understand that. My wife—my ex-wife—doesn't understand that.

"That's not an option. Because I love my country. I recognize that for all its faults we have a lot of great potential here. Somebody said to me last week that he doesn't like the war but he doesn't make policy. He knows that war crimes happen and he's powerless to stop it. He asked me, why should he care about what happened at Haditha.[6] I said to him, 'The reason you should care about what happened in Haditha is because it's your war. It's your incident.' He said, 'Well, I've been opposed to this war from the beginning.'

"And I said, 'Okay, I've been opposed to the war since I came home from it. But it's still my war, because it was done in my name with my

money. Those bullets that went into that three-year-old girl and the praying man and up to thirty or fifty other people—those bullets were paid
for with your tax dollars. It's your war. Those are our armed forces and
we have to recover them no matter what the cost is. That's not an option.
That's not negotiable. That's what we have to do.'"

Conclusion
Six Soldiers

These six are at once ordinary and extraordinary.

These six soldiers—or, more precisely, three soldiers, one sailor, one Marine, and one Guardsman—are ordinary American citizens. Like the United States today, they are of diverse racial and ethnic backgrounds, religions, sexual orientations, and political beliefs. We have heard that they grew up in close-knit families as well as troubled ones. They had loving parents and absent ones, lots of siblings and none. Like many in the country, their families did not have much wealth, so money for college was a big draw to the military for all these young people. For Garett, who became a father perhaps before he was quite ready, supporting his new daughter added to the allure of joining the Army; it definitely beat low-paying work with no benefits or apparent future.

Most people sign up in the military for promised job training and college money, not to go to war. Recruiters rarely discuss the killing for which they will be trained. But it surely wasn't only about the money for these six. Military recruiters sometimes strike gold when they also appeal to young people's more idealistic side. The call to service was powerful for many; as Charlie enlisted, he thought: "I was serving something that was greater than myself." On the other hand, this idealism may have been one reason these six were more disillusioned by Iraq than others: they had higher expectations to begin with. What they did share with many was the lure of the recruiting-ad promise that soldiers are the manliest men because they go to war for their country.

At first, though, boot camp training proved more brutal and sadistic than any of the six had imagined possible. All nonetheless emerged with a sense of pride in having accomplished something very significant. It was easy to imagine that the worst was now behind them. When Tina joined, before 9/11, as she said, there were no wars, and "I thought I'd do four years and get out. . . . I was just curious to do my four years and get out with my money for college."

Tina, Garett, and Charlie were sent to Kosovo. There they had mixed experiences with a local and foreign population they were expected to control, though both Tina and Garett, at least, felt they were doing something noble and useful in Kosovo. Not every soldier had an overseas posting before being thrown into Iraq—and even when they did, their duties were often far removed from combat. Ricky spent his time learning French and interrogation techniques; Chris enjoyed driving new military vehicles in the California desert. For troops with no prior experience like Kosovo, landing in Iraq would prove all the more shocking.

Ricky began the first in a series of chats with Army chaplains in hopes that his doubts about the war would be clarified. Charlie, too, looked to the Bible for guidance on going into combat. After leaving the service, all six looked back and realized that they had had all sorts of questions about the U.S. military and its actions abroad even before deployment to Iraq. A couple of them learned about conscientious objector status and thought about filing for it, but except for Chris none was yet close to refusing orders or deserting. If Iraq was in the cards for them, well, they would just see what happened.

What happened immediately to the five who were sent to Iraq was the shock and blood of coming face to face, literally, with what "invasion" and "occupation" look like. They were stunned with the reality of humiliation, abuse, and random killing of the people of Iraq, combatants or not. And for young men and women who come overwhelmingly from the working poor in the United States, it is one thing to train to kill and wound an abstract "enemy" and quite another to be face to face with people who look as if they, too, are poor and relatively powerless in their own societies. "They are a normal population of people," Ricky concluded, and that's why "I just kind of hit a brick wall."

That slow recognition that their officers and some of their fellow enlisteds seemed either not to care or to actively encourage indifference to the suffering their own actions brought on Iraqi civilians engendered growing disillusionment with the U.S. military and the war. "My reality was shattered. My whole perception of America, and the U.S. Army, and what I was doing in the Army," continued Ricky, "was broken up." That's when the naked inequalities of who was fighting and dying and who was calling the shots from the safety of government buildings in Washington and Baghdad became unbearable. For Demond, going out on each mission only increased his empathy for the people he saw. He realized, "We were destroying people's lives." Garett joined IVAW.

Although the military is often regarded as a tightly controlled institution that demands and receives conformity and obedience from its rank and file, it turns out that joining the military can be a radicalizing experience. It certainly was for these six veterans. They were those the military called "the best Americans" (and the manliest men), those who answered the call to fight and kill and die to project America's strength abroad. Yet they were also widely seen by the more privileged as a dumping ground for society's unwanted and otherwise unemployable youth. There is indeed more dissent in the military than is commonly understood by those who have never been in it.

They became radicalized through the war because their experiences in Iraq were punctuated by moments of human connection with Iraqis—with their translators, with their own prisoners, with people on the street, even, as for Demond, with Iraqis in Internet chat rooms. In those moments of empathy, they began to see the world through Iraqi eyes. They began to see themselves, in Garett's words, as the Nazis. Their radicalization led them to read books they had never heard of before they were in the military—by Henry David Thoreau, Frederick Douglass, and Howard Zinn—and these books made them understand the war as motivated by much uglier realities of pride and profit than the recruiters had suggested. They became angrier and, inspired by what they read about histories of disobedience and conscience, became more determined to do something to change their situation. As they felt increasingly betrayed by their politicians and their commanders, by the chaplains who seemed willing to say anything in order to get them back into the fight, by civilians who did not get it, and by equipment and training that did not work, a storm of righteous indignation began organizing inside each of them.

By the time they returned home, as glad as they were to be out of the war zone, their combat experience was far from over. Tina crawled into bed with her mother when the nightmares became too much to bear. Jackhammers, helicopters, traffic jams, and dark city streets could cause uncontrollable panic in Garett and Charlie. The VA diagnosed PTSD, hoping that by labeling and medicating a soldier's suffering he or she might learn to cope better with the aftermath of what was seen and done in Iraq. But dissident veterans, as we have seen, do not easily swallow such pills. As Garett remarked, "They try to make it your problem. And it's not your problem. It's society's problem." Society's problems came to include, for Chris and Charlie, difficult divorces, as they have for veterans of war in general, along with higher rates of unemployment, homelessness, suicide, and domestic abuse. No easy pills for these.

What happens to a soldier when military targets become human beings, says Demond, is you ask even more intently what you are doing in the country and on that mission: "You had to find that reason. And all you could come up with was ugly."

ORDINARY FUTURES

If you walked into a middle school in any working-class community in the United States today, you would find children who, in five short years or so, will be of military age. Are they going to be sent or enticed into the next chapters of the wars in Iraq, Afghanistan, or one of the many other somewheres that are already "rifle-ready"? And when unemployment rolls balloon and long-term economic troubles become the norm, military jobs seem sweeter to more and more young people. No wonder enlistment goes up in times of economic downturn. So it is sensible to ask: Will these children of thirteen and fourteen themselves be going to war in a few years?

They will be if not enough people question the idea that the military is the solution to any problem. These children will become the next generation sent off to war because, we will be told, "It's still a dangerous world out there," "Diplomacy is for wimps," "Some people don't understand anything but force," "We can prevent another 9/11 by taking the battle overseas preemptively," and "These are extraordinary times, and they require extraordinary military measures and sacrifices."

Well, yes and no. Military incursions by the U.S. Armed Forces and their proxies were all too ordinary long before 9/11, from the invasions of Haiti, Panama, Honduras, Nicaragua, and Cuba earlier in the twentieth century, to Lebanon in 1958 and 1982, to the Dominican Republic in 1965, to Vietnam, Laos, Cambodia through the early 1970s, to Grenada, Panama, and Somalia and innumerable missile attacks on Libya, Sudan, Kosovo, and Bosnia in the years following. Such invasions and occupations are fairly called the American way of life as it is experienced by millions of people in uniform—to say nothing of hundreds of millions of citizens of other countries invaded and occupied.

The enormous human and financial costs of sending young people to war and occupation duty are all too commonly "factored in" to foreign policy plans and federal budgets, with military outlays exceeding one trillion dollars a year.[1] It is taken for granted, made normal and unremarkable, that this country has invested in building a military more powerful than all the other militaries in the world massed together.

Like everyone else, the children in any school in America today have been taught that our role as citizens is not to question why but only to "support" the men and women who conduct the military mission or to aspire to join them. Odd as it may seem, then, these same children may unlearn these lessons in the very military missions they are sent to carry out. Over the long run, volunteer armies are only as good as their will to fight. And when soldiers and veterans begin to break ranks and oppose military strategies, tactics, and the missions overall, no amount of hype or promised rewards can make up for this unlearning.

EXTRAORDINARY LIVES

The five men and one woman whose lives are recounted in this book might not have stood out, a few years ago, among the millions of other kids in schools all across the United States, dreaming of what they might be as they grew up. They grew up poor, working class, or with some middle-class comforts. In some ways, they have little in common besides their current antiwar convictions. Even after all their parallel experiences of recruitment, training, deployment, and leaving the military, they have a range of opinions about the U.S. military and military service. But they are united in opposition to the wars in Iraq and Afghanistan, and several extend that sentiment to U.S. foreign military interventions of any kind.

What made them extraordinary? Partly it was their extra measure of empathy for Iraq's civilians. Partly it was an unwillingness to simply live with the sense that they were participating in something wrong. A commitment to—and empathy for—the other members of their units, whose lives depended on them as well, kept most of them at their posts, but they found themselves unable to cordon off contradictions between what they had been taught about America and its military and what they saw happening on the ground in Iraq. First they read—and then they made—history, joining a long column of dissenters in the U.S. military.[2]

No amount of political and journalistic spin can make idealistic soldiers believe in their mission to save the peoples of other countries when those peoples so clearly despise the soldiers' presence. The war in Iraq quickly moved from an aerial and tank assault to a counterinsurgency war, and such wars are bloody assaults inside neighborhoods, villages, homes, markets, and schools. Such wars require troops who are loyal to the overall mission, not just to their comrades-in-arms.

How extraordinary are these six? They are, in fact, like thousands of other veterans who have spoken out publicly against the war, and they undoubtedly speak for still many others unwilling or unsure as yet of what to do with their own discontent.

They are among the millions of U.S. citizens who have spoken out in one way or another against the wars in Iraq and Afghanistan. As soldiers and veterans they have put even more on the line by their dissent. Ricky lost his benefits. Chris lost the ability to be with his family and country. Tina and Charlie suffer daily from PTSD. They are only a few people, to be sure, but they clearly represent many more veterans who have not risked their benefits and comforts but nonetheless agree in spirit with the radical opposition of these six. Because of their outspoken stands, their experiences in the military, and the risks they take in dissent that civilians often do not, they are surely among the most audacious and inspiring of antiwar leaders. Because of their personal knowledge, they are among the most authoritative figures arguing against such invasions and occupations.

Much is made in the United States of the fact that the United States has a volunteer force. That millions join is seen as an index of high national levels of patriotism. But it also presents a puzzle when we see the class and race composition of the military and when we try to explain why these and many other soldiers object to the war and want to leave the military, sometimes as soon as they begin basic training. The people getting off the bus for basic training today in the United States are overwhelmingly from poorer families and disproportionately from African American and Latina/o communities, young people who have made the choice to join for complex practical and romantic reasons.

Critics sometimes call the volunteer military "a poverty draft." This tag captures important aspects of class inequalities in the United States — the poverty of prospects as well as income — and the fact that although no one is technically drafted, it is no coincidence that few children of the rich or even middle class join the military. When young people visit the recruiter to talk about their options, it is often their only option left, and of this they are well and often cynically aware.

But the notion of a poverty draft also misses a significant point. In the minds of the young men and women who make the decision to join, in circumstances far beyond their abilities to control, enlisting also means they have decided to change their lives for the better, to make something of themselves other than what they've been and what they see their friends becoming. Many times they join over and above the objections of friends and family. The dissent and discontent that emerge so often—and that shaped the lives of these six people—can be explained only by the power of military advertising and the false front of the recruiting office.

As we go to press, the United States has moved tens of thousands of troops from one disastrous war, in Iraq, to another one, in Afghanistan. For the young people of the United States, especially of the working class, those who are sooner or later to be recruited into the military, these deployments have serious consequences. They are more than abstract geopolitics or ideas about spreading democracy and fighting terrorism. What civilian leaders and the Pentagon plan on paper, those young people will be expected to implement, living or dying with what they are asked to do.

Throughout the United States, every day sees thousands of people consider military enlistment. Before they sign up for war, they need to hear from the men and women who came before them; yesterday's recruits who are from families and communities just like theirs. They will want to hear about the extraordinary journeys of Demond, Ricky, Tina, Garett, Charlie, and Chris, who have refused to accept that war, or a war like that in Iraq, should be the ordinary experience of each new generation of Americans.

Acknowledgments

Our first debt is naturally to the six people whose words are at the core of this book. While the reader would be right to see them as individuals who undertook great physical risks in training for and going to war, we recognize their bravery in taking on the risk of rejection by their peers and superiors—those who had often become, up to that point in their lives, deeply important in validating not only their self-worth but their very ability to grasp what was real and right. These six people, and many more like them, have displayed this blazing social courage. We thank them for this, and for their stories.

We would also like to thank the other forty men and women who contributed long interviews from which those in this book were selected. Their remarkable stories, conducted in connection with the GI Rights Oral History Project in 2005 and 2006, inform our understanding of how soldiers come to dissent in a climate that can be deeply hostile to it. Their words are now on permanent record in the Southern Historical Collection of the University of North Carolina at Chapel Hill, in the interview series entitled "Military Dissenters: Veterans, Military Families, and the Iraq and Afghan Wars."

A deep debt of gratitude is owed to the oral historian Betsy Brinson, who conducted most of those initial interviews and who invited us to work them into a book. It was Betsy's initiative, tireless travels, and questioning that led to those stories now being available, and to our meeting the six veterans whose stories are here.

We would also particularly like to thank the anthropology graduate student Jose Vasquez, also a leader of Iraq Veterans Against the War, for his support of this project. He gave us detailed and extremely helpful comments on each page of the manuscript. His support of this project and of the veterans' witnessing against the wars and occupations in Iraq and Afghanistan has been unstinting.

Along the way, we also counted on the good counsel of several colleagues, including Philippe Bourgois, Louise Lamphere, William Simmons, Kay Warren, and Zoë Wool. We are especially grateful as well to Aaron Glantz and Stan Goff for their support and to Andrew Bickford, Keith Brown, Roberto González, Kate McCaffrey, Larry Minear, and Robert Rubinstein for reading the entire manuscript with a helpful and critical eye. Our editor at University of California Press, Naomi Schneider, has been our trusty collaborator throughout the project.

Background research and careful transcription of each word spoken in our collective interviewing were contributed by several dedicated research assistants from among Brown University's undergraduates, including Anna Christensen, Lindsay Cunningham, Spencer Amdur, Lindsay Mollineaux, and Jenna Williams. Eric Rodriguez and Scott Ewing, themselves Brown University veterans of the Iraq War, provided valuable background for understanding the predicaments, thinking, and experiences of their fellow vets. Finally, help from Zachary Stone and Rachel Starr in the late editing process sped the book to press.

We would also have had a much more difficult time completing this manuscript without the expert administrative help of Matilde Andrade, Katherine Grimaldi, Deborah Healey, and Marjorie Sugrue.

Mention also should be made of the soldiers, Marines, airmen, and sailors of Operation Dewey Canyon III, who made history in front of the Capitol in April 1971 by hurling back the military ribbons and medals that they had been awarded for their actions in the Viet Nam War. Among those who stood near the microphone as witness to their conscientious objection was Matthew, then a seventeen-year-old boy. Those veterans' example helped inspire this book.

We also gratefully acknowledge a fellowship grant from the American Council of Learned Societies and a leave from Brown University to Matthew, which provided an essential year of time for interviewing and writing, as well as Michael Kimmel and Lesley Gill for midwiving the process. We thank Brown University for providing the leave time for Catherine to write and for funding that supported the project throughout.

.   .   .   .   .

In the end, this was a collaborative project in many respects: we sent a rough draft of the entire manuscript to each of the six veterans and received comments back from each of them. We hope the end result does honor to them and the many others like them, both in Iraq and in the United States, who have said no to this war. Given their involvement with the organization, the royalties from this book are being donated to Iraq Veterans Against the War.

Notes

INTRODUCTION

1. In reprinting these soldiers' stories, we have used each person's words
as originally spoken wherever possible. We have deleted some throat clearing or
placeholding words and have occasionally shifted some sentences from present
to past tense for stylistic reasons. But how these veterans see the war and the
world is embedded in each word and sentence they spoke, so they are faithfully
rendered here.

2. A corpsman is an enlisted medical specialist.

3. Interview with Vice President Dick Cheney, NBC, *Meet the Press*, tran-
script for March 16, 2003, www.mtholyoke.edu/acad/intrel/bush/cheneymeetthe-
press.htm.

4. Neta C. Crawford et al., "The Real 'Surge' of 2007: Non-combatant Death
in Iraq and Afghanistan," Carnegie Council, January 22, 2008, www.cceia.org/
resources/articles_papers_reports/0003.html; Hannah Fischer, "Iraqi Civilian

Deaths Estimates," Congressional Research Service Report for Congress, August 27, 2008, www.fas.org/sgp/crs/mideast/RS22537.pdf.

5.   Maggie Farley, "Report Notes Toll of Cluster Bombs, Strikes in Iraq," *Los Angeles Times*, December 12, 2003.

6.   Gilbert Burnham et al., "Mortality after the 2003 Invasion of Iraq: A Cross-sectional Cluster Sample Survey," *Lancet* 368 (October 21, 2006): 1421–28.

7.   Office of the UN High Commissioner on Refugees, "UNHCR Doubles Budget for Iraq Operations," news release, July 12, 2007, www.unhcr.org/cgi-bin/texis/vtx/media?page=home&id=469630434.

8.   Steven Lee Myers, "Many Investors Still Avoid Risks of Iraq," *New York Times*, September 27, 2009.

9.   These numbers are based on a CBS News investigation, conducted after the Veterans Administration released suspiciously low numbers; "Suicide Epidemic among Veterans," November 13, 2007, www.cbsnews.com/stories/2007/11/13/cbsnews_investigates/main3496471.shtml, and "Statement of Stephen L. Rathbun, Ph.D.," in House Committee on Veterans' Affairs, "The Truth about Veterans' Suicides," hearing, May 6, 2008, http://veterans.house.gov/hearings/Testimony.aspx?TID=41682&Newsid=237&Name=%20Stephen%20L.%20Rathbun,%20Ph.D. An e-mail subsequently came to light, written by the VA's mental health director, Dr. Ira Katz, to Ev Chasen, the agency's chief communications officer (February 13, 2008, www.cbsnews.com/htdocs/pdf/VA_email_021308.pdf), stating that there were approximately one thousand suicide attempts *per month* among all veterans seen by the VA system. The CBS study of death registries in forty-five states found that at least 6,256 suicides had occurred among all veterans in 2005, and that among veterans twenty to twenty-four years of age the suicide rates were almost three to four times higher than among comparable civilians. See also Benjamin R. Karney et al., "Invisible Wounds: Predicting the Immediate and Long-Term Consequences of Mental Health Problems in Veterans of Operation Enduring Freedom and Operation Iraqi Freedom," working paper, Rand Corporation, Center for Military Health Policy Research, April 2008.

10.   Joseph E. Stiglitz and Linda Bilmes, *The Three Trillion Dollar War: The True Cost of the Iraq Conflict* (New York: W. W. Norton, 2008).

11.   James Risen, "Use of Iraq Contractors Costs Billions, Report Says," *New York Times*, August 11, 2008; Pratap Chatterjee, *Iraq, Inc: A Profitable Occupation* (New York: Seven Stories Press, 2004); Antonia Juhasz, *The Bush Agenda: Invading the World, One Economy at a Time* (New York: HarperCollins, 2007).

12.   James Risen, "Controversial Contractor's Iraq Work Is Split Up," *New York Times*, May 24, 2008.

13.   Office of the Special Inspector General for Iraq Reconstruction [SIGIR], "Hard Lessons: The Iraq Reconstruction Experience," December 13, 2008, http://projects.nytimes.com/reconstruction#p=1; James Glanz and T. Christian Miller,

"Official History Spotlights Iraq Rebuilding Blunders," *New York Times*, December 13, 2008. An early report from this same source described waste on a monumental scale, with contracts canceled on account of mismanagement or poor-quality work costing the U.S. $600 million. SIGIR, "Iraq Reconstruction Project Terminations Represent a Range of Actions," Report No. 09–004, October 27, 2008, www.sigir.mil/reports/pdf/audits/09–004.pdf.

14. Juhasz, *Bush Agenda*.

15. Scott Keeter and Robert Suls, "Awareness of Iraq War Fatalities Plummets," news release, Pew Research Center, March 12, 2008, http://people-press.org/reports/pdf/401.pdf.

1.   RECRUITING VOLUNTEERS

1. That Chris would eventually join the military was in part determined by the fact that the islands of his home state bristle with major military installations—Pearl Harbor, which has the world's most advanced warships, and thirteen others, which house forty-six thousand soldiers, sailors, and Marines. Junior Reserve Officer Training Corps (JROTC) programs are supported throughout the island schools, local media coverage of the military is overwhelmingly positive, and the bases host regular community events like air shows, complete with kiddy attractions and hot dogs. Hawai'i is by any measure one of the most militarized spots on earth.

2. The 442nd Infantry unit was composed of mostly Japanese Americans from Hawai'i who fought in Europe in World War II. (Many of their families were imprisoned in Japanese internment camps on the mainland during the war.) Twenty-one of its soldiers and officers were awarded the Medal of Honor.

3. This has been quite common, with judges reasoning that national security needs trump those of the justice system and that military service can "straighten out" young people.

4. For most eighteen-year-olds in the States, the answer to such a question is "right around the corner," because there are over 8,200 recruiters for the Army alone and 2,850 for the Marines. The military's total recruiting and advertising budget, which was already a monumental $4 billion in 2003, exploded to $20.5 billion in the 2009 budget. The rise went toward more recruiters, more recruitment bonuses, more advertising money to Madison Avenue firms, and more "outreach" activities, particularly to the people—like parents and coaches—known as "influencers" in military marketese. Joseph Stiglitz and Linda Bilmes, *The Three Trillion Dollar War: The True Cost of the Iraq Conflict* (New York: Norton, 2008).

5. With recruiting shortfalls, the military was now taking more and more

young people they would have previously rejected. Recruits without high school diplomas went up from 6 percent in 2003 to 29 percent in 2007, and the percentage of what the military terms "high-quality" recruits—high school graduates who also score above the mean on their aptitude test, the ASVAB—had dropped to 45 percent in 2007. The recession that began in 2007, with the massive unemployment it brought, made Pentagon recruiters' jobs much easier.

6. Damien Cave, "For a General, a Tough Mission: Building the Army," *New York Times,* February 5, 2006.

7. One-fifth of students in New York City high schools surveyed in 2007 had class time taken by military recruiters. Sewell Chan, "Report Finds Little Monitoring of Military Recruiting in Schools," *New York Times,* September 6, 2007.

8. See "Freakley Supports Using Facebook for Military Recruitment," October 31, 2008, FORA.tv, http://fora.tv/2008/09/11/Freakley_Supports_Using_Facebook_for_Military_Recruitment.

9. Around 31 percent of the nation's population of comparable age are from these same racial and ethnic groups.

10. From 1942 until 1945, during World War II, Navajo code talkers served in the Marines in the Pacific transmitting messages by telephone and radio in their native language. Their transmissions were never deciphered by the Japanese.

11. Catherine Lutz and Lesley Bartlett, *Making Soldiers in the Public Schools: An Analysis of the Army JROTC Curriculum* (Philadelphia: American Friends Service Committee, 1995); Gina Perez, "How a Scholarship Girl Becomes a Soldier: The Militarization of Latino/a Youth in Chicago Public Schools," *Identities* 13 (2006): 53–72.

2. TRAINING

1. "Army's Rising Promotion Rate Called Ominous," *Los Angeles Times,* February 11, 2006.

2. Demond was like many young people who thought of the National Guard as a part-time job. He was one of the approximately forty thousand National Guard soldiers who were soon to find themselves, full time, in Iraq; Thomas E. Ricks, "Wars Put Strain on National Guard: Fire, Flood Relief Efforts Threatened," *Washington Post,* June 6, 2004.

3. Waterboarding is a form of torture that has been employed by the U.S. military against certain prisoners to get information from them. The torture consists of pouring water over the face of a prisoner who is tied down, inducing suffocation and the feeling of drowning.

4.   Before it was exposed in the media in April 2004, U.S. military personnel routinely carried out torture, rape, and even homicide against prisoners held at Abu Ghraib prison near Baghdad. Though low-level personnel alone were charged with crimes against the prisoners, the abuse at Abu Ghraib was ordered and supported at top levels of the U.S. Armed Forces, the CIA, and the White House.

5.   *Towelhead* is a derogatory term for Arabs, some of whom wear a cloth covering on their heads.

6.   This is an especially stark illustration of the more general militarization of schooling in the United States, including JROTC at the secondary level and extensive military funding of research at colleges and universities; Henry Giroux, *The University in Chains: Confronting the Military-Industrial-Academic Complex* (New York: Paradigm, 2007).

7.   All Marines are compelled to memorize the Eleven General Orders for a sentry on duty: "To talk to no one except in the line of duty," for example. The "Twelfth General Order" mentioned here does not actually exist but is an inside joke for servicemen.

8.   Thomas Ricks, *Making the Corps* (New York: Scribner, 1998).

9.   In 1999, DEP recruits were dropping out in record numbers (15,800 or 20 percent of all recruits) before they reached basic training; James Knowles et al., "Reinventing Army Recruiting," Interfaces 32, no. 1 (2002): 78–92. The Navy has lost between 16 and 25 percent of its DEP recruits in recent years; Marian Lane, "Predictors of Attrition from the U.S. Navy Delayed Entry Program," paper presented at the International Military Testing Association Conference, 2006, www.internationalmta.org/Documents/2006/2006070P.pdf.

10.   Stan Goff, *Full Spectrum Disorder: The Military in the New American Century* (New York: Soft Skull Press, 2004); Stan Goff, *Sex and War* (New York: Soft Skull Press, 2006).

11.   E1 is for "Enlisted 1" and is the lowest rank of private. A private first class, for instance, is an E3, and a sergeant is an E5.

3. FIRST MISSIONS

1.   The bubble Garett talks about is the very intentional effect of the U.S. military's operation of a vast media network: its Armed Forces Network runs television and radio stations and Internet sites that are ubiquitous sources for U.S. troops around the world. The military publishes hundreds of newspapers and magazines, many on the Web as well, from *Bavarian News* at U.S. bases in Germany to the *Desert Voice Newspaper* in Kuwait to Fort Hood's *Sentinel* in Texas; see Nick Turse, *The Complex: How the Military Invades Our Everyday Lives* (New

York: Metropolitan Books, 2008). And the military spent $1.1 billion just on its contracts with private advertising and public relations firms in the three years from 2003 to 2005, working to convince the public that the war in Iraq and the U.S. military were righteous; see U.S. Government Accountability Office, "Media Contracts: Activities and Financial Obligations for Seven Federal Departments," report to Congress, January 2006, www.gao.gov/new.items/do6305.pdf.

2.   The term *re-up* is military slang for "reenlist." There is often a large monetary bonus for soldiers who re-up, since the military prefers to retain experienced soldiers, especially highly trained specialists, rather than train new recruits.

3.   Amnesty International, "Croatia: Briefing to the Human Rights Committee on the Republic of Croatia," January 21, 2009, index no. EUR 64/001/2009, www.amnesty.org/en/library/info/Eur64/001/2009/en.

4.   Chris was not alone, of course; the U.S. military has made strenuous efforts to foster this belief among the general public by banning photographers on U.S. bases from covering the arrival of coffins of the war dead (though the order was reversed in 2009), requiring embedded U.S. journalists to submit their stories for prepublication review, erasing their footage of civilian deaths, and refusing to release their data on civilian casualties. "ACLU Releases Navy Files on Civilian Casualties in Iraq War," American Civil Liberties Union press release, July 2, 2008, www.aclu.org/natsec/foia/35878prs20080702.html.

5.   Associated Press, "US Army Desertion Rates Rise 80 Percent since 2003 Iraq Invasion," *International Herald Tribune*, November 16, 2007. An unauthorized absence (UA) is essentially the same as the more familiar infraction absent without leave (AWOL) in terms of severity. In general, the Army and Air Force use *AWOL* while the Marines and Navy prefer the term *UA*.

6.   The year-by-year figures for the Army are 4,399 (2001), 3,971 (2002), 2,610 (2003), 2,450 (2004), 2,659 (2005), 3,301 (2006), and 4,698 (2007). See "Army Desertion Rate Soaring," November 16, 2007, www.cbsnews.com/stories/2007/11/16/national/main3513410.shtml?source=mostpop_story, and "As Desertions Rise, U.S. Military Makes Little Effort to Track Down Those Who Flee," *North County Times*, June 28, 2007, www.nctimes.com/articles/2007/06/29/military/10_86_256_28_07.txt.

4.   INSIDE IRAQ, ON THE OUTSKIRTS OF REALITY

1.   The prayer of St. Francis reads:

Lord, make me an instrument of your peace. Where there is hatred, let me sow love; where there is injury, pardon; where there is doubt, faith; where there is despair, hope; where there is darkness, light; and where there is sadness, joy.

O Divine Master, grant that I may not so much seek to be consoled as to console; to be understood as to understand; to be loved as to love.

For it is in giving that we receive; it is in pardoning that we are pardoned; and it is in dying that we are born to eternal life.

2. "President George W. Bush Addresses the Nation on the Start of War with Iraq," March 19, 2003, www.c-span.org/executive/warwithiraq.asp.

3. National Guard units were in fact often given inferior equipment, such as unarmored trucks, when there were not enough to go around. This made them more vulnerable as well as more resentful of regular Army units.

4. After Viet Nam, the military realized the problem of alienation for black and Latino troops in such a context and eventually prohibited the use of racial epithets in basic training, but the practice persists unofficially.

5. As has been frequently pointed out, service members' access to cyberspace makes this war much different from previous wars in that it has eroded the distance and distinctiveness of home versus battle space; Keith Brown and Catherine Lutz, "Grunt Lit: The Participant Observers of Empire," *American Ethnologist* 34, no. 2 (2007): 322–28.

6. Neither story about the Abu Ghraib scandal really held elites more broadly responsible for creating the larger climate for torture and the situation of occupation. See Lila Rajiva, *The Language of Empire: Abu Ghraib and the American Media* (New York: Monthly Review Press, 2005).

7. There were two major battles in Fallujah early in the war. The first followed shortly on the killing and mutilation of four security contractors working for the United States. The civilian death figures given here are from the widely respected site Iraq Body Count, which also noted that U.S. military officials at the time said they were doing "everything possible to protect noncombatants." There were eighty-three U.S. military casualties during Operation Vigilant Resolve (in the spring of 2004) and ninety-two casualties during Operation Phantom Fury later that same year. Ricky is referring here to the second battle, in November and December 2004.

8. By one estimate, by five years post-invasion the U.S. military had imprisoned seventy-seven thousand Iraqis and released fifty-three thousand of them (Bing West, "A Report from Iraq," *Atlantic Monthly,* January 2008). By another estimate, one hundred thousand Iraqis had passed through the U.S. prison system in Iraq by the end of 2008 (Amit R. Paley, "In Iraq, 'a Prison Full of Innocent Men,'" *Washington Post,* December 6, 2008). As of the beginning of 2008, the United States was holding nearly twenty-five thousand Iraqis in prisons in that country; 80 percent of the Iraqis who had been detained were Sunni (West, "Report from Iraq").

9. Prisoners have had few legal rights or oversight: they are typically not formally charged with crimes, allowed to confront the evidence held against them, or allowed to have lawyers represent them. This was all facilitated by the

Bush administration's reclassification of their imprisoned population in Afghanistan as detainees or enemy combatants. Use of these terms was carried over to Iraq and in both cases was designed to allow the Department of Defense to avoid the term *prisoner of war*, a category of person expressly protected by the Geneva Convention. The military in Iraq now calls their prisoners Persons Under Control, or PUCs. Human Rights Watch, "Torture in Iraq," *New York Review of Books,* November 2005; see also Paley, "In Iraq."

10. This particular technique, along with many other forms of torture, was specifically ordered from the highest Pentagon levels, with the ACLU citing a memo signed by General Ricardo A. Sanchez calling for "yelling, loud music, and light control used to create fear, disorient detainee, and prolong capture shock." Other well-documented tactics in U.S. prisons in Iraq include beatings, long periods of solitary confinement, exposure to extreme cold, use of dogs to intimidate blindfolded detainees, humiliating treatment, rape, restraint for prolonged period in "stress positions," prolonged standing, and waterboarding. ACLU, "Letter to Attorney General Gozales Requesting Investigation of Possible Perjury by General Ricardo A. Sanchez," March 30, 2005, www.aclu.org/safefree/general/17554leg20050330.html. Human Rights Watch also reports that the U.S. military regularly used music-based torture methods to disorient prisoners and deprive them of sleep; see Human Rights Watch, "No Blood, No Foul: Soldiers' Accounts of Detainee Abuse in Iraq," Human Rights Watch Report, July 2006, www.hrw.org/reports/2006/us0706/2.htm; Amnesty International, "Beyond Abu Ghraib: Detention and Torture in Iraq," March 6, 2006, www.amnesty.org/en/library/asset/MDE14/001/2006/en/dom-MDE140012006en.html.

11. Loren Baritz, "Military Mismanagement," in *Light at the End of the Tunnel: A Vietnam War Anthology,* ed. Andrew J. Rotter (Lanham, MD: Rowman and Littlefield, 1999).

12. What is commonly referred to as Camp Anaconda is the joint base that is a combination of the Balad Airbase (formerly run by the Air Force) and Logistical Support Area Anaconda (formerly run by the Army); Thomas E. Ricks, "Biggest Base in Iraq Has Small-Town Feel," *Washington Post,* February 4, 2006; see also Tom Engelhardt, "Iraq as a Pentagon Construction Site," in *The Bases of Empire: The Global Struggle against U.S. Military Posts,* ed. Catherine Lutz (New York: New York University Press, 2009).

13. Tom Vanden Brook, "DOD Data: More Forced to Stay in Army," *USA Today,* April 21, 2008.

14. With the first agreement signed in 1864, there are today four Geneva Conventions, all last revised or ratified in 1949. They are meant to protect wounded and sick members of the armed forces, prisoners of war, and civilians in time of war.

15. See "Bush Jokes about WMD," June 10, 2007, http://youtube.com/watch?v=nKX6luiMINQ&feature=related.

16. "America's Medicated Army," *Time Magazine,* June 5, 2008. The study was conducted in fall of 2006, and its results were released in May 2007. Journalists report rampant dispensing or street purchase of Valium, Vicodin, Benadryl, Paxil, Wellbutrin, and Percocet, for example, used to medicate all manner of anxiety, panic, and despair. Anne Usher, "High-Stress Duty," *Milwaukee Journal-Sentinel Online,* November 26, 2006; Amy Schlesing, "Drugs, Booze Easy for GIs to Get in Iraq," *Arkansas Democrat-Gazette,* January 3, 2005.

17. Meanwhile U.S. munitions, including depleted uranium and unexploded ordnance, were turning areas of Iraq into wastelands; Barbara Nimri Aziz, "Gravesites: Environmental Ruin in Iraq," in *Anthropologists in the Public Sphere,* ed. Roberto Gonzalez (Austin: University of Texas Press, 2004).

5. FACE TO FACE WITH IRAQI CIVILIANS

1. Iraq Veterans Against the War, Aaron Glantz, and Anthony Swofford, *Winter Soldier, Iraq and Afghanistan: Eyewitness Accounts of the Occupations* (Chicago: Haymarket, 2008); Trish Wood, *What Was Asked of Us: An Oral History of the Iraq War by the Soldiers Who Fought It* (New York: Little, Brown, 2006); Chris Hedges and Laila al-Arian, *Collateral Damage: America's War against Iraqi Civilians* (New York: Nation Books, 2008).

2. Plastic strips used as handcuffs by U.S. soldiers because they're cheaper than metal handcuffs and don't need a key.

3. On Haditha, see Julian E. Barnes and Tony Perry, "Photos Indicate Civilians Slain Execution-Style," *Los Angeles Times,* May 27, 2006.

4. On Diyala Square, see James Glanz and Alissa J. Rubin, "From Errand to Fatal Shot to Hail of Fire to 17 Deaths," *New York Times,* October 3, 2007; and Jeremy Scahill, *Blackwater: The Rise of the World's Most Powerful Mercenary Army,* 2nd ed. (New York: Nation Books, 2008).

5. Scahill, *Blackwater.*

6. M-4s are assault rifles; M-249s are light machine guns also known as SAWs; RPKs are Soviet-origin light machine guns; AK-47s are Soviet-origin assault rifles. The feelings of respect Demond and his unit had for their adversaries is something that has been widely reported among warriors in many other contexts, including the Viet Nam War, when U.S. soldiers reported often grudging or full-out respect for the North Vietnamese they fought against.

7. White phosphorus is considered by many to be an illegal weapon, banned by the Chemical Weapons Convention. The United States at first denied using it in Iraq but later admitted it had done so; Andrew Buncombe, "Incendiary Weapons: The Big White Lie," *Independent of London,* November 17, 2005.

8. News reports about these "condolence payments" usually cite the Iraqi custom of *solatia* (actually the practice of *diya*), which is the tradition of offering

financial compensation for injury or loss of property. U.S. payouts are done on an ad hoc basis so that responsibility is never officially taken and apologies are never officially given, and many Iraqis remain outraged and bitter about how the system is administered and the seemingly universal American dismissal of Iraqi hardship. "For Iraqis in Harm's Way, $5,000 and 'I'm Sorry,'" *New York Times,* March 17, 2004, www.nytimes.com/2004/03/17/international/middleeast/17CIVI. html?ex=1219377600&en=188c4eba4ac02739&ei=5070. A former JAG who served in Iraq reports on Iraqi reaction to the system: "Every Iraqi I spoke with on the issue expressed shock and disbelief I could only offer $2,500 for the death of a human being." Captain Jonathan Tracy (U.S. Army, Ret.), "Condolence Payment Memo," July 2006, www.civicworldwide.org/storage/civic/documents/condolen ce%20payments%20current.pdf.

9. The insurgency in Iraq is obviously more elusive and more complex in composition and goals than any one soldier's ability to experience directly; Ahmed Hashim, *Insurgency and Counterinsurgency in Iraq* (Ithaca: Cornell University Press, 2006).

6. AWAKENINGS

1. The U.S. media were willing accomplices in the campaign to convince civilians and soldiers that the war was justified. Mainstream media, like the *New York Times* and *Washington Post,* have admitted their failings in this; "Leading US Daily Admits Underplaying Stories Critical of White House Push for Iraq War," August 12, 2004, Agence France Presse, www.commondreams.org/head-lines04/0812-01.htm. Polls have shown that some news sources, especially Fox News, have been especially culpable for the miseducation of millions about the war. Regular viewers of Fox were much more likely to erroneously believe that Saddam Hussein was behind the 9/11 attacks; World Public Opinion.org, "Misperceptions, the Media, and the Iraq War," October 2, 2003, www.worldpu-blicopinion.org/pipa/articles/international_security_bt/102.php.

2. Troops' political positions varied by service, rank, and age. Marines were more likely than the Army who were more likely than reserves or the Guard to believe an extended stay in Iraq was necessary; "U.S. Troops in Iraq; 72% Say End War in 2006," February 28, 2006, www.zogby.com/news/readnews.dbm?id=1075. Troops of higher ranks were also much more likely than lower ones to support the war, and men were much more likely than women to do so ("Annual Year-End Polls and Special Surveys," 2004, *Military Times,* www.militarycity.com/polls/). Those troops with "high" or "very high" morale at the lower enlisted levels (E1 to E4) were 3 percent in 2003, up to 11 percent in 2007. The *Military Times* polls also showed that while disaffection with the war in Iraq was growing among the

troops, they remained relatively happy with their military jobs ("Annual Year-End Polls," 2006, www.militarycity.com/polls/).

3. In his speech at the Pentagon memorial service on October 11, 2001, George Bush said, "Today, we are a nation awakened to the evil of terrorism, and determined to destroy it. That work began the moment we were attacked; and it will continue until justice is delivered. . . . The hijackers were instruments of evil who died in vain. Behind them is a cult of evil which seeks to harm the innocent and thrives on human suffering. Theirs is the worst kind of cruelty, the cruelty that is fed, not weakened, by tears. Theirs is the worst kind of violence, pure malice, while daring to claim the authority of God. We cannot fully understand the designs and power of evil. It is enough to know that evil, like goodness, exists. And in the terrorists, evil has found a willing servant. For us too, in the year 2001, an enemy has emerged that rejects every limit of law, morality, and religion. . . . The terrorists have no true home in any country, or culture, or faith. They dwell in dark corners of earth. And there, we will find them." "President Pays Tribute at Pentagon Memorial," *September 11 News*, October 11, 2001, www.september11 news.com/PresidentBushPentagon.htm.

4. Claymores are what the U.S. military refers to as "antipersonnel" mines that shoot shrapnel up to one hundred yards after being detonated. Armed aerial drones, including the Hunter and Predator systems, are used for both reconnaissance and attack.

5. A *fatwā* is a religious edict or ruling in Islam.

6. Miles Moffeit and Amy Herdy, "Female GIs Report Rapes in Iraq War," *Denver Post*, January 25, 2004.

7. IVAW is active in forty-eight states, Washington, D.C., and Canada. The organization has developed a three-point program with the goal of bringing troops home from Iraq as soon as possible, and this program involves speaking and recruiting at military bases, protecting military men and women who put themselves at risk by speaking out against the war, and providing a more honest and realistic perspective on military service to potential recruits at recruiting centers and schools. IVAW also campaigns for more comprehensive support and health care for returning veterans and reparations for the destruction that has occurred in Iraq.

7. HOMECOMING TRAUMAS

1. *Casualties* refers to both the injured and the dead. The figures are from Joseph Stiglitz and Linda Bilmes, *The Three Trillion Dollar War: The True Cost of the Iraq Conflict* (New York: W.W. Norton, 2008).

2. PTSD is an affliction resulting from exposure to traumatic events that,

according to the American Psychiatric Association, have "involved actual or threatened death or serious injury, or threat to the physical integrity of self or others." The cause here, of course, is exposure to combat itself, more universal among the troops in this than any previous U.S. war. Factors that exacerbate PTSD include frustration and anger because of insufficient preparation, equipment, and training; the feeling that there is no end in sight; discomfort and deprivations of life in a war zone; worries about career and family back home; racism and sexual harassment within the military; and extended tours of duty. The Vanderbilt rehabilitation program at Fort Campbell specifically identifies "post-traumatic vision syndrome," which involves light sensitivity. Melissa Norton Carro, "When War Comes Home," Summer 2008, www.vanderbilt.edu/maga zines/vanderbilt-magazine/2008/07/when-war-comes-home/. Light sensitivity is also a common symptom of traumatic brain injury.

3.   U.S. Department of Veterans Affairs, *Fifth Annual Report of the Department of Veterans Affairs Undersecretary for Health Special Committee on Post-Traumatic Stress Disorder,* cited in William B. Brown, "Another Emerging 'Storm': Iraq and Afghanistan Veterans with PTSD in the Criminal Justice System," *Justice Policy Journal* 5 (Fall 2008): 13; Terri Tanielian and Lisa H. Jaycox, eds., *Invisible Wounds of War: Psychological and Cognitive Injuries, Their Consequences, and Services to Assist Recovery* (Santa Monica, CA: RAND Corporation, 2008).

4.   The GI Rights Hotline can be contacted at www.objector.org/girights/contact.html or 1–800–394–9544.

5.   Talk at Sacramento State College, October 16, 1967.

6.   This is just one of the factors that help to account for higher rates of unemployment and often subsequent homelessness among cohorts of veterans. See Bureau of Labor Statistics, "Employment Situation of Veterans Summary," March 20, 2009, www.bls.gov/news.release/vet.nro.htm, and "Surge Seen in Number of Homeless Veterans," *New York Times,* November 8, 2007.

7.   Charles Hoge et al., "The Occupational Burden of Mental Disorders in the U.S. Military: Psychiatric Hospitalizations, Involuntary Separations, and Disability," *American Journal of Psychiatry* 162 (2005): 585–91; Philip Dine, "Many Soldiers Get Boot for 'Pre-existing' Mental Illness," *St. Louis Dispatch,* September 30, 2007.

8. SPEAKING OUT

1.   Watada's first court-martial ended in a mistrial. A second one was stayed on grounds of double jeopardy, and the Army finally dropped its appeals in 2009 and discharged him from the military "under other than honorable conditions."

2.   Jose Vasquez, "Groundswell: The Veterans' and Survivors' March from

Mobile to New Orleans," unpublished manuscript, 2008, in possession of the authors.

3. The Stryker is an eight-wheeled all-wheel-drive armored combat vehicle produced by General Dynamics.

4. A variety of attempts have been made, in fact, to do just this by indicting Bush, Cheney, and other key players in the invasion of Iraq and Afghanistan. The legal system of Belgium indicted them, and the Greek Bar Association filed a complaint against Bush and Cheney in the International Criminal Court (ICC) for crimes against humanity and war crimes (Marjorie Cohen, National Lawyers Guild). A lawsuit was also brought against Rumsfeld in Germany in 2006; Adam Zagorin, "Exclusive: Charges Sought against Rumsfeld over Prison Abuse," *Time*, November 10, 2006, www.time.com/time/nation/article/0,8599,1557842,00. html. Nothing has come of these efforts so far, in part because the United States threatened retaliation (for example, of pulling NATO headquarters out of Belgium if that country proceeded with its legal efforts) and in part because the United States does not recognize the ICC.

5. Jay Price, "Deserter May Fare Worse Because of Flight," *Raleigh News and Observer*, August 17, 2008. Robin Long, the first deserter to be deported from Canada, was sentenced to fifteen months in prison. Approximately forty deserters in Canada have filed asylum claims; "Military Deserters Once Again Flock to Canada," *Dallas Observer*, March 11, 2009.

6. All charges were dropped against seven of the eight Marines charged in connection with the Haditha killings of twenty-four Iraqi civilians. The charges against Frank Wuterich, the leader of the squad which went on the killing spree, remained pending in early 2010; Mark Walker, "Military: Chessani Prosecution May Be Over," *North Country Times*, May 5, 2009, www.northcountytimes.com/articles/2009/05/05/military/z36bf7cbe425ec638882575ad0055cf5a.txt.

CONCLUSION

1. This is by conservative estimate. The figure includes the regular Department of Defense budget, the supplementary budgets for the wars in Iraq and Afghanistan, spending on nuclear weapons and arms transfers in the Departments of Energy and State budgets, the budget for the Department of Veterans Affairs, some military items in the Department of Homeland Security budget, and some portion of the interest on the national debt incurred for past wars. Winslow T. Wheeler, "The Chaos in America's Vast Security Budget," Center for Defense Information, February 4, 2008.

2. See David Mayers, *Dissenting Voices in America's Rise to Power* (Cambridge: Cambridge University Press, 2007); Andrew Bacevich, *The Pentomic Era:*

The U.S. Army between Korea and Vietnam (Washington, DC: National Defense University Press, 1986); Marjorie Cohn and Kathleen Gilberd, *Rules of Disengagement: The Politics and Honor of Military Dissent* (Sausalito: Polipoint Press, 2009); David Cortright, *Soldiers in Revolt: GI Resistance during the Vietnam War* (Boston: Haymarket Books, 2005); Shirley Castelnuovo, *Soldiers of Conscience: Japanese American Military Resisters in World War II* (New York: Praeger, 2008).

Glossary

Abu Ghraib	A prison in Iraq that has been the site of torture and prisoner abuse committed by members of the 372nd Military Police Company of the U.S. Army
AK-47	Soviet-origin assault rifle
AWOL	Absent without leave
CO	Conscientious objector
DFR	Dropped from the [military] rolls
IED	Improvised explosive device
IVAW	Iraq Veterans Against the War
JROTC	Junior Reserve Officer Training Corps
M-4	Assault rifle
M-249	Light machine gun, also known as SAW
MOS	Military Occupational Specialty
MRE	Meal, Ready-to-Eat
NCO	Noncommissioned officer

PTSD	Post-traumatic stress disorder
RPK	Soviet-origin light machine gun
Stop-loss	A program that forces soldiers to stay in the service past their scheduled separation date
UA	Unauthorized absence (Marine term for what the Army calls AWOL)
VA	Veterans Administration
WMD	Weapons of mass destruction

Text:	10/14 Palatino
Display:	Univers Condensed Light and Bauer Bodoni
Compositor:	BookComp, Inc.
Printer and Binder:	Maple-Vail Book Manufacturing Group